"Steven Tungate has produced a rich, comparative study that explores the similarities between the theologies of John Wesley and the mystics Juan de Avila and Miguel de Molinos. What emerges from such an engaging work is a bold invitation to recognize in a fresh way the undoubted influence of mysticism on Wesley's theology especially at its lowest depths as well as at its highest reaches. Kudos to Tungate!"

—KENNETH J. COLLINS,
professor of historical theology and Wesley studies,
Asbury Theological Seminary

"In *The Almost Mystic*, Steven P. Tungate offers an expert overview of many key aspects of John Wesley's theology such as theological authority, epistemology, soteriology, prayer, spiritual growth, and suffering. He also brings fresh insight and energy to the crucial and neglected study of John Wesley's work as an editor in this detailed and careful analysis of the work of Juan de Ávila and Miguel de Molinos in his *Christian Library*. Highly recommended!"

—KEVIN M. WATSON,
director of academic growth and formation, Asbury Theological Seminary

"Here is a very useful and thorough analysis of key Roman Catholic mystic sources that John Wesley used in his understanding and articulation of the perfecting work of God's Spirit in Christian experience. Attentive readers will learn much not only about Wesley, but also about Spanish Christian mystics who form an important part of the Christian tradition. The book also helps readers grasp the nature and significance of Wesley's *Christian Library*—the fifty-volume resource Wesley published to help serious Christians in their life and witness."

—HOWARD A. SNYDER,
author of *The Radical Wesley and Patterns for Church Renewal*

"The vast *Christian Library*, assembled, edited, and promoted by John Wesley has been generally ignored by his spiritual descendants. Now, Steven Tungate makes important contributions to Wesley and English literary studies by undertaking this analysis. His work is significant for its methodological approach as well as its findings. It will be a standard work for understanding Wesley's approach to theology and mysticism and as a case study on reading and editing of literature in eighteenth-century England."

—**DAVID BUNDY,**
associate director, Manchester Wesley Research Centre,
Nazarene Theological College

"By closely examining John Wesley's nuanced relationship to the Spanish Catholic mystical tradition, Steven Tungate sheds new light on Wesley's theology of suffering and Christian perfection. A work of refreshing scholarship, *The Almost Mystic* invites readers to reflect on a most fascinating subject—mystical union with God!"

—**JASON E. VICKERS,**
professor of theology and Wesleyan studies, Truett Seminary, Baylor University

The Almost Mystic

The Almost Mystic

John Wesley's Editing of the Spanish Mystics, Juan de Ávila
and Miguel de Molinos, in His *Christian Library*

STEVEN P. TUNGATE

☙PICKWICK *Publications* · Eugene, Oregon

THE ALMOST MYSTIC
John Wesley's Editing of the Spanish Mystics, Juan de Ávila and Miguel de Molinos, in His Christian Library

Pickwick Publications
An Imprint of Wipf and Stock Publishers
199 W. 8th Ave., Suite 3
Eugene, OR 97401

www.wipfandstock.com

PAPERBACK ISBN: 978-1-6667-8155-7
HARDCOVER ISBN: 978-1-6667-8156-4
EBOOK ISBN: 978-1-6667-8157-1

Cataloguing-in-Publication data:

Names: Tungate, Steven P., author.

Title: The almost mystic : John Wesley's editing of the Spanish mystics, Juan de Ávila and Miguel de Molinos, in his Christian library / Steven P. Tungate.

Description: Eugene, OR : Pickwick Publications, 2024 | Includes bibliographical references.

Identifiers: ISBN 978-1-6667-8155-7 (paperback) | ISBN 978-1-6667-8156-4 (hardcover) | ISBN 978-1-6667-8157-1 (ebook)

Subjects: LCSH: Wesley, John, 1703–1791—Contributions in mysticism. | Wesley, John, 1703–1791. | Mysticism—Spain. | Mystics—Spain. | John, of Avila, Saint, 1499?–1569. | Molinos, Miguel de, 1628–1696.

Classification: BX8495.W5 .T71 2024 (paperback) | BX8495.W5 .T71 (ebook)

07/25/24

To Billy Abraham (1947–2021), a brilliant scholar, philosopher, theologian, and prophetic voice who generously mentored with compassion and encouragement.

You have now reached life's telos and will be sorely missed.

Contents

Abstract

The Almost Mystic: A Study of John Wesley's Editing of the Spanish Mystics, Juan de Ávila and Miguel de Molinos, in His *Christian Library*

Steven P. Tungate

JOHN WESLEY, EIGHTEENTH-CENTURY Church of England priest and founder of Methodism, was strongly influenced by the works of Roman Catholic mystics early in his ministry. These writings helped shape his widely known doctrine of *Christian perfection* or *entire sanctification*. The mystics inspired Wesley to advocate for a lofty spiritual goal which he believed to be attainable in this life. In time, however, he developed many contentions with some extremes as well as many particulars found in the mystical tradition.

Beginning in 1749, Wesley began to publish his *Christian Library*—a fifty-volume compilation of abridged works which he believed to be among the best writings on divinity that had been published in the English language. Among this vast collection, he included three works originally written in the Spanish language. One was a biography titled *The Holy Life of Gregory Lopez*; the others included a sampling of letters by Juan de Ávila and the *Spiritual Guide* by Miguel de Molinos.

This thesis examines Wesley's editing of the non-biographical works by Ávila and Molinos as a way of evaluating Wesley's theology in comparison and contrast with the Spanish mystics. The original seventeenth-century English publications of both works were compared side-by-side with Wesley's edited versions. Wesley's alterations were carefully noted and categorized by topic. The available corpuses of each of these authors were then consulted to examine their respective theological perspectives. A comparative study ensued.

The themes to which Wesley made alterations include theological authority, self-knowledge and epistemology, soteriology, spiritual growth, suffering and divine withdrawal, prayer, meditation, contemplation, mystical language, and the spiritual climax or *telos*. The chapters are arranged topically to address these themes. Each chapter draws from Ávila's body of writings to examine his perspective on the theme, followed by Wesley's editing of Ávila on that topic, then looks at Molinos's understanding of the idea recorded in his works, followed by Wesley's editing of Molinos on the matter, then explores Wesley's views on the subject found in his broader corpus, and concludes with a comparative study of the preceding.

Key Terms: John Wesley, Juan de Ávila, John of Ávila, Miguel de Molinos, Methodism, Catholic Mysticism, Historical Theology, Stages of Spiritual Growth, Christian Spirituality, Meditation, Contemplation, Wesley's *Christian Library*, Molinos's *Spiritual Guide*, *Guia Espiritual*, Soteriology, Suffering, Divine Withdrawal, *Telos*

Preface

EARLY IN MY MINISTRY, I faced some unexpected challenges that left me wounded and perplexed. While I was working through the hurt, I came across an abridgement to the writings of John of the Cross. There was something about his description of the *dark night of the soul* with which I identified at that stage of my own life. With this introduction to Spanish mysticism, I knew I wanted to dive deeper into these writings. A few years later, I enrolled in a doctor of ministry program in Christian spirituality with the intent of writing a dissertation on the stages of spiritual growth comparing the writings of John of the Cross with Theresa of Ávila. After writing a couple of chapters, I desired to explore their perspectives in relation to my own Methodist tradition, so I included a comparison with John Wesley. This began my exploration of Spanish Mysticism and John Wesley's reading of the mystics—which could be described as a bit of a love-hate relationship.

Upon completion of a doctor of ministry degree from Fuller Theological Seminary, I half-jokingly said to my wife, Rachel, that it was time to start looking at PhD programs. She playfully retorted, "No more degrees for seven years." I agreed that the timing was not right, so I quietly placed the dream on the back burner.

As time passed, the academic itch reemerged. To satisfy this yearning, I applied for a two-week visiting ministers fellowship at the Bridwell Library at Southern Methodist University to study Wesley's editing of the writings of Juan de Ávila in his *Christian Library*—a more direct look at Wesley and Spanish Mysticism. While there, I wanted to meet Billy Abraham to pick his brain a bit. Within a few short minutes of arriving in the library, Billy walked past. Upon introducing myself, he invited me to lunch. This was the first of a few conversations that transpired over the course of the two weeks. At the conclusion of my time in Dallas, I saw Billy at a restaurant. I finished my lunch, then stopped by his table to thank him for his time. He invited me to sit down. Billy proceeded to ask if I would consider developing my study into a PhD dissertation and invited me to join the Polycarp Fellows under his tutelage. This was an opportunity that I couldn't pass up. It also just so happened to be seven years after the completion of my doctor of ministry. This began the work that resulted in the dissertation contained in this book.

I am deeply grateful for Jim Bradley of Fuller Theological Seminary, whose contagious love for historical theology and gentle encouragement gave me the desire to further my studies. Likewise, I am thankful for what I see as a divinely arranged appointment with Billy Abraham and for the impact he had in my life over these past five years. As I write this, I feel the grief of his sudden passing just a few short days ago. Words cannot begin to express the depth of gratitude I feel. He will be deeply missed.

Early in the process, I consulted a number of scholars to help me formulate the right questions and to establish the trajectory of this thesis. I appreciate the time and wisdom shared by Ken Collins at Asbury Theological Seminary, Liam Brockey at Michigan State University, Daniel Keating and Robert Fastiggi at Sacred Heart Major Seminary, Bernard McGinn at the University of Chicago, Barry Bryant at Garrett Evangelical Theological Seminary, Ted Campbell at Southern Methodist University, and my dear friend Joe Cunningham at Eureka College. In many of these meetings, Bob Tuttle's name emerged as one who has written on John Wesley and Mysticism, as well as Wesley's *Christian Library*. Even though Bob taught at Asbury Theological Seminary where I received a master of divinity degree, I had not personally met him up to that point, yet I knew much about him. I am deeply grateful for Bob's willingness to meet, to video conference, to email, and to give careful feedback on each chapter. I am also appreciative of Bob's ministry nearly fifty years ago when he preached in the church of my childhood, Clarkston United Methodist Church, and the impact he had on the lives of my parents. I was raised in the faith as a result of his ministry and he continues to encourage me in the faith today.

Lastly among the scholars, I would like to thank Mokhele Madise of the University of South Africa for mentoring me through the PhD thesis. His feedback was valuable and always encouraging. I appreciate his careful interaction with the chapters submitted and the guidance provided throughout. More than a paper for submission, this has been a part of my spiritual journey complete with many guides along the path.

The library staffs of the Bridwell Library at Southern Methodist University, Michigan State University, Sacred Heart Major Seminary, Garrett Evangelical Theological Seminary, Trinity Evangelical Divinity School, Mundelein Seminary, and Greenville University have all been immensely helpful in responding to questions, locating resources, and doing whatever they could to assist.

Finally, I want to thank my wife, Rachel, and daughters Natalie and Alana. They are a tremendous joy! Rachel has encouraged me every step of the way through this project, listened to my external ponderings, and supported my big ideas. She has a sacrificial care for others that often seeks to help others thrive, a care that reaches through and beyond family. I have enjoyed walking life's path and growing together through many of the stages referenced in this thesis. I love finding those moments of closeness in the everyday of life from our evening walking of the dog to the meaningful conversations while doing chores. She remains my bride and my closest friend for whom I am immeasurably grateful.

There aren't many teenagers with whom one can discuss a PhD thesis. Natalie is one of those exceptions. I love our intellectual musings and opportunities to share in an excitement for all things historical. Her intellect is uniquely matched by her kindness. I write this just after returning home from seeing her off to university overseas for the first time. I am proud of the woman whom she is becoming.

Alana fills our home with song, dance, and laughter. She works hard toward her goals but knows how to have fun. She is loyal and compassionate. I enjoyed holding her as a baby while reading for my DMin and now I love the playful study breaks, which often include an appointment with the Mario Brothers, and the deep conversations which she provides. I am also proud of the young woman whom she is becoming.

Introduction

AREA OF INVESTIGATION

In 1749, John Wesley began releasing his *Christian Library: Extracts from and Abridgments of the Choicest Pieces of Practical Divinity Which Have Been Published in the English Tongue*, a fifty-volume collection of the writings which Wesley desired all to read. This collection covered a broad range of eras and traditions from the fourth century Macarius to Wesley's contemporaries like Bishop Reynolds (1674–1743); from the German Lutheran theologian John Arndt (1555–1621), forerunner of the pietist movement, to the Spanish Catholic mystic Juan de Ávila (1499–1569), prominent figure in the counter-reformation, and many more authors covering a wide breadth from various Christian traditions which preceded and accompanied Wesley's time. In developing this collection, Wesley drew from already existing English translations and the primary sources of texts originally written in English. In bringing this sampling into publication, Wesley served as a meticulous editor, presenting the messages and theology that he wanted conveyed while editing out the themes, philosophies, and theological perspectives that he did not wish to perpetuate.

Analysis of such duteous editing provides a glimpse into Wesley's thought. Like the approach of the centuries-old apophatic tradition, sometimes it is easier to affirm what something *is* by first understanding what it *is not*. This thesis delves into what Wesley's theology *is*, especially regarding the themes of spiritual development and mysticism, based on that which he edited out of the works of two Spanish Catholic mystics. Specifically, the thesis observes and analyzes Wesley's editing of the *Letters* of the sixteenth-century priest Juan de Ávila (1499/1500–1569) and the *Spiritual Guide* of the seventeenth-century priest Miguel de Molinos (1628–96). Thus, it interacts some writings from the counter-reformation and early-modern period in Spain with the early-modern British writings of John Wesley.

Juan de Ávila, known as the "Apostle of Andalusia," was a well-respect-
ed preacher, spiritual director, founder of a number of colleges and schools,
key spokesman in the counter-reformation, and influential supporter of the
fledgling Jesuit movement. Juan de Ávila is often categorized among the
Catholic mystics; however, his writings did not take him as far down that
path as some of his contemporaries like John of the Cross or the next century's Miguel de Molinos. However, some mystical themes did emerge in his
writings—themes which Wesley carefully edited.

Ávila maintained a close friendship and correspondence with Ignatius
of Loyola, the founder of the Society of Jesus. He served as a strong influence upon Ignatius's founding of the new order. Wesley wrote often in his
journal regarding some of the negatives he found in the Jesuits of his time.
However, he also included the writings of Ávila in his *Christian Library*.
Wesley had a way of critically sorting through differing theologies while
learning, keeping, and gently setting aside various aspects of their nuanced
teachings. This is precisely what he did with Ávila.

Miguel de Molinos falls very definitively into the Catholic mystical
tradition. In his writings, one can find the basic patterns (and countless allusions to the patterns) of the three-fold way of purgation, illumination, and
enlightenment laid out by Pseudo-Dionysius the Areopagite, often referred
to as the father of the Christian mystical tradition. Molinos also expressed
the language of mystical union with God, and a description of suffering
that reflects the *Dark Night* experiences explained by the sixteenth-century
Spaniard John of the Cross. Early English translations of the writings of
Molinos had a profound effect on John Wesley's contemporary setting, the
"Long Eighteenth Century" in England. The writings of Molinos, with their
emphasis on contemplative prayer and remaining silent before God, led to
England's Quietist movement, a movement which Wesley at first embraced,
but later wrote emphatically against.

Wesley wrote extensively about the dangers of Quietism in his journal. In a letter to his brother Samuel dated November 23, 1736, he declared
that he almost shipwrecked his faith upon the mystics. He also confronted
the mystical understanding of suffering in his sermons *Heaviness through
Manifold Temptations* and *The Wilderness State*, yet he praised mystics like
Madame Guyon, encouraged people to read the early works of William Law,
and included in his *Christian Library* the mystical works of Fénelon, Molinos, Ávila, and de Rentry, and, arguably, drew from the mystical theology of
union with God to formulate some of his doctrines on Christian Perfection
or Entire Sanctification.

In addition to analyzing Wesley's editing of the works of Juan de Ávila
and Molinos, this thesis explores the theological motive behind Wesley's

editorial alterations, argues that there existed a strong link between Catholic Mysticism and Wesley's doctrine of Christian Perfection, displays historically where Wesley conflicted with the Quietist movement and its accompanying roots in Molinos's writings (especially demonstrated in the Quietist controversy of 1740), makes a case that it was the writings of Molinos that inspired Wesley to develop his counter-response found in his sermons on *Heaviness* and *Wilderness*, and points out specifically where Wesley differed from Ávila and Molinos in their teachings more broadly.

Gregory Lopez

This thesis focuses specifically on the Spanish mystics in Wesley's *Christian Library* including Ávila and Molinos. Wesley did, however, include one other Spanish mystic in his *Library* not included in this thesis. Wesley edited an English translation of the *Life of Gregory Lopez* by Francisco de Losa. Gregory Lopez was a Spanish mystic who made his way to the Americas as a monastic hermit. Since the abridgement on Lopez which appears in Wesley's *Library* is a biography and not a theological treatise, it is not included in this thesis as theological content is somewhat limited.

JUSTIFICATION FOR THIS STUDY

Wesley's life and teachings were under rigorous scrutiny even while he was alive. In the centuries following, countless volumes of books, articles, tracts, and modern-day blogs have addressed Wesley's works, ministry, teachings, and impact. However, relatively little work has been done on Wesley's editing in his *Christian Library*, with the exception of Robert G. Tuttle's PhD dissertation and follow-up book *Mysticism in the Wesleyan Tradition*, and a few short articles or chapters by other authors.

Likewise, little work has been done in the English-speaking world on the works of Juan de Ávila. There are many translations of his letters and smaller treatises, a biography by Longaro Degli Oddi, but little beyond that. The secondary texts in English concerning Ávila are limited to an academic work by Rady Roldan-Figueroa and a popular work by Denise Clare Oliver. A relatively large amount has also been written on Miguel de Molinos and Quietism. However, very little work has been done on the direct interchange between the writings of Molinos and Wesley's response. Wesley's response to Molinos has great implications on his theological perspectives and his relationship to the Quietist movement of his time. While contributing original research in this area, this thesis may also serve as a catalyst for further study personally for this author and corporately for the broader community of Wesley scholars.

AIMS AND OBJECTIVES

The primary aim of this work is to provide a clearer understanding of the theology of John Wesley, especially in relation to the Catholic mystical tradition and Quietism. Secondarily, by analyzing Wesley's editorial approach in his *Christian Library*, this study seeks to advance current, while promoting future, scholarship of Wesley's anthological collection. Thirdly, this thesis develops further scholarship regarding Juan de Ávila and Miguel de Molinos in the English-speaking world in regard to their relationship to early Methodism and their influence upon the eighteenth-century religious climate of England.

RESEARCH METHODS

A major guide followed for the research methodology and writing structure of this work includes the second edition of *Church History: An Introduction to Research Methods and Resources* by James E. Bradley and Richard A. Muller.[1] Since the main thrust of this thesis is looking at John Wesley's editing of Juan de Ávila and Miguel de Molinos, there are three primary sources that remain crucial to the study: Wesley's edited version of these two authors, and the two respective English translations which Wesley used in compiling his version. Two publications have been made of Wesley's *Christian Library*—his original publication in 1749 through 1755 and a later production in 1821. This study makes use of the former as it was solely the result of Wesley's editorial work, whereas the second printing underwent further editing at the hands of others. Wesley drew from the most recent publications of his time including an English translation of the letters of Juan de Ávila published in 1631 and an English translation of the *Spiritual Guide* of Miguel de Molinos published in 1688. Original Spanish editions were also consulted for clarity on the thought of Ávila and Molinos.

Analysis of these writings took place through a side-by-side comparison, noting the alterations made by Wesley. These alterations were then categorized topically and described in this thesis according to these topics. Next, applying an inductive approach, interpretations were made based on these observations looking at *why* Wesley made such changes; this was

---

1. Published by Eerdmans in 2016.

done by also interacting his editorial changes with the broader writings of Wesley's corpus. The primary sources consulted include the multi-volume bicentennial critical edition of the works of Wesley by Abingdon Press, the 1938 publication of Wesley's *Journal* by Curnock (originally published in 1916), and Wesley's *Letters* published by Telford in 1931. Other collections of the works of Wesley were also consulted including the 1959 edition by Thomas Jackson (originally published between 1829 and 1831), the 1991 and 1996 reprints by Baker Books of the 1872 publication of Wesley's works, and the online collections of Wesley's works at the Christian Classics Ethereal Library and the resources of Northwest Nazarene University.

From there, secondary source materials were consulted to trace the current trends and conversations pertaining to Wesleyan Theology. Dialogue with these resources ensued as directed by the findings of this research. For example, some debate exists over the level to which entire sanctification, according to Wesley, is more process based or instantaneous. Randy Maddox from Duke University, for example, emphasizes the former, while Ken Collins from Asbury Theological Seminary stresses the latter, while both ultimately take a "both/and" approach. Collins also sees the influence of Western Christian thought on Wesley's understanding of justification and sanctification, while others believe his perspective on sanctification was influenced more by the Eastern church. This study shows the connections of Wesley's theology with the Western Catholic tradition in a broad sense, and particularly how the concept of mystical union relates to Wesley's understanding of sanctification.

Setting the three authors in their respective historical context is important for understanding their writings, while a look at their broader writings will also help to illumine their theological perspectives. Because the historical context is crucial, but not the major thrust of the thesis, several current secondary source materials were consulted in order to arrive at a relatively clearer understanding of the surrounding issues of their time period. However, in understanding their respective theological points of view, it was important to go directly to the source. Thus, in addition to the works of Wesley mentioned above, the breadth of primary source materials available pertaining to Ávila and Molinos were also consulted. These include the Spanish critical edition of the works of Ávila edited by Luis Sala Balust and Francisco Martin Hernandez published in Madrid in 1970. Consultation of English translations of Ávila and Molinos's work included in the bibliography were also utilized. Much of the work of Molinos available remains limited to his *Spiritual Guide*. The bibliography also lists examples of this work available for research.

In order to trace the development of availability of the Spanish masters to Wesley, publication records were consulted to see when and where these works were published, thus arriving at an understanding of *how* and *why* Wesley came across them in the first place. For example, Ávila's *Audi, Filia* was first translated into English in 1620. This coincides with a British treaty made with Spain that same year in connection to the marriage of the Prince of Wales with Infanta Maria Anna. This allowed for Spanish Catholic writings to make their way into Protestant England. Likewise, the translation of Molinos's *Spiritual Guide* into English in 1688 corresponded with the Declaration of Indulgence made by King James II through which greater freedoms were granted to Roman Catholics in Britain.

REVIEW OF LITERATURE

Although many sources were used to gain a clearer understanding of the respective historical contexts represented, along with many primary sources to arrive at a clearer picture of the respective theological perspectives of the three authors studied, this thesis is designed to delve into the theological perspectives of John Wesley. Therefore, the following literature review focuses on Wesleyan theology, specifically on the contributions and gaps pertaining to Mysticism, Quietism, and the *Christian Library*.

The Person and Theology of John Wesley

Regarding the primary sources of Wesley, the approach of this thesis adheres closely to the method laid out in the introductory material of Thomas Oden's four volume systematic essays titled *John Wesley's Teachings*.[2] In the preface found in volume 1, Oden explained an order of authoritative editions of the works of Wesley. The most recent and critical edition of Wesley's works can be found in the bicentennial edition published by Abingdon.[3] Many volumes of this set have been made available to the public, yet several volumes remain in process. For this thesis, where possible, the primary source references to Wesley come from the bicentennial edition. Where not available, quotes from Wesley's *Journal* were extracted from Curnock's edition and references pertaining to his *Letters* came from Telford's publication. Other primary source material was extracted from a printing of the

2. Zondervan, 2012.

3. 1984 to present.

fourteen-volume set compiled by Thomas Jackson, *The Works of the Rev. John Wesley*, and subsequent publications.[4]

The secondary works pertaining to John Wesley from both theological and historical perspectives are numerous. In relatively recent years, there has been a resurgence of interest in Wesley in the wake of the studies of the twentieth-century theologian Albert Outler, who brought the founder of Methodism back into the forefront of theological discussion. Since that time, many colleges, universities, and theological seminaries in the Wesleyan tradition have appointed professors to posts and endowed chairs of research in Wesleyan theology. Since the field is vast, this literature review will highlight a sampling of resources available in Wesleyan theology, broadly defined, then focus more intently on the literature pertaining to the specific themes found in this thesis. Therefore, the following is not exhaustive, but it is representative to the whole.

Biographies pertaining to Wesley emerged early from John Whitehead's *The life of the Rev. John Wesley: M.A. some time Fellow of Lincoln-College, Oxford. Collected from his private papers and printed works*, first printed in 1793 with multiple editions to follow, to Thomas Coke and Henry Moore's *The life of the Rev. John Wesley: A.M. including an account of the great revival of religion, in Europe and America, of which he was the first and chief instrument* printed a couple years later. Samuel Bradburn also added his perspective on Wesley that year in his work titled *A farther account of the Rev. John Wesley, M.A.* Other printings of Wesley's life continued through the 1800s, including Robert Southey's *The Life of John Wesley* published in 1820, a large two-volume composition on Wesley. In volume 1, he began writing biographically, but soon shifted to unpacking many of Wesley's doctrines in a systematic format. In the middle portions covering both volumes, he also looked topically at the theological writings of the early Methodist preachers. This work, however, was not without its critics. Not least of these was Richard Watson's retort, which had already seen six editions by 1835.

In 1870, Hodder and Stoughton published a three-volume set by Rev. L. Tyerman titled *The Life and Times of the Rev. John Wesley, M.A., Founder of the Methodists*. In this set, Tyerman tracked Wesley's life and ministry year-by-year, drawing from the breadth of Wesley's works and his correspondence with others, along with the publications against Wesley to show his ministry and theological leanings. In the pages of this collection, Tyerman provided his own commentary while also including lengthy quotes directly from Wesley and his contemporaries.

4. London, 1829–31.

In 1891, B. W. Bond made the life of Wesley accessible to a popular audience in his work *Life of John Wesley*, published by the Publishing House of the M. E. Church, South in Nashville, Tennessee. In the preface, Bond praised the work of Tyerman, but labeled it "too voluminous." Bond, although tracing Wesley's life chronologically, organized his material more thematically to record the influential life experiences, organization of the Methodists, and theological emphases. A similar approach was taken that same year in J. H. Overton's *John Wesley*.

After his 1890 publication on the *Life of John Wesley; The Mission of Methodism* (The Fernley Lecture for 1890), in 1896, Richard Green shifted the secondary literature on Wesley beyond biography as he traced the publication records of both John and Charles in his work *The Works of John and Charles Wesley: A Bibliography Containing an Exact Account of All the Publications Issued by the Brothers Wesley Arranged in Chronological Order, With a List of the Early Editions, and Descriptive and Illustrative Notes.* This lengthy title accurately describes the thrust of the book. Green arranged his book following a year-by-year assessment, identifying the works published for that year, with a brief description of the publication, along with a relevant quote from Wesley's journal where available.

It didn't take long for interest in Wesley to reach beyond the realm of his ministry. For example, in 1868, Matthew Lelievre wrote his work *John Wesley, Sa Vie et Son Oeuvre*. A later French work of interest also included a look at Wesley in the context of the Reformation from the perspective of the Roman Catholic priest and historian Maximin Piette titled *Réaction de John Wesley dans l'Evolution du Protestantisme*, later translated by J. B. Howard as *John Wesley in the Evolution of Protestantism*.[5] Piette's three-volume work covered an in-depth look at the Reformation, the historical context of Protestantism in England, and Wesley and the Methodist movement in relationship to this context. The nineteenth and twentieth centuries also found many publications considering the life and theology of Wesley written in German, not least of which include the works by Martin Schmidt *John Wesley* and *John Wesley: A theological biography*.[6]

Biographical work in the English-speaking world continued into the twentieth century. The Methodist bishop Hurst wrote *John Wesley the Methodist: A Plain Account of His Life and Work*, with the title utilizing the language of Wesley's *Plain Account of Christian Perfection*.[7] Interestingly,

---

5. Published in 1937.

6. Published in 1953 and translated into English by Norman Goldhawk in 1962, respectively.

7. Hurst's work was published in 1903.

Hurst originally published this work anonymously under the authorship of "a Methodist Preacher." In many ways, this work served like any ordinary biography following a chronological account of the Methodist founder. However, Hurst made great and deliberate use of some of the earliest sketches, paintings, and tintypes to visually place Wesley in his historical context. A few years later in 1906, C. T. Winchester added to the conversation with the publication of *The Life of John Wesley*.

Throughout the twentieth century, Wesleyan scholarship began to focus more intently on specific aspects of Wesley, as opposed to the broad-sweeping histories, with key transition points found in the 1920s, 1950s–60s, and again in the 1980s with each era, by and large, moving toward a narrower focus. In the early 1900s, there was a bit of a transition toward this movement with biographical work presenting a particular emphasis. For example, S. Parks Cadman published his 1916 work titled *The Three Religious Leaders of Oxford and Their Movements: John Wycliffe, John Wesley, and John Henry Newman*. Here, Cadman took a strictly biographical approach; however, he uniquely placed Wesley in his Oxford context showing prior and posterior reform movements.

J. S. Simon followed this trend by publishing the biography *John Wesley, the master-builder* in 1927 and *John Wesley, the later years* in 1934, and began with the more narrowly focused *John Wesley and the Religious Societies* in 1921. This followed suit with the key turning points of Methodist scholarship mentioned above.

A few years later in 1928, J. Ernest Rattenbury wrote about the broader influence and long-lasting impact of Wesley's teaching and ministry in his *Wesley's Legacy to the World: Six Studies in the Permanent Values of the Evangelical Revival*. The six studies include a look at what shaped Wesley's life and understanding, the doctrines pertaining to God, Wesley's pragmatism, his influence on the broader Christian community, his impact on society and social issues, and his effect on and through music. That same year found the publication of *John Wesley among the Scientists* by Frank W. Collier. This work evaluated Wesley's scientific publications, showed the development of his scientific thought, while also interacting his perspectives with some of the scientific issues contemporary to Collier's time. To some extent, however, it seems that Collier projected later scientific perspectives back onto the times of Wesley.

The 1920s also saw its publications of broad-sweeping biographies written for a popular audience including *John Wesley* by W. H. Hutton in 1927 and *The Lord's Horseman: John Wesley the Man* by Umphrey Lee in 1928 and republished in 1954. A few years later, however, Lee also followed the emerging pattern of scholarship toward the theological evaluation of

Wesley in his 1936 book *John Wesley and Modern Religion*, where he tackled topics of soteriology, ecclesiology, affect, sanctification, and others in comparison and contrast to the theological climate of Wesley's time and Lee's contemporary setting.

The title of George Croft Cell's 1935 work on Wesley, *The Rediscovery of John Wesley*, seems to capture the reason for the developments of Wesleyan scholarship that developed throughout that century. Here Cell offered a thorough, if not systematic, critical analysis of Wesley's theological thought. In this work, Cell challenged some of the contemporary writings on Wesley while drawing from the primary sources. For example, pertaining to Calvinism, Cell traced Wesley's early leanings toward and later leanings away from Calvinism while showing that Wesley did not fit nicely into the bounds of Arminianism as Cell believed his contemporaries pushed too frequently.

Maldwyn Edwards later addressed the political thought of Wesley setting him in his contemporary environment in *John Wesley and the Eighteenth Century: A Study of His Social and Political Influence.*[8] He evaluated Wesley's philosophical approach to politics, Wesley's interaction with events like the American fight for independence and the French Revolution, and Wesley's perspective on issues of his day like slavery, education, and prison reform.

Even during this shift toward thematic accounts of Wesley, the place of the chronological biography was not anathematized. In fact, the mid-twentieth century saw an increase of interest in Wesley's life. This may be seen in the number of books published, including Francis McConnell's *John Wesley* in 1939, *The Long Quest: The Story of John Wesley* by Harry Harrison Kroll in 1954, *The Young Mr. Wesley: A Study of John Wesley and Oxford* by V. H. H. Green in 1961, also that year, a translation of the Norwegian work by Ingvar Haddal *John Wesley: A Biography* in 1961, a later and broader work by Green, *John Wesley* in 1964, and the short overview *John Wesley* by Dorothy Marshall in 1965.

However, even many of the biographies started to shift from broad-sweeping chronologies toward biographical accounts revolving around a specific theme or topic. An example of this includes Leslie Church's *Knight of the Burning Heart: The Story of John Wesley.*[9] Church followed a chronological ordering of the life of Wesley, but the primary focus was on the formative early experiences in Wesley's life that led to the making of the leader of a great movement. Similarly, Frederick Gill produced a biography some years later in 1962 that emphasized the places of Wesley's life, categorizing

8. Published in 1933 and 1955.
9. Published in 1938.

Wesley's life into certain towns and cities. Gill combined photographs, narratives, and primary quotes to tell of the Anglican preacher's life in context of place. The book is aptly titled *In the Steps of John Wesley.*[10] Likewise, *The Burning Heart: John Wesley, Evangelist* by A. Skevington Wood covered the biographical development of Wesley while focusing specifically on his development as an evangelist.[11]

In the year of Gill's second printing, 1963, A. B. Lawson added to the conversation of Wesley's theological perspectives in *John Wesley and the Christian Ministry: The Sources and Development of His Opinions and Practice.* This would not be the last work to study the progression of Wesley's thought over time, or of the narrowing focus of study pertaining to the eighteenth-century reformer. A unique angle on Wesleyan scholarship was introduced by George Lawton in his publication of *John Wesley's English: A Study of His Literary Style.*[12] Here, Lawton gave a thorough analysis of Wesley's linguistic work, his introduction of new words and phrases, his use of traditional rhetoric like simile, hyperbole, metaphor, alliteration, etc., among others.

Another example of thematically focused scholarship from the mid-1900s includes Robert Monk's *A Study of the Christian Life: John Wesley, His Puritan Heritage.*[13] This work has related interest to this thesis. The book is divided into three parts: part 1 looks at Wesley's interaction with Puritanism by analyzing his abridging of Puritan works in the *Christian Library,* similar to the way this thesis looks at Wesley's editing of the Spanish mystics.

This movement toward more specific themes pertaining to the theology and the history of Wesley continued as the twentieth century progressed, especially toward the end of the millennium and on into the 2000s. Examples of the shift regarding the teaching of Wesley include Richard E. Brandley's *Locke, Wesley, and the Method of English Romanticism* where he explored, in his theory, the influence of Locke's epistemology on Wesley's philosophical theology, especially as it related to the role of experience.[14] Also that decade, Warren Thomas Smith produced a work looking at *John Wesley and Slavery.*[15] A few years later, in 1989, Tore Meistad published his dissertation work comparing the perspectives of Reformer Martin Luther with Wesley regarding Jesus's Sermon on the Mount. This book later became

10. Published in 1962 and 1963.
11. Published in 1967.
12. Published in 1962.
13. Published in 1966.
14. Published in 1984.
15. Published in 1986.

part of the twenty-seven-volume *Pietist and Wesleyan Studies* series, which explores the deep connections between the two traditions—again, showing the emphasis on specific and narrowing themes of Wesley's theology. Topics within this series also look at Wesley's views on affections (volume 1), Pentecost (volume 15), abolitionism (volume 20), and ecclesiology (volume 27), among others.

Other examples of narrowing themes may include Joel Green and David Watson's *Wesley, Wesleyans, and Reading Bible as Scripture.*[16] This serves as a compilation of essays by many of the leading Wesley scholars of the day on the theme of Wesley's bibliology and the ensuing perspectives of later Methodists and those from various Wesleyan traditions. From this general time period, even some books that may appear broader have a focus on specifics. For example, *John Wesley: Contemporary Perspectives* edited by John Stacey consists of a compilation of nineteen essays that examine very narrow aspects of Wesley's theology and practice.[17] Examples of these essays include Heitzenrater's "Wesley and His Diary," "Wesley's Chapels" by Christopher Stell, and "Health and Healing in the Ministry of John Wesley" by Morris Maddocks, among others.

For a look at the pragmatic side of Wesley, Howard Snyder's *The Radical Wesley and Patterns for Church Renewal* serves as a thorough look at Wesley's ecclesiology and practical structuring of the Methodists.[18] Snyder described Wesley's view of *ecclesiola in ecclesia,* "little churches within the church," as inspired by the Moravians and further developed through the Methodists. In true Methodist pragmatism, Snyder concluded the book by describing how these principles can prove useful today.

The histories pertaining to Wesley also followed this trend of narrowing thematically at the transition of the new millennium. For example, Frank Baker's lengthy book *John Wesley and the Church of England* examined Wesley's career-long relationship with his mother church, examining Wesley's loyalty, ensuing struggles, and the pending separation of the Methodists after his death.[19] Released in 1990, Henry Abelove's *The Evangelist of Desire: John Wesley and the Methodists* examined some of the specific influences Wesley had in England and abroad. Abelove looked not only at what Wesley taught but examined what was retained by the early Methodists—the aspects of his person and ministry that "stuck." In 2014, Oxford University Press released Geordan Hammond's *John Wesley in America:*

---

16. Published in 2012.

17. Published in 1988.

18. Published in 1980.

19. Published in 1970.

Restoring Primitive Christianity. Here, Hammond explored the experience, theological formation and emphasis, and historical dynamics of Wesley in Georgia. Hammond looked at Wesley's attempt to restore primitive Christianity, the influence of the Moravians upon this young Anglican priest, the mission to the Native Americans, along with the many struggles Wesley faced during his time in America. As another example, Samuel Rogal introduced his *The Wesleys in Cornwall, 1743–1789: A Record of Their Activities Town by Town* in 2015. This was his fifth such book following his publications which looked at the Wesleys in London, Scotland, Ireland, and Wales.

Given this thematic narrowing among Wesleyan scholarship, like at the turn of the nineteenth to twentieth centuries, it did not completely eliminate the place for broad-sweeping biographies and histories. Examples of the continuation of such publications include Bonamy Dobree's *John Wesley* in 1933, where he described the "holy monotony" of Wesley's life; and *Reasonable Enthusiast: John Wesley and the Rise of Methodism* by Henry Rack in 1989 and 1992. In the latter, Rack examined Wesley's life chronologically in three parts from Wesley's early days to the rise of Methodism, to what he called "The Consolidation of Methodism." However, Rack also inserted between these parts interludes that unpack some of the more generalized themes that emerged during the respective time periods. Other examples include Kenneth Collins's *A Real Christian: The Life of John Wesley* in 1999, where he looked at Wesley's life thematically; *John Wesley: A Biography* by Stephen Tomkins in 2003, where John's life was evaluated chronologically; Richard Heitzenrater, also taking a chronological approach in his *Wesley and the People Called Methodists* in 1995; and Roy Hattersley's *A Brand from the Burning: The Life of John Wesley* in 2002 where he followed a chronological flow from beginning to end, but categorized each smaller time period around the themes which surfaced from Wesley's life.

In 1978, Robert G. Tuttle Jr. brought the historical and theological examinations of Wesley together in his book *John Wesley: His Life and Theology*. Tuttle, writing in the first person as if from Wesley's pen, showed the development of Wesley's theology in direct connection to the historical events surrounding his writings. In this work, Tuttle explained how some of Wesley's seeming contradictions were often a matter of a shifting of emphasis based on the immediate needs around him.

As referenced above, in 2012 Thomas Oden released a systematic analysis of the writings of Wesley. This served as an expansion of his previous work *John Wesley's Scriptural Christianity: A Plain Exposition of His Teaching on Christian Doctrine*, published in 1994. In the more recent addition, Oden laid out his study following the classic categories of systematic theology. Volume 1 examined Wesley's teaching on *God and Providence*, volume 2, *Christ and Salvation*, the third volume *Pastoral Theology*, and the set concludes with an examination of the Anglican priest's teaching on *Ethics and Society*. Oden's intent was to make a case for Wesley as an intentional, systematical (or, perhaps better stated, methodical) theologian, dispelling claims that Wesley was merely a pragmatist. In so doing, Oden also demonstrated the consistency of Wesley's teaching over time, with only slight and few variations.

Where Oden emphasized Wesley's consistency over time, Kenneth J. Collins examined the development of Wesley's perspectives over the course of his writings and ministry in the book *John Wesley: A Theological Journey.*[20] Collins explored Wesley's theological development by looking at the early influences upon the young minister including the writings of William Law, Thomas à Kempis, and Jeremy Taylor, along with the family's pietistic background and Anglican commitments, and the influence of the Moravians. Collins traced the "three rises of Methodism" from the Oxford Holy Club to the Georgia mission on through the Fetter Lane Society and Aldersgate conversion. Collins then delved into various theological topics, explaining ways in which Wesley's views changed over time and the ways in which he maintained consistency throughout his life.

For a solid overview of Wesleyan theology, the *Cambridge Companion to Wesley* serves as a summary of the life, times, and theology of Wesley.[21] Specifically pertinent to this thesis is Isabel Rivers's chapter on "John Wesley as Editor and Publisher." In this fifteen-page essay, Rivers addressed the originality of Wesley's editorial methods, an analysis of the legitimacy of Wesley's approach to liberal editing, while describing the breadth of his publications and insights into his theology as expressed through his publications.

Wesleyan scholarship continues to produce massive amounts of volumes on the influential preacher, his ministry, teaching, contemporary setting, and many aspects of his life. Scholars like Henry Rack, Ken Collins, Richard Heitzenrater, Randy Maddox, and many others continue to flood the shelves with resources pertaining to the founder of Methodism. There are also many academic peer-reviewed journals advancing Wesleyan scholarship including the *Arminian Magazine* (published by the Fundamental Wesleyan Society), *The Asbury Journal* (published by Asbury Theological Seminary), *Caminhando* (published by the Methodist University of São Paulo, Brazil), *Epworth Review* (published by the Methodist Church in Britain), *Holiness* (a publication of Wesley House-Cambridge), *Methodist*

---

20. Published in 2003.
21. Published in 2010.

History (published by the General Commission on Archives and History of The United Methodist Church), *Methodist Review* (an online, open-access journal), *Wesley and Methodist Studies* (published by Penn State University Press), and the *Wesleyan Theological Journal* (published by the Wesleyan Theological Society). Given the vast research, however, relatively little has been produced regarding Wesley and his relationship with mysticism and even less on Wesley's *Christian Library* as I will demonstrate below. Therefore, this thesis and future work on the theme remains important to advancing scholarship in Methodist studies.

Wesley and Mysticism

As this thesis explores Wesley's editing of two Spanish mystics, the topic of Wesley and Mysticism will serve as an important theme of exploration. Two of the most thorough works on this were written by Robert G. Tuttle Jr. The first was his PhD dissertation in which he analyzed Wesley's editing of the mystics in the *Christian Library*. This thesis builds upon that work by focusing more deeply and specifically on the two Spanish authors. The second is Tuttle's work *Mysticism in the Wesleyan Tradition*, an edited version of his dissertation in which he traced the back-and-forth interaction of Wesley with Mysticism. Here, Tuttle demonstrated how what appears to be an ebbing and flowing of Wesley's high acceptance of Mysticism to Wesley's strong rejection of the same was really a long process of Wesley "mining the gold" of the mystical "spiritual discipline, holiness, and communion with God" while eliminating the dross of speculation, darkness, passivity, and self-centeredness.[22]

In 1945, J. Brazier Green published his work *John Wesley and William Law*. Green looked at Wesley's interactions with Law from a historical and theological perspective serving as one of the earlier examinations of Wesley and mysticism. One of the key doctrinal issues Green addressed was their varied teachings on the atonement. The book climaxes with the final two chapters exploring Wesley and mysticism more broadly and finally Wesley's distinctive doctrine of Christian Perfection. Green showed the influence of mysticism on this defining doctrine of Methodism. In 1973, G. E. Clarkson also pursued this topic in his article "John Wesley and William Law's Mysticism" in *Religion in Life* 42.

Other resources of note on Mysticism and the Methodist founder include Chet Cataldo's book *A Spiritual Portrait of a Believer: A Comparison between the Emphatic 'I' of Romans 7, Wesley and the Mystics* published 2010;

22. Tuttle, *Mysticism*, 185.

the dissertation by David D. Wilson for Leeds University, *The Influence of Mysticism on John Wesley* in 1968; along with the following journal articles: Kenneth Collins's "John Wesley's Assessment of Christian Mysticism" published in 1993, John Falkner's "Wesley the Mystic" from 1930, Thorvald Kallstad's "John Wesley Och Mystiken" in 1988, Stephen Martyn's "The Journey to God: Union, Purgation and Transformation within the Ascent of Mount Carmel and a Plain Account of Christian Perfection" of 2012, Mark Olson's "The Stillness Controversy of 1740: Tradition Shaping Scripture Reading" published in 2011, E. E. Turner's "John Wesley and Mysticism" in 1930, and David Wilson's "John Wesley and Mystical Prayer" from 1968.

The Christian Library

As the thrust of the comparative study in this thesis is drawn from Wesley's editing of the *Christian Library*, it is important to look at this work somewhat broadly. Both printings of the library, Wesley's original published in 1749–55 and the posthumous edition in 1821, are readily available online. However, the secondary material on this topic remains very limited. In fact, the topic is relegated to a relatively few sporadic chapters or journal articles. As mentioned above, Rivers's chapter in the *Cambridge Companion* offers some insights. In 1940, Thomas Walter Herbert published his dissertation for Princeton University under the title *John Wesley as Editor and Author*. His fourth chapter looked specifically at Wesley's *Christian Library*. Here, Herbert offered a broad-sweeping overview of the process of Wesley's publication from the inception of the idea and counsel from others to the editing and publication. Herbert's view is quite disparaging of the work, however. He labeled it a "dismal failure" as financially it lost money and never saw many customers.[23]

WESLEY'S EDITING PROCESS

Wesley's first level of editing included making the texts more reader friendly to his cultural context. He edited spellings and sentence punctuation to fit more closely with the style of his contemporaries. For example, one of the more common spelling changes included dropping the final *e* used in Middle English, changing *losse* to *loss*, *wee* to *we*, *itselfe* to *itself*, *feare* to *fear*, *sinnes* to *sins*, etc.

---

23. Herbert, *Wesley as Editor*, 25.

Wesley also removed redundant or unnecessary words and some adjectives for brevity. Examples of this include "the pure love of Jesus" reduced to "the love of Jesus"; "these words are to be weighed, and feared withal . . ." was condensed to "these words are to be weighed . . ."; "his divine love" became simply "his love" as God's divinity is assumed; "tears in our eyes" was edited merely to "tears" as their location is a given; these were among countless other inconsequential examples of his editing.[24] In addition, Wesley also omitted adjectives and titles that, perhaps, ought to be a given or understood by implication, especially as they relate to Jesus or the Godhead. Wesley often edited out "our Lord" when it appeared after "Christ." This may have been an act of economy of words and brevity, or perhaps Wesley was moved by a deeper theological conviction that prevented him from using *our* for readers whom he did not know if Christ was truly their Lord. The latter possibility is further supported by Wesley's deliberate removal of the phrase regarding Jesus "and is, in fine, your lord" in an address to a woman at advent time.[25]

Where Ávila quoted from Latin texts, which the translator of the 1631 edition kept in Latin, Wesley translated the words into English. We see this, for example, where Ávila urged his readers to "pray to our lord & say *Deus meus illumine tenebras meas,*" Wesley stated as, "Pray to our Lord and say, *My God enlighten my Darkness.*"[26]

The British cultural avoidance of extremes and the Church of England's "middle way" was reflected in the way Wesley toned down the language by removing strong words and phrases like *extremely, profound, certain, great, infallibly true, heart-breaking, severe and nothing delicate, high repose, a more hideous thing, most cruelly,* and *abundantly.*[27]

Also regarding Wesley's inconsequential editing, we see a few word choice preferences used by Wesley over specific words used by the earlier English translator of Ávila. For example, he changed *tepidity* to *lukewarm, benediction* to *blessing, saciety* to *true satisfaction, profoundest of our harts* to *Bottom of our Hearts, pusillanimity* to *Backwardness,* and *affected and frequented* to *allowed.*[28]

---

24. Ávila, *Selected Epistles,* 89, 93, 112.

25. Ávila, *Selected Epistles,* 133.

26. Ávila, *Selected Epistles,* 53; Wesley, *Christian Library* (Ávila), 46:267.

27. Ávila, *Selected Epistles,* 18, 50, 57, 67, 70, 87, 113, 121, 175.

28. Ávila, *Selected Epistles,* 19, 22, 49, 55, 92, 125, 135; Wesley, *Christian Library* (Ávila), 46:260, 262, 264, 268, 283, 294, 298.

Another phrase used often by Ávila that Wesley omitted was "to the end that."[29] This may, perhaps, be an inconsequential removal of an over-used empty phrase, or it may reveal a deeper conviction within Wesley concerning that which is involved in reaching the *telos*, or end, of such things. Although Wesley's intent in examples like this may remain ambiguous, and others, like those stated above, may show themselves as clearly inconsequential, there are still other examples of Wesley's editing through omissions and alterations that very clearly and deliberately demonstrate Wesley's theological positions. In fact, some of the most subtle of changes prove to be quite consequential toward the theological implications they represent.

Editing of Molinos

Similar to his editorial work on Juan de Ávila, John Wesley meticulously edited Miguel de Molinos's *Guia Espiritual*, or *Spiritual Guide*. Though a great deal of his editing was executed with intentional precision to convey his theological perspective through the writings of others, some of his trimming was done for the sake of brevity of the abridgement, or an updating of the language to fit his contemporary audience. Simple spelling changes and changes in punctuation are not considered in this thesis as they are categorized as inconsequential to the theological message of Molinos and that which was relayed through Wesley's anthology. Some, however, will be considered as they capture Wesley's person and thought.

In Molinos's text, Wesley was consistent in removing phrases like "it is clear that," "it is necessary," "know that," "it must be known," and "you must know that."[30] Though it is somewhat speculative to conjecture reasons for Wesley's removal of such phrases, it may serve as an insight into his thought, especially pertaining to his epistemology. Wesley often promoted a moderate approach to his dogmas such that words of certainty should be reserved only for those beliefs of which one can be certain, for example, Trinitarian doctrines, salvation through Jesus, etc. One example of this includes Wesley's counsel to people who believe to be hearing from God; he advised that they should preface their statements with words like "perhaps" or "I believe" when asserting that God is speaking.

Elsewhere, Wesley was likewise sure to remove phrases that contained language pertaining to the memory like "consider how," "all this time remember," and "remember well what follows."[31]

29. Ávila, *Selected Epistles*, 20, 50, 61, 124.

30. Wesley, *Christian Library* (Molinos), 38:253, 260, 283, 271, 288.

31. Wesley, *Christian Library* (Molinos), 38:261, 267, 282.

Though Wesley's editing of these phrases point to significant insights into Wesley's epistemological perspectives, they do remain inconsequential to the meaning of the text presented. In other words, such editing did not alter or diminish the teaching of Molinos, so for that reason, they are here deemed as inconsequential editing.

Redundant Language Adjectives and Adverbs

Likely for the sake of brevity, or perhaps as a way of avoiding repetitive language, Wesley removed nearly seventy words or phrases that were redundant in their respective contexts. Likewise, just over a dozen times, John Wesley removed adjectival or adverbial wording leaving the concept at hand in its simplest form without added description. For example, as Miguel de Molinos encouraged his readers to "keep thine Heart in Peace" so as to be prepared to face the trials that would come through the "envious Enemy" including "grievous persecutions," Wesley removed the words *envious* and *grievous*.[32] Although this and the examples that follow may be somewhat inconsequential to the overall message being conveyed, these editorial changes tell us something about John Wesley. These changes demonstrate the value Wesley placed on matter-of-fact speech and frankness.

Other examples include a reference to the fruits that one may reap from a season of dryness where Molinos refers to the dryness as "that great dryness"; however, Wesley removed the words "that great," thus leaving it at "dryness."[33] Wesley may have removed these words because he believed that dryness is not great, or for the mere sake of redundancy in that it goes without saying that there is a greatness in such a season of dryness. Given the overall pattern of adjective removal, it is likely that Wesley simply left the descriptive commentary out of the writings where the reader could determine for oneself whether the dryness is good or bad, great or insignificant.

In the tenth chapter of *The Spiritual Guide* (the latter part of chapter 5 in Wesley's version), Molinos described the purifying nature of temptation as the "Furnace of terrible and grievous Temptation."[34] Wesley preserved this overall concept; however, he removed the wording "terrible and grievous."[35] This may be due to the redundancy of stating that temptation is terrible and grievous as this goes without saying.

32. Wesley, *Christian Library* (Molinos), 38:250.

33. Molinos, *Spiritual Guide*, 14; Wesley, *Christian Library* (Molinos), 38:255.

34. Molinos, *Spiritual Guide*, 28.

35. Wesley, *Christian Library* (Molinos), 38:261.

Similarly, in that same chapter, Molinos explained that saints arrive at holiness by enduring a "doleful valley of temptation" and that there is a direct correlation between the level of sainthood and the depth of temptations endured.[36] Wesley kept Molinos's description of this association, but simply removed the word *doleful*.[37] Again, this was likely due to the repetitive nature of the adjective as valleys of temptation are indeed doleful.

Wesley not only removed the adjectives that Molinos used to add emphasis to the negative experiences, but Wesley also eliminated the words which made the positive things more emphatic. For example, Wesley removed the word *great* connected with the happiness of a soul subdued as described by Molinos.[38] Likewise, where Molinos described the state of the "servants of God" who passed through tribulation, Wesley edited out the word *sweet* where *valiant* and *constant* were already used.[39] He also left out the word *sweet* in relation to the "weight of [God's] loving presence."[40] Though other examples exist, these serve as a sampling of the way in which Wesley dealt with redundant adjectives.

Wesley's practice of editing consisted mostly of the removal of words or phrases; however, on occasion he did change the wording. He did this about sixteen times to the writing of Molinos. An example of this may be found where Molinos described how the ability to triumph to find victory over the enemies and trials is found "within thine own soul" through "Divine aid and Sovereign Succour."[41] In Wesley's edition, he changed the word "succour" to "strength."[42] Wesley did not stress that God gives relief from such difficulties; rather his emphasis was on God's ability to provide strength for his people to stand up under such trials.

Later in the next chapter, Molinos described how spiritual advancement—which include nearness to God and understanding "Divine Doctrines"—happens through "Darkness and Dryness" over and above one's own effort. Wesley changed the outcome of understanding "Divine Doctrines" to understanding "Divine Teachings."[43] This was likely due to a perspective that, to Wesley, the doctrines are necessary to salvific belief whereas understanding the broader teachings from God is an ongoing outcome of

---

36. Molinos, *Spiritual Guide*, 29.

37. Wesley, *Christian Library* (Molinos), 38:262.

38. Wesley, *Christian Library* (Molinos), 38:123.

39. Wesley, *Christian Library* (Molinos), 38:126.

40. Molinos, *Spiritual Guide*, 135; Wesley, *Christian Library* (Molinos), 38:278.

41. Molinos, *Spiritual Guide*, 2.

42. Wesley, *Christian Library* (Molinos), 38:250.

43. Molinos, *Spiritual Guide*, 6; Wesley, *Christian Library* (Molinos), 38:252.

spiritual progress. Many other such examples exist, like the way Wesley changed the word *sentiment/s* to *joy* three times.[44] However, as noted, these alterations remain relatively inconsequential, so they are not addressed exhaustively in this thesis.

THESIS STRUCTURE

After determining the alterations which Wesley made to the writings of Ávila and Molinos, the changes were categorized by theme. These themes determined the breakdown of the chapters. The chapters were then arranged based on the overall order of spiritual progression as described by the authors. Each chapter follows the same format, beginning with an introductory summation, then following with a look at Ávila's perspective on the theme, Wesley's editing of Ávila, Molinos's perspective, and Wesley's editing of Molinos. Each chapter then concludes by analyzing Wesley's views on the respective topic and addressing the potential reasons for Wesley's alterations followed by a comparative summation. When quoting from the seventeenth-century texts, original spellings and punctuation were preserved to highlight Wesley's editing without belaboring the inconsequential details.

---

44. Wesley, *Christian Library* (Molinos), 38:254, 255, 264.

1

Theological Authority

CHRISTIANITY MAY BE VIEWED analogically as a tree with its many branches representing the various denominations, traditions, and expressions that have emerged over time. In the field of historical theology, the emphasis can easily remain on that which is above the surface while taking each branch individually and focusing on that which grows, or has grown, out of that particular branch. However, there also exists that which rests beneath the surface—the root system with its many tendrils drawing from multiple sources to nourish the branches. For every branch, there are multiple roots that actively form and inform the development of the branch. As this thesis examines the theology of John Wesley as seen in his interaction with the Spanish mystics Juan de Ávila and Miguel de Molinos, this chapter explores the authoritative roots from which the latter two drew in the development of their respective perspectives. Additionally, Wesley's reactions to their writings pertaining to theological authority, as well as some of the various roots from which Wesley drew to form his own doctrinal perspectives, will be explored.

JUAN DE ÁVILA ON THEOLOGICAL AUTHORITY

Juan de Ávila adhered closely to the standard Catholic doctrine and practice of his time on many issues, and particularly on his perspectives of theological authority. It is clear in his writings that Ávila found high value in the biblical text and called upon it as an authoritative voice. Likewise, he also quoted frequently from those whom the church had deemed as worthy of the title of saint as another voice of authority to the doctrines about which he wrote. Through his involvement in the Council of Trent, his editorial alterations to his own writings which clarified his teachings to the inquisition, his increasingly intentional rejection of Lutheranism over time, and the reasons laid out below, he demonstrated his respect for the authoritative position of the Roman Catholic Church and the papacy.

Scripture

Juan de Ávila held in high esteem the role of the Bible in faith and deeds. This can be seen in many ways, not least of which was demonstrated in the way he based the structure of his entire treatise *Audi Filia* on Ps 45:10–11, "Listen, O daughter, incline your ear and see; forget your people and your father's house, and the king will desire your beauty." In a general sense, he took an allegorical approach to its application, seeing the passage not as a love poem for a wedding, but as a call for the church to love God in this fashion. Juan did not write the book as a commentary on the text per se; rather he used the various clauses as section headings and expounded upon the verbs as they relate to one's relationship with God. For example, in his first section, "Listen, O Daughter," Juan wrote forty-four chapters about how to listen to God and to hear his voice. Taking an apophatic approach, Juan began by discussing the voices to which one should *not* listen, i.e., languages of the world, the flesh, and the devil. From there, he described how one ought to listen to God with faith being the primary means through which listening may occur.

Not only did Juan structure his book around a passage of the Bible, but he made multiple quotes, allusions, and references to the biblical text—the writings of Paul in particular. He also spoke of the great gift of the Scriptures while warning against those who interpret the Scriptures by "the winds of the earth (their own talents and studies)."[1] All this demonstrates Juan's high view of the Bible as an authoritative voice for faith. However, Juan wrote severely against the *sola scriptura* approach of his contemporary Martin Luther. In the *Audi Filia*, Juan stated, "You should be aware that the exposition of divine scripture is not to be done according to the mind or ingenuity of each person." He later continued stating, "Only the Catholic Church has the privilege of interpreting and understanding the divine scripture, because the same Holy Spirit who spoke in the scripture dwells in her."[2]

---

1. Ávila, *Audi, Filia* (Gormley), 153.
2. Ávila, *Audi, Filia* (Gormley), 147.

Church

Juan de Ávila saw the church as the authoritative voice of doctrine. This may be seen most notably in the way in which he became more vocal about his disdain for Martin Luther, even though Juan embraced a strong emphasis on faith as the entry point into one's relationship with God, perhaps even influenced by the early writings of Luther. Later, however, as the church condemned the writings and person of Luther, Ávila began to take on a not so favorable view on the reformer. In his *Audi Filia*, he condemned the followers of Luther as being *engañados*, or *deceived*, and to Luther himself as a *mal hombre*, or *bad man*, or even "evil man" as translated by Gormley.[3] A few chapters later, he referred to Luther's teachings as heresy and to Luther himself as *perverso*, or *perverse*, for which Gormley opted to use the word *wicked*, and described him on the same level as Mohammed.[4] This growing animosity toward Luther and his students shows his loyalty to the authoritative role of the church in the formulation and continuance of doctrine.

Saints

Though Ávila did not necessarily make statements concerning the role of saints in the formulation of doctrine or regarding their authority to shape belief, he modeled what it looks like to give the saints of old a place of authoritative prominence through his many quotes, references, and allusions to their works. Perhaps the most potent place where this may be observed is found in his discussion on the need to seek spiritual counsel from others, laid out in his *Audi Filia*. In just a few short paragraphs he quoted from and/or referenced the works of Augustine, John Climacus, Jerome, Vincent, Bernard, Bonaventure, as well as many biblical texts.[5] In doing so, he placed the claims of these saints at or near the same level of authority as the biblical writers. Elsewhere and throughout his *Audi Filia*, he continued to quote from these authors as well as the Saints Catherine of Sienna, Origen, Richard of St. Victor, John Chrysostom, Gregory, Dominic, Francis, Basil, Athanasius, Anthony, and Ambrose.

---

3. Ávila, *Audi Filia*—Spanish, capítulo 46; Ávila, *Audi, Filia* (Gormley), 148–49.
4. Ávila, *Audi Filia*—Spanish, capítulo 49; Ávila, *Audi, Filia* (Gormley), 155.
5. Ávila, *Audi, Filia* (Gormley), 166.

JOHN WESLEY'S EDITING OF ÁVILA ON THEOLOGICAL AUTHORITY

Scripture Quotes

Although John Wesley was well read in many subjects, especially divinity, his view of the Bible was so strong that in the preface to his sermons, he claimed his desire to be *"homo unius libri"*—"a man of one book."[6] Given such a view on the authority of Scripture, it is interesting that he removed so many Scripture quotes, references, and allusions from the writings of Ávila. In fact, there were twenty-four such references edited out of these letters. Some were removed for more obvious reasons. For example, Bible passages quoted or alluded to from the so-called apocrypha were predictably left out of Wesley's publication. This is seen in Wesley's editing out of the Tobias quote in the ninth epistle stating, "What joy cann I have in this life, since I cannot see the light of heaven."[7] He also removed two references to Ecclesiasticus or Sirach. The first of these references was found toward the end of the ninth epistle where he quoted, "There is no profitt in such sadness"; the second appeared in the fifteenth letter stating, "By that which is in thy selfe, thou shalt come to know that which is in they neighbour."[8] Wesley did, however, preserve one quote from Ecclesiasticus, also found in Ávila's fifteenth letter claiming that "the soule is as changeable as the moone."[9] Wesley may have felt liberty to maintain this quote because it is not referenced, although it is labeled with the term *Scripture*, and it would align with Wesley's perspective of the un-regenerated soul.

Secondly, Wesley seems to have eliminated any Scriptures where Ávila applied allegorical or typological interpretation. At least seven such cases exist. The first such reference may be found in the seventh letter where Ávila described that when Jesus "placed him selfe in the midst of them," that is, when he appeared to his disciples after his resurrection as found in Luke 24, it was to show that "he is in the midst of us" in the present.[10]

In Ávila's ninth epistle, he alluded to Jesus' teaching on prayer found in the eleventh chapter of Luke, specifically verses five through eight where Jesus gave the example of a friend who goes to the home of another friend asking for bread because of an unexpected visitor. In the letter, Ávila provided

---

6. Wesley, *Works* (Outler), 1:105.

7. Ávila, *Selected Epistles*, 68.

8. Ávila, *Selected Epistles*, 72, 115.

9. Ávila, *Selected Epistles*, 113.

10. Ávila, *Selected Epistles*, 51.

a typological analysis of this text by equating the neighbor to "God made man." Wesley omitted this portion of the paragraph.[11]

As Ávila described the benefits given from God, he urged his reader to find safety and security in these benefits. In order to support this idea of safety, he offered an allegorical interpretation of Jacob placing the "wife and those children whom he least loved" at the front of his company in order to keep everyone else safe.[12] Wesley maintained much of the description of benefits but removed the allegorical reference to Jacob.

In a letter to a great lord, Ávila began by quoting Augustine as saying, "Grant to mee, O Lord, that I may know thee, & that I may know my selfe"; he proceeded to describe how Solomon's Temple had two parts, the lesser holy, through which one arrives at the holy of holies.[13] He then explained typologically how the lesser holy part is self-knowledge and the holy of holies is knowledge of God. Wesley kept the quote from Augustine showing that he did not have issue linking knowledge of God with knowledge of self. However, Wesley removed the entire remainder of the paragraph that pertained to the typological understanding of the temple. So, this was most likely not an issue of theme or content as it was an issue of hermeneutics.

Later in that same letter, Wesley removed a description from the book of Mark concerning a young boy, brought to Jesus by his father, who was prone to being thrown into a fire or into water by an evil spirit. Ávila continued, stating that "the same happens to us. Sometimes wee fall into the fire of covetousness, of wrath, & of envy, at other tymes into the water of carnality, of tepidity, and of malice."[14] This entire portion did not find its way into Wesley's version. Again, this is likely due to the allegorical approach taken by the Apostle of Andalusia.

As this letter continued, Wesley removed a lengthy portion of the epistle. Two entire pages, to be precise. These two pages primarily consisted of Bible passages followed by Ávila's commentary.[15] In each, Ávila applied a Platonic reading of the texts, seeing allegory, typology, and analogy in the words of Scripture. On these pages, Ávila used Mount Hermon and the other hills mentioned in the Old Testament typologically as representing Mount Calvary. This connection was made by stating that the former was the place where the Law was given; the latter was the place where law-breakers were executed. He then continued to support this typological approach

11. Ávila, *Selected Epistles*, 64–65.

12. Ávila, *Selected Epistles*, 97.

13. Ávila, *Selected Epistles*, 107.

14. Ávila, *Selected Epistles*, 113.

15. Ávila, *Selected Epistles*, 119–20.

by quoting from Gal 3, stating, "Christ was made malediction that so his benediction might be communicated to the Gentiles."[16]

Ávila described a sorrow for sin that leads to cleansing or repentance—to which Wesley altered the wording. Wesley preserved this discourse; however, he removed Ávila's statement that "this we are taught by holy Scripture, which relates how Hester kissed the end of Assuerus rod."[17] Again, this was another removal of an allegorical interpretation of the biblical text.

Wesley also used such scrutiny in editing Ávila's interpretations of the seventh chapter of Matthew. Wesley removed a portion from the twenty-first letter of Ávila that interpreted portions of Matthew chapter 7 allegorically. To the Spanish mystic, the path "which he calls streight, and saith, that it leades men to life" is the path of suffering. He continued to urge his reader to have such a mind to be with Christ in such suffering. Wesley did not remove Ávila's statements about the role of suffering, but he did eliminate the use of this passage to support such views. Elsewhere, in Ávila's fifteenth letter, Wesley preserved the reference to the seventh chapter of Matthew stating, "Let noe man thinke, that Christ our Lord, will *measure to us with any other measure then what we measure to others.*"[18] Ávila continued with a straightforward interpretation and application of this text which Wesley kept in his reprinting of the letter. However, on the next page, Ávila once again quoted this passage with a lengthy explanation which Wesley deleted. Where the former had a straightforward and literal interpretation of the text, the latter shifted to implications of wantonness to others and to God that move beyond the text.

There also exist numerous biblical references which Wesley removed, seemingly for the reason of context. There are some passages eliminated from their scriptural context while others do not necessarily support the point being made by Ávila in his letters. The former takes the quote out of its original context, while the latter places the biblical text in a context in which it does not fit. In addition, Wesley also removed some Scripture references where the wording may have been different enough from his understanding, or where Ávila's interpretation differed from that of Wesley. In these latter cases, Wesley deleted the quote from the Bible along with the accompanying interpretation laid out by Ávila.

One such reference omitted by Wesley pertaining to context may be found in Ávila's third letter. In it, he called for the removal of all impediments, a composing of heart, and an expectation of Christ's comforting

16. Ávila, *Selected Epistles*, 120.

17. Ávila, *Selected Epistles*, 188.

18. Ávila, *Selected Epistles*, 116.

presence. In order to support this exhortation, he referenced the Psalms, saying, "For David saith of him, Our Lord heard the desire of the poore, and his eares harkened to the preparation of his hart."[19] This passage contextually pertained to David; it was not an overarching command. Ávila did not develop this broader connection but stated it in such a way as to seem obvious to readers. Wesley's careful removal of this text may indicate a disagreement with its usage.

There appear two passages from the Bible to which Ávila referenced in his ninth letter which Wesley removed, also likely for reasons of context. The first appears within a paragraph where Ávila offered comfort to his reader for her ill health. He alluded to God not reaping where he does not sow, implying that God was the source or giver of her affliction. Wesley preserved Ávila's pastoral words of comfort but edited out any reference to God being the cause. This is also found later in the paragraph where Wesley removed the words "God chastises us now for the thing which wee inordinately desired before."[20]

The second removal of Scripture based, perhaps, on context may be found a couple of pages later. This paragraph continues the theme of suffering, specifically about remaining faithful to God in the midst of suffering. Ávila described the comfort one receives from remaining faithful in trials. Because of this comfort, according to Ávila, one may live in hope and be assured that the outcome will be enjoying "our beloved." He then supported this assertion by quoting from Paul's statement in the fifth chapter of Romans, saying, "Patience breedes hope."[21] In some ways, it is a bit perplexing as to why Wesley removed this biblical reference. The context found in Romans chapter 5 is directly connected with facing trials. However, the broader context deals with justification by faith. Ávila's use of the text seems to indicate that hope is found in the comfort received in tribulation. Whereas to Wesley, the hope is found in justification.

Ávila described in his thirteenth epistle the process people go through when God gives them "both the knowledge of their sinnes; and of his divine love."[22] Wesley preserved most of this description, removing a few shorter statements related to a hardness of heart. However, he also removed a sentence which described rich people as "being killed with hunger" along with its accompanying quote from Luke 16 stating that the righteous man "was

19. Ávila, *Selected Epistles*, 24.

20. Ávila, *Selected Epistles*, 68–69.

21. Ávila, *Selected Epistles*, 71.

22. Ávila, *Selected Epistles*, 93.

afflicted with thirst."[23] Two matters that emerge here of which Wesley may have taken issue were the idea of hunger being a divine punishment and the quote referring to Jesus' thirst on the cross being linked to a punishment of others.

Two other Scriptures which Wesley removed based on context may be found in Ávila's fifteenth letter. Two biblical texts which appear within the same paragraph were removed while the surrounding context was preserved. In both cases, Ávila discussed one's relationship to "Christ our Lord" and then supported it with an Old Testament quote. The first discussed how one who goes to Christ "for the cure of his inconstancy, shall obtaine a perseverance," then referenced Anna, Samuel's mother, as an example as found in the opening chapter of First Kings. The second referenced how one "who dwells in Christ our Lord, doth not wander hither and tither but stands fast in goodness," which he then followed with a quote from Ecclesiasticus stating "that such a one is ever clean like the sunne; and that his light is not diminished."[24] In both cases, a relationship to Christ is supported with an example referencing a specific person in the case of the former, and a group of people in the case of the latter, who existed prior to the incarnation. Thus, the biblical texts may not have been the best support to the point Ávila was making.

Issues of differing wording of the biblical text may be observed in the twelfth letter of Ávila where he quoted from the first chapter of Nahum as stating "that God doth not punish a man for the same thing twice."[25] Wesley edited out this text while preserving the surrounding instructions. However, other translations from Wesley's time tended to use the word *affliction* instead of the idea of punishment (i.e., King James Version, 1611). This may have been enough of a variation for Wesley to delete the reference.

Another alteration of a biblical text may be seen in Ávila's use of 2 Pet 2:21 in his thirteenth letter.[26] Wesley did not remove this quote, but he did alter it by removing two phrases. These two phrases were not found in the biblical text, but did appear in the original English translation of Ávila's letter. Therefore, Wesley's editing brought the quote more in line with the Scripture.

An example of differing interpretation may be noted in the beginning of Ávila's thirteenth letter. Here, Ávila quoted from Job's longing to have

23. Ávila, *Selected Epistles*, 94.

24. Ávila, *Selected Epistles*, 124.

25. Ávila, *Selected Epistles*, 88.

26. Ávila, *Selected Epistles*, 92.

things as they were in his youth.[27] Ávila then proceeded to describe how this referred to a deep communication with God that Job must have had in earlier days.[28] Wesley omitted both the biblical text and the accompanying interpretive description.

In Ávila's fifteenth epistle, he described a process of applying self-awareness to the way in which one treats one's neighbor. For example, knowing what hurts or offends oneself allows a person to be aware of that which may hurt or offend another and to make the appropriate behavioral changes so as not to hurt or offend another. In support of this relational approach, he then quoted from or referenced the fifth chapter of Matthew stating that "the mercifull, shall obtaine mercie," then from the twenty-first chapter of Proverbs pointing out that "he whoe shutts his eare against the vow of the poore, that man shall cry out, and not be heard."[29] Wesley eliminated these Scripture references, likely not because of the passages themselves, but because of the preceding sentence. Along with these biblical texts, Wesley eliminated the statement that "he who practises this point of mercy with his neighbour; may safely passe on to the knowledge of Christ our Lord."[30] Although Wesley strongly elevated the role of works as a necessary expression of faith, works do not produce knowledge of Christ. Rather, to Wesley knowledge of the Divine comes through revelation, the inner witness of the Holy Spirit, and attending to the means of grace, as will be explored in a later chapter.

In a letter to some friends who were going through persecution, Ávila encouraged his readers not to allow "the menaces of them who threaten you, breede you any trouble"; he then continued to explain how he knew what they were facing because he had preached the gospel in that town. In describing the persecutors, Ávila referenced 2 Corinthians chapter 4, stating, "The God of this world, which is the devil, did blinde the soules of the Infidells; to the end that the glory of the gospell, might not shine upon them."[31] Wesley preserved the paragraph but eliminated this Bible reference. At first glance, the context within Ávila's letter seems to align with the meaning of the Pauline quote. However, to Wesley, this passage seems to refer more to the understanding and lack of belief than the source of persecution.

27. See Job 29.
28. Ávila, *Selected Epistles*, 91.
29. Ávila, *Selected Epistles*, 116.
30. Ávila, *Selected Epistles*, 116.
31. Ávila, *Selected Epistles*, 178.

In his *Explanatory Notes on the New Testament*, Wesley summarized this blinding as "not only veiled, the eye of their understanding."[32]

Mary and the Saints

Although within the letters of Juan de Ávila which Wesley kept in the *Christian Library* there is little mention of Mary, Wesley carefully removed the few statements that perhaps aligned too far, in his perspective, with Catholic Marian doctrines. For example, when Ávila reflected upon the blows which Christ received, he stated that these blows also had their effect upon "the most Blessed virgin" whom he also referred to as "that other second stone of heaven."[33] Wesley eliminated these statements, leaving the focus here solely on Christ. Elsewhere, Ávila offered a prayer for open eyes to consider Christ "descending out of the bosome of thy Father; and entering into that of thy virgin mother."[34] Wesley ended the sentence with Christ "descending out of the bosom of thy Father," while leaving off the portion about entering the virgin mother.[35] Finally, and most significantly, Wesley omitted altogether a lengthy statement highly exalting Mary made by Ávila where he stated:

> What a day will that be, when that true Mary, the virgin of virgins, shall go before with her Timbrell, which is her sacred body, praying God both in body and soule and singing thus, *come magnifye our Lord with mee, and let us exalt his name in mutuall sacieting with one another.*[36]

In some regards, it is interesting that Wesley edited out these references to Mary as they do not make any direct statements concerning the Roman Catholic doctrines with which Protestants might disagree. For example, in these statements Ávila did not make claim to the perpetual virginity of Mary, her immaculate conception, or her sinlessness, or other dogmas which Wesley deemed inaccurate, as will be discussed later.

Wesley also did some significant editing around Ávila's quoting of other saints of the church. Four times where Ávila quoted from some of the saints, Wesley preserved the quote but removed the name of the person who stated it. Although keeping the quotes, Wesley eliminated Gregory's name altogether. For example, in Ávila's first letter, Wesley preserved the quote

32. Wesley, "Notes on St. Paul's Second Epistle," ch. 4.

33. Ávila, *Selected Epistles*, 87.

34. Ávila, *Selected Epistles*, 138.

35. Wesley, *Christian Library* (Ávila), 46:300.

36. Ávila, *Selected Epistles*, 348.

"Noe man feeles the weight of dihonour, but he who loves his owne honour," yet eliminated the words preceding, "for as S. Gregory saith."[37] He did the same with another quote by Gregory in Ávila's eighth epistle.[38]

Where Wesley completely removed Gregory's name, he was selective in the use of Bernard. In the thirteenth epistle of Ávila, Wesley completely eliminated one quote from Bernard, yet later preserved a smaller quote, but removed Bernard's name; thus not giving credit to the one from whom the quote came.[39] However, in the ninth epistle, Wesley maintained the quote and credit to Bernard concerning the unnecessity of hell conditioned to the ceasing of "our proper will."[40]

In Ávila's twelfth letter, Wesley maintained a statement from Ignatius, kept the attachment of Ignatius's name to it, but removed the description of Ignatius stating "this saith that Saint, as one who knew well and did much love our lord Jesus Christ; and who saw that all was well employed, which could be disbursed for the gaying of him."[41]

At the end of a letter to one who has grown cold in virtue, Ávila concludes with a list of recommended books. These include "*Confessions*, and *Meditations* of S. Augustine; *The Moralls* of S. Gregory; the *Summe of the mysteries of our faith* by Titileman, and Dionisius Carthusian."[42] Although like Ávila, Wesley was not shy about recommending a good book, as demonstrated through the publishing of his *Christian Library*, he did omit this list.

Ávila addressed the recipient of his forty-fifth epistle to trust the word of Christ, assuring her that Christ's word was trustworthy as demonstrated through "S. Katherine, S. Agnes, S. Barbara, and S. Lucy, and to innumerable other Lady virgins."[43] Wesley, however, reduced this list down to state "innumerable others."[44] Wesley did not seem to hesitate, however, in keeping intact the three quotes from Augustine along with the attachment of his name to the statements.[45]

---

37. Ávila, *Selected Epistles*, 7.

38. Ávila, *Selected Epistles*, 57.

39. Ávila, *Selected Epistles*, 95.

40. Ávila, *Selected Epistles*, 66.

41. Ávila, *Selected Epistles*, 89.

42. Ávila, *Selected Epistles*, 98.

43. Ávila, *Selected Epistles*, 348.

44. Wesley, *Christian Library* (Ávila), 46:325.

45. Ávila, *Selected Epistles*, 65, 67, 107.

MIGUEL DE MOLINOS ON THEOLOGICAL AUTHORITY

Since Molinos did not write as a systematic theologian, he did not lay out his ecclesiology or sources of spiritual authority in an orderly manner. However, by observing his practice of biblical hermeneutics and quotations from the saints, it remains rather clear that Molinos held to an equal or near to equal place of authority for Scripture and the tradition of the saints. Interestingly, however, he was not as quick to refer to the authority of the church, church councils, or the pope as were Ávila or many of his contemporaries.

In reading the *Spiritual Guide*, it doesn't take long to see that Miguel de Molinos was relatively well read in Roman Catholic and broader Christian traditions. His introductory words lay the groundwork of *apologia* for the work to follow. In defense of his teachings, Molinos quoted broadly accepted authoritative voices of saints that preceded him, arguing that his teachings were well in line with theirs. To create an exhaustive list and dialogue concerning these hagiographical influences would deter from the task at hand but referencing some key examples will help to understand the unfolding theological perspectives of this controversial Quietist.

In his introductory notes to the reader, Molinos laid out his argument. The first spiritual authority whom he quoted was the apostle Paul. In doing so, he offered a biting critique of his attackers while aligning his own teachings with the biblical witness. He argued that those who condemned the spiritual matters of which he wrote were functioning out of their "animal man" and ran the risk of condemning themselves.[46] He immediately followed this with a reference to Pseudo-Dionysius—often referred to as the founder of the Christian mystical tradition—asserting that these men are not granted wisdom from God.

From there, Molinos continued by claiming that his teachings were in agreement with such greats as Teresa of Ávila, Augustine, Gregory, Bernard of Clairvaux, Thomas Aquinas, and Bonaventure.[47] The most frequently quoted include Thomas Aquinas and Teresa of Ávila, followed by Bernard of Clairvaux and Francis de Sales, then Augustine and Gregory. Bernard McGinn pointed out that in addition to these spiritual authorities, he also quoted from and referenced Francis of Assisi, Jean Gerson, Peter Alcantara, Jane de Chantal, Juan Falconi, Gregorio Lopez, and many others who covered the gamut of older, recent, and contemporary writers.[48] Not least among these was John of the Cross, whose perspectives on meditation and

---

46. Molinos, *Spiritual Guide* (Baird and McGinn), 51.

47. Molinos, *Spiritual Guide* (Baird and McGinn), 52.

48. Molinos, *Spiritual Guide* (Baird and McGinn), 28–29.

contemplation along with the role of suffering, or *dark night* experiences, seem to echo throughout the pages of the *Spiritual Guide*. He was also quick to turn to Catherine of Sienna, Dominic, Ignatius, and Chrysostom as writers of spiritual authority. When not quoting directly, Molinos set various people up as examples to follow, like John Tauler and Henry Suso, for example.[49]

With Molinos's strong affirmation of mystical theology, it is interesting that his citing of Pseudo-Dionysius is relegated to his opening defense, but then tapers off throughout the remainder of his corpus, whereas the references to Thomas Aquinas and Teresa of Ávila carry throughout his three books. That being said, even among those from whom he quoted with relative frequency, all such secondary sources seem to fall away midway through the third book as he stuck more closely to the development of his own theological perspective. The exception to this is his occasional biblical quotes and allusions which carry all the way to the end of his treatise.

The allegorical interpretation of Scripture was an acceptable Christian practice going back to Origen in the Greek-speaking world and later Ambrose in the Latin-speaking portion of the church, both who applied the four-fold levels of understanding a text as used in classical critical approaches to literature which included the literal, moral, allegorical, and anagogical interpretations.[50] Like Ávila, Molinos was apt to apply this hermeneutical approach. Although, Molinos did not seem to do this as frequently as Ávila as reflected in the smaller number of editorial changes made by Wesley in their respective texts. However, this may be due to Molinos's less frequent use of Scripture overall compared to Ávila.

JOHN WESLEY'S EDITING OF MOLINOS ON THEOLOGICAL AUTHORITY

Use of Scripture

Wesley did not make too many alterations to the writings of Molinos regarding the use of Scripture, just five in all, but some do point to significant differences in the theology and/or hermeneutical practices between Wesley and Molinos. As was his practice with the writings of Juan de Ávila, Wesley removed Scripture passages that pointed to an allegorical interpretation. Although a long-standing practice, Wesley disagreed with this hermeneutical approach. This led him to eliminate the phrase in which Molinos used

49. Molinos, *Spiritual Guide* (Baird and McGinn), 103–4, 132.
50. Colish, *Medieval Foundations*, 19.

the imagery of Jonah being cast into the sea as an opportunity to urge his readers to "cast the Jonas of sence into the sea" as a means of purification.[51] Similarly, Wesley also removed the text where Molinos encouraged people to "imitate the Woman of Canaan, who being rejected and injured, did importune and persevere."[52]

Wesley also removed the quote from 1 John 3:18 where Molinos argued for a love with few words. Wesley preserved the call to this type of love but eliminated the Scripture that Molinos used to support the argument.[53] This may have been done to remove scriptural support of Quietism, or perhaps to deemphasize the role of deeds.

There were a couple of places where Wesley preserved the Scripture texts used by Molinos but altered the use of references. In one place, Wesley added a reference that Molinos neglected to include.[54] Elsewhere, Wesley changed the reference from Matt 24:26 to Luke 9:23 in order to correct an inaccurate reference used by Molinos in connection with a biblical quote.[55]

Catholic Language

Similar to his editing of Ávila, Wesley removed language that would hint at some of the differences held by Roman Catholics of his time. Many of these alterations of Molinos and Ávila included certain references to some of the saints and Mary. For example, Wesley removed three quotes attributed to St. Teresa of Ávila. Following a description of the spiritual attacks that ensue in order to disquiet the soul, Molinos gave a three-paragraph description of how Teresa affirmed what he had just described.[56] Interestingly, Wesley preserved the description given by Molinos, but completely eliminated the three paragraphs pertaining to Teresa with the exception of one sentence.[57] Perhaps, Wesley saw this as redundancy and simply let Molinos's description stand alone without requiring the reinforcement of the saint, or perhaps it was a direct issue Wesley had with Teresa. The former reason may be supported by Wesley's similar views on spiritual attack as found in his sermon "Satan's Devices."[58] The latter may be the case as Wesley also removed other

51. Molinos, *Spiritual Guide*, 13.

52. Molinos, *Spiritual Guide*, 134.

53. Molinos, *Spiritual Guide*, 57.

54. Wesley, *Christian Library* (Molinos), 38:252.

55. Wesley, *Christian Library* (Molinos), 38:272.

56. Molinos, *Spiritual Guide*, 33–34.

57. Wesley, *Christian Library* (Molinos), 38:264.

58. Wesley, *Works* (Outler), 2:138–51.

quotes attributed to Teresa used in later chapters by Molinos. One of the latter quotes may have been removed by Wesley perhaps because of who wrote it, Teresa, or perhaps because of the content which called for a repose in this life—the concept of which Wesley rejected. The third quote consisted of a two-paragraph description of Teresa appearing to someone after her death instructing the person about suffering in quiet and resignation and the ensuing rewards that would follow.[59] The removal of such a quote was likely due to the theological content.

Elsewhere, Wesley preserved the summary of Francesca Lopez's perspective on internal recollection but removed the descriptions of her as "the Venerable Mother" and "a religious of the Third Order of St. Francis."[60] This alteration indicates that Wesley was not opposed to Lopez or her thoughts, necessarily. Rather, this likely points to Wesley's issue with the veneration of people and certain aspects of polity in the Catholic church. That being said, Wesley's issue was not a broad rejection of Catholic saints, as he preserved the quotations of so many of them. This is also demonstrated in his preservation of a reference to Bernard of Clairvaux pertaining to the place of suffering evil and doing good in service to God.[61]

In reflecting upon people in the midst of difficulties, Molinos warned of the problems that may ensue if such people consult an inexperienced confessor. Wesley maintained this caution; however, he changed the word *confessor* to *pastor*. This is likely due to his position on the role of confession.

JOHN WESLEY ON THEOLOGICAL AUTHORITY

The Quadrilateral and Its Problems

From the time of the earliest *Book of Common Prayer*, the text setting forth the liturgy for the Church of England, a three-fold foundation for doctrine was followed including Scripture, tradition, and reason. As a priest in the Church of England, John Wesley drew from this triad in the development of his own theological beliefs. However, as someone who was influenced by the Reformation writings of Martin Luther, he also placed a higher value on the role of Scripture, if not holding to a *sola scriptura* approach to doctrine. As stated earlier, in his introduction to his *Standard Sermons*, published in 1746, he proclaimed that he wanted to be "*homo unius libri*," a "man of one

---

59. Molinos, *Spiritual Guide*, 134–35.

60. Wesley, *Christian Library* (Molinos), 38:265.

61. Wesley, *Christian Library* (Molinos), 38:272.

book" regarding the Bible.[62] In a letter to John Newton, he stated that "the Bible is my standard of language as well as sentiment."[63]

In his preface to a publication containing some of Wesley's writings, Albert Outler described Wesley's theological development as drawing from Scriptures and Patristics in "a theological fusion of faith and good works, Scripture and tradition, revelation and reason" in what he referred to as "evangelical catholicism."[64] In time, Outler established his understanding of Wesley's doctrinal development by adding *experience* to the *Book of Common Prayer* triad of Scripture, tradition, and reason, coining the term *Wesleyan Quadrilateral*. Robert Wall attributed Wesley's Oxford training in Aristotelian empiricism along with his affirmation of John Locke's empiricism to his affirmation of experience, properly scrutinized.[65]

Outler's approach to the quadrilateral later came under scrutiny however, and Outler himself later lamented his use of the quadrilateral, citing the overemphasis on experience that emerged as a point of contention. This quadrilateral may be relatively helpful in understanding some of Wesley's hermeneutical approach; however, it must not be separated from the Lutheran influence which elevated the place of Scripture. More accurately stated, Wesley's approach to theological authority begins with the Bible as understood throughout history, following a logical reading and plain interpretation, and informed by experiential revelation.

The Bible

In a chapter on "Wesley as biblical interpreter" in *The Cambridge Companion to John Wesley*, Robert Wall pointed out that "Wesley never wrote a treatise or preached a sermon on the doctrine of Scripture" due to the largely assumed authority of the Bible held at the time.[66] Wall's point is well made that Wesley did not produce a systematic theology regarding the inspiration of Scripture, or any other doctrine pertaining to doctrines of Scripture. However, the word *never* is not quite accurate as Wesley did produce a brief one-page argument for his belief in the divine inspiration of the Bible titled *A Clear and Concise Demonstration of the Divine Inspiration of Holy Scriptures*. In his treatise, he offered four components to an argument for divine inspiration: "miracles, prophecies, the goodness of the doctrine, and

62. Wesley, *Works* (Outler), 1:105.

63. Maddox and Vickers, *Cambridge Companion to Wesley*, 114.

64. Wesley, *John Wesley* (Outler), iv.

65. Maddox and Vickers, *Cambridge Companion to Wesley*, 115.

66. Maddox and Vickers, *Cambridge Companion to Wesley*, 113.

thc moral charactcr of thc penmen," as all four of these originate in divine action.[67] He then proceeded to state a very brief three-fold logical analysis that led him to his conclusion, as follows in its entirety:

> The Bible must be the invention either of good men or angels, bad men or devils, or of God. 1. It could not be the invention of good men or angels; nor they neither would nor could make a book, and tell lies all the time they were writing it, saying, "Thus saith the Lord," when it was their own invention. 2. It could not be the invention of bad men or devils; for they would not make a book which commands all duty, forbids all sin, and condemns their souls to hell to all eternity. 3. Therefore, I draw this conclusion, that the Bible must be given by divine inspiration.[68]

Although Wesley's treatises on a doctrine of inspiration were seriously limited, likely to this one-page example, his hermeneutical style and philosophy may be observed through his sermons, notes on the Bible, and the occasional statements made in his letters and journal. Wesley sought to communicate "plain truth for plain people" and often rejected Plato's approach to reading sacred texts as including the plain understanding, allegorical interpretation, and spiritual level meaning.[69] For example, regarding allegorical interpretation of the Bible, in his treatise *The Advantage of the Members of the Church of England, Over Those of the Church of Rome,* Wesley stated concerning those in the Roman Catholic Church:

> That their souls are not edified by sermons and catechizing out of the word of God, the Scriptures being cited very sparingly in their sermons, and generally in a strained and allegorical sense: That they are not permitted to search the Scriptures at home, and seek food for their souls therein: That the common people are by this means purposely kept in the grossest ignorance and superstition.[70]

He criticized allegorical interpretation, and called for the "naked Bible," or a direct interpretation of the plain text, as he stated in the preface of his *Explanatory Notes upon the Old Testament.*[71]

In his preface to the *Standard Sermons,* Wesley laid out a simple outline of biblical hermeneutics beginning with the plain reading, then if

67. Wesley, *Works* (Jackson), 11:484.

68. Wesley, *Works* (Jackson), 11:484.

69. Wesley, *Works* (Outler), 1:104.

70. Wesley, *Works* (Jackson), 10:137.

71. See Wesley, "Preface to the Old Testament Notes."

doubts arose, he turned to prayer for wisdom, followed by consulting parallel texts, trailed by careful meditation, and concluded with consultation with knowledgeable people both living and dead.[72] Robert Wall summarized Wesley's interpretive technique as including ten components—the *intuited text*, which he defined as "an intellectual faculty brought to maturity over time by rigorous study and spiritual discipline"; *the naked text*, which includes a straightforward reading and interpretation, but not without the application of solid biblical criticism and hermeneutics; *the canonical text*, which includes an integration of the whole of the Bible in the interpretation of individual texts; *the community's text*, involving an act of understanding Scripture within the framework of the broader interpretation of others; *the salvific text*, the united metanarrative; *the ruled text*, the unfolding message of salvation; *the preached text*, the interpretation of the biblical message through contemporary proclamation; *the responsive text*, the lived-out application of the text; *the performed text*, an application of the message to contemporary issues; and *the sacramental text*, passing on the words of Scripture through his biblically saturated sermons.[73] Here, Wall captured the breadth of Wesley's hermeneutical practices as both a scholar and a pragmatist as he combined his University of Oxford training with a passion to see the biblical text lived out through the people.

The Church and the Pope

John Wesley's perspectives on the Roman Catholic Church were complicated—paradoxical, if not contradictory. As this thesis will demonstrate, he drew heavily from Roman Catholic mystics in the formulation of some key doctrines, later felt that his immersion into the mystics was detrimental to his faith, yet continued to reference them, publish them, and praise them later in life. He was often critical of the pope, papists, and Jesuits, but he himself was pejoratively christened a papist and a Jesuit by some of his contemporaries. He attacked doctrines of the Roman Catholic Church but wrote to affirm commonality and solidarity across the Protestant-Catholic divide.

Wesley frequently used strong words of opposition to the Catholic church. In various places throughout his journal, he spoke of the "grievous errors" of Roman Catholics, he called the Catholic church "the mother of abominations," and referred to their "many erroneous opinions . . .

---

72. Wesley, *Works* (Outler), 1:106.

73. Maddox and Vickers, *Cambridge Companion to Wesley*, 122–28.

numberless superstitious and idolatrous modes of worship."[74] In his *Treatise on the Doctrine of Original Sin*, he wrote of the "errors of Popery . . . the novel corruptions" and the "vices and villainies of the Romish nations," and in a letter to Mr. John Stretton he called Popery "that deadly enemy of true religion."[75] These examples span from as early as 1737 to as late as 1785. Other such criticisms may be found before and after these dates too; thus, his harsh criticism of Catholicism remained relatively consistent throughout most of his ministry.

Although Wesley maintained a degree of objectivity toward the popes as he affirmed some good qualities in a couple of the papal leaders, he was quick to assert that their goodness was not good enough. In his journal article dated Wednesday, July 14, 1773, Wesley offered brief commentary on his reading of *The Life of Sextus Quintus*. In his reflections, Wesley affirmed Quintus's genius, his accomplishment of great things, and his possession of *excellent qualities*. Yet, he quickly followed up his compliments with judgments questioning Quintus's Christianity and likening him to Henry VIII and Oliver Cromwell.[76] In a journal entry for Sunday, July 23, 1786, Wesley affirmed the late pope, but quickly criticized the office with the words, "strange, that such a man should be suffered to sit two years in the Papal chair!"[77]

In his treatise *A Word to a Protestant*, Wesley offered a definition of the term *Papist* as "one who holds the Pope or Bishop of Rome . . . to be head of the whole Christian Church; and the Church of Rome, or that which owns the Pope as their head, to be the only Christian Church."[78] Wesley took strong issue with the structures that allowed such power over the church to belong to one man. Interestingly, amidst Wesley's harsh critique of the papal office, if not the pope himself, Wesley was often criticized for being as a pope over the Methodists in a sort of *tu quoque* argument. If not accused of being a pope, he was touted as a Papist. In his journal entry dated August 27, 1739, Wesley stated, "The report now current in Bristol was, that I was 'a Papist, if not a Jesuit.' Some added, that I was 'born and bred at Rome,' which many cordially believed." Wesley's retort included his preaching of the doctrine of "justification by faith alone" as a defining distinction between the

74. Wesley, *Works* (Ward and Heitzenrater), 18:182; *Works* (Ward and Heitzenrater), 19:89; Wesley, *Works* (Outler), 3:470.

75. Wesley, *Works* (Maddox), 12:190; Wesley, *Works* (Jackson), 13:137.

76. Wesley, *Works* (Ward and Heitzenrater), 22:384.

77. Wesley, *Works* (Ward and Heitzenrater), 23:410.

78. Wesley, *Works* (Jackson), 11:188.

Methodists, as Protestants, and the Roman Catholics.[79] Similar indictments may be found referenced in a letter of response to Rev. Mr. Church dated February 2, 1744/45.[80] The records of cases where the allegations against Wesley went beyond that of being sympathetic toward Roman Catholics and moved to charges of setting himself up as a pope may be found in the *Minutes of Several Conversations between the Rev. Mr. Wesley and Others from the Year 1744 to the Year 1789* as recorded in the eighth volume of Jackson's *Works of John Wesley*, and in a letter to Mr. Downes dated November 17, 1759.[81] To all of these, Wesley argued the free will of the Methodist preachers and lay members and the adherence to the authority of Scripture.

In order to set himself apart from these claims, in 1744, Wesley signed the "declaration against Popery" in order to satisfy the Surrey justices.[82] Although Wesley's critique of Catholicism spanned much of his ministry, the accusations of his "popery" seems primarily relegated to the 1740s through the 1750s.

Wesley expressed ten main points of contention with Roman Catholic doctrine and honed in on two additional items of conflict. He pointed out these ten in a letter to a Catholic priest which he included in a journal entry dated Monday, August 27, 1739. They include:

> 1. Seven sacraments; 2. Transubstantiation; 3. Communion in one kind only; 4. Purgatory, and praying for the dead therein; 5 Praying to saints; 6. Veneration of relics; 7. Worship of images; 8. Indulgences; 9. The priority and universality of the Roman Church; 10. The supremacy of the Bishop of Rome.[83]

Wesley both preceded and concluded this list with the reason for his disagreement, asserting that these were added to that which may be found in the Bible. He also nearly reproduced most of this list in *A Word to a Protestant*.[84]

Interestingly, Wesley did not include in this list the two issues that remained recurring throughout his writings on the subject. These two include salvation by faith *and* works, and the mystical teachings on suffering. These two will be addressed later in this thesis, but they are worth mentioning briefly here as they pertain to Wesley's relationship with the Roman

79. Wesley, *Works* (Ward and Heitzenrater), 19:89.
80. Wesley, *Works* (Davies), 9:107–8.
81. Wesley, *Works* (Jackson), 8:313; Wesley, *Works* (Davies), 9:363.
82. Wesley, *Works* (Ward and Heitzenrater), 19:18.
83. Wesley, *Works* (Ward and Heitzenrater), 20:92.
84. Wesley, *Works* (Jackson), 11:188.

Catholic Church and his sources of spiritual authority. These ten, plus two, points of issue highlight Wesley's perspective on the authority of Scripture. He rejected the authority of the Roman Catholic Church based primarily on the areas where he felt that they taught beyond or contrary to the biblical texts. Based on these, he strongly rejected any accusations of being a Papist himself. However, in a journal entry dated Monday, August 27, 1739, he attested to essentially being a Papist for ten years, early in his ministry, based on his tendency to preach faith and works as the means to salvation.[85]

Although Wesley maintained a harsh criticism of Roman Catholicism throughout his ministry, he was also able to acknowledge the points of commonality and to call for an ecumenical approach to ministry. In fact, in *A Letter to a Roman Catholic* written in 1749, Wesley sought a relationship between Catholics and Protestants that called for "softening our hearts towards each other, the giving a check to this flood of unkindness and restoring at least some small degree of love among our neighbours and countrymen."[86] After his initial call for mutual respect, grace, and kindness, Wesley continued to address their points of commonality on theology proper, Christology, pneumatology, ecclesiology, and soteriology based on the creeds, before addressing the points of contrasting perspective.

Likewise, in his sermon "Catholic Spirit," Wesley began by calling those of differing opinions concerning the worship of God to be one in love and spirit, though they be of differing thoughts. He continued, through rhetorical interrogation, asking his audience if their hearts were right with God and if they were living out their faith. He then made a key statement that captures the thrust of his message:

> "If it be, give me thy hand." I do not mean, "Be of my opinion." You need not. I do not expect or desire it. Neither do I mean, "I will be of your opinion." I cannot. It does not depend on my choice. I can no more think than I can see or hear as I will. Keep you your opinion, I mine; and that as steadily as ever. You need not even endeavor to come over to me, or bring me over to you. I do not desire you to dispute those points, or to hear or speak one word concerning them. Let all opinions alone on one side and the other. Only "give me thine hand."[87]

Here we see that Wesley kindly made allowances for differing opinions, and though his own opinions were strong against some of the teachings of

---

85. Wesley, *Works* (Ward and Heitzenrater), 19:89.
86. Wesley, *John Wesley* (Outler), 493.
87. Wesley, *Works* (Outler), 2:89.

the Roman Catholic Church, he ultimately called for a unity and working together.

Wesley's Ecclesiology

In Wesley's ecclesiology, he believed that "every follower of Christ is obliged, by the very nature of the Christian institution, to be a member of some particular congregation or other, some church, as it is usually termed."[88] He went on to state that he once believed this to be based on place of birth, but later came to believe that the congregation to which one belongs may be based on choice and matter of conscience. In this, he gave his affirmation of the Reformation. Thus, to Wesley, one ought to be under the authority of a church; however, the Roman Catholic Church and thus the pope do not serve as everyone's spiritual authority.

Wesley captured a bit of his ecclesiology in a sermon titled "Of the Church." This message was preached in Bristol in response to some of the opposition he received to his ordaining of Coke, Whatcoat, and Vasey for ministry in the Americas.[89] Here, he laid out his definition of the church while interacting with the Apostle's Creed and the *Articles* of the Church of England. Albert Outler observed that Wesley's "conclusions are neither Anglican, Lutheran, nor Calvinist"; rather he described them as "an unstable blend of Anglican and Anabaptist ecclesiologies."[90]

To Wesley, the church is about the people, those who are "called out."[91] He believed that the word *church* may be applied to any one of three groupings of "called out" ones. These include the church universal, or those throughout the world; a regional reference, for example the church at Rome, the Church of England, the Ephesians, etc.; and the church particular, for example the two or more who meet in a particular home or place of worship.[92] Wesley, however, saw the church regional and particular as always a part of the greater church universal. In fact, in his sermon "On Schism," he emphatically stated that schism "is not a separation *from* any church . . . but a separation *in* a church" regardless of it occurring at the regional, denominational, or particular levels.[93] In other words, schism occurs within the universal church, not a removal and formation of a separate entity.

88. Wesley, *Works* (Outler), 2:86.

89. See Outler's introductory comments, Wesley, *Works* (Outler), 3:45.

90. Wesley, *Works* (Outler), 3:46.

91. Wesley, *Works* (Outler), 3:47.

92. Wesley, *Works* (Outler), 3:50–51.

93. Wesley, *Works* (Outler), 3:60.

Wesley took time in his sermon to interact a bit with the Church of England's definition of the church, which stated, "The visible church of Christ is a congregation of faithful men, in which the pure word of God is preached, and the sacraments be duly administered."[94] Here, Wesley raised the question regarding the degree to which accurate preaching and the right administration of the sacraments play into the allowance of a particular group to be counted among the church universal. Although he didn't delve fully into this issue to the point of drawing a conclusion, he raised the question nonetheless.

Wesley's definition of the church universal, which then carries into the church regional and particular, was based on his exposition of Eph 4:1–6. He summarized his ecclesiology stating that:

> the catholic or universal church is all the persons in the universe whom God hath called out of the world as to entitle them to the preceding character; as to be "one body," united by "one spirit"; having "one faith, one hope, one baptism; one God and Father of all, who is above all, and through all, and in them all."[95]

One brief statement here was critical to Wesley's definition, "to entitle them to the preceding character." To Wesley, being part of the *church* is not merely a membership status, but a lived experience. He concluded his sermon "Of the Church" with a relatively lengthy description of the lived holiness to be exhibited by those who are "called out."

Thus, to Wesley, the church universal is composed of followers of Jesus who have been "called out" from the world. Thus, the church universal is more of an organic composition of people and less about a systematic structure or organization. Likewise, the church regional and local or particular is also composed of the same people. However, to Wesley, it is at these levels in which structures, organization, and leadership come into play. Therefore, he did not adhere to the authority of the pope, but allowed for people to be submissive to a regional bishop or local pastor.

Mary and the Saints

Wesley's interaction with the Catholic saints in his writings may be deemed as selective. At times, he held various saints as authoritative, quoting frequently from the church historic and publishing edited works of many in his *Christian Library* and other publications. Elsewhere, however, he expressed

94. Wesley, *Works* (Outler), 3:51.
95. Wesley, *Works* (Outler), 3:50.

deep skepticism. Ultimately, he held the voices of Scripture as the primary authoritative written word.

His skepticism may be seen clearly in his letter to a priest:

> I have neither time nor inclination for controversy with any, but least of all with the Romanists. And that both because I can't trust any of their quotations, without consulting every sentence they quote in the originals, and because the originals themselves can very hardly be trusted, in any of the points controverted between them and us. I am no stranger to their skill in *mending* those authors who did not at first speak home to their purpose, as also in *purging* them from those passages which contradicted their emendations.[96]

In spite of this cynicism, Wesley did not hesitate to call upon the words of some saints, and even a few popes, to support his disagreements with Roman Catholicism in his *A Roman Catechism, Faithfully Drawn Out of the Allowed Writings of the Church of Rome, with a Reply Thereto.* For example, he appealed to Cyprian to refute the claim that Peter was the first pope, he quoted Pope Pius II to argue for equality between Rome and Constantinople with Jerusalem being the mother city of the church, and he referenced Tertullian and Augustine to proclaim the sufficiency of Scripture.[97] In addition, Saints Cyril, Basil, Jerome, Chrysostom, Austin, Cyprian, Gregory Nazianzus, Ambrose, and Origen served as quotable authorities on other points of contention between Wesley and Roman Catholic doctrines. In this treatise, he also was quick to reference the Council of Trent, Popes Paul III and Julius III, and Cardinal Quignonius.

Since as a general rule, Wesley referenced passages of the saints a bit more sparingly, it may be concluded that his abundant use of quotations in this treaty was strictly as an appeal to his audience—Roman Catholics. As stated earlier, to Wesley, Scripture serves as the ultimate authoritative written voice. This also comes through clearly in his reply to the catechism. In nearly all of his replies to the various Catholic doctrines, Wesley referenced passages of the Bible to refute the church's teachings. Thus, the saints have their voice, but Scripture has the final word for Wesley.

Regarding Mary among the other saints, Wesley saw her as someone deserving special honor, but differed with some of the Catholic teachings about her. His response to these doctrines are articulated in his *Catechism . . . with Reply.* There he stated:

---

96. Wesley, *Works* (Ward and Heitzenrater), 19:90–91.
97. Wesley, *Works* (Jackson), 10:88–90.

> We honor this blessed Virgin as the mother of the holy Jesus, and as she was a person of eminent piety; but we do not think it lawful to give that honor to her which belongs not to a creature, and doth equal her with her Redeemer.[98]

In this response, Wesley altered the wording of "mother of God" to "mother of the holy Jesus." He went on to argue against the dogmas of Mary's bodily assumption, placement on a throne above angels, assignment as the queen of heaven, advocating for sinners, among others.[99] Concerning Mary and the saints, Wesley held that there is only one mediator, Jesus, between humans and God, but many intercessors. Though he was open to Mary and the saints serving as possible intercessors, he maintained, "For though the angels and saints may intercede for us in heaven, that no more makes them such intercessors as we may pray to."[100] It could be concluded that Wesley valued Mary and many of the church's saints, but thought veneration went too far.

SUMMARY OF WESLEY'S EDITING ON THEOLOGICAL AUTHORITY

Ultimately, Wesley's editorial alterations pertaining to spiritual authority boiled down to three key issues: the authority of Scripture—if not *sola scriptura*—and his accompanying hermeneutical approach, papal or Roman supremacy, and the level of authority of various saints. For Wesley, the biblical text serves as the prime authority for doctrine, the saints may have a supporting voice with limited authority, while the Roman Catholic Church and the pope do not hold authority over the universal church—defined as the entirety of those "called out." Molinos and Ávila, on the other hand, both held to the authoritative voice of Scripture, and the saints, and the pope, and the Roman Catholic Church, all on nearly equal levels. It was primarily on these matters out of which Wesley made his editorial changes concerning authority. By including all of those "called out" as comprising the church universal, Wesley was able to assign a degree of authority to the writings of the saints as they too were persons "called out" by God and vital members of the church. However, through the lenses of *sola scriptura*, Wesley kept a critical eye on their writings, assessing them through the scrutiny of the biblical texts.

98. Wesley, *Works* (Jackson), 10:106.

99. Wesley, *Works* (Jackson), 10:106–7.

100. Wesley, *Works* (Jackson), 10:105.

COMPARISON AND CONTRAST

These three authors shared a degree of agreement as to *what* held spiritual authority. They all demonstrated through their writings, if not direct affirmation, that the Bible, saints of old, and the church held spiritual authority for informing doctrinal understanding. They differed, however, on the order and level to which these remained authoritative.

All of them clearly held the Bible in high regard, respected its authoritative voice, and believed the text to be divinely inspired. The differences remained in their understanding of the level of biblical authority in comparison to other authoritative voices. Wesley held a near *sola scriptura* as influenced by the Lutheran Reformation, while Ávila and Molinos kept the writings of the saints on nearly the same plane as the Bible with the church being the authoritative voice of interpretation. Ávila and Molinos referenced texts that Wesley would have classified as apocryphal as they followed the canon of the Roman Catholic Church.

These three also differed in their hermeneutical approach. Whereas Ávila and Molinos were quite comfortable with allegory and typology, Wesley called for the plain or face-value understanding of the written word. Wesley was also a proponent of interpreting the text in context both immediate and in relation to the whole.

These authors clearly valued the teachings of the church historic and many of the writers from the past. Ávila in particular as well as Molinos were much more comfortable drawing from a breadth of those whom the Roman Catholic Church deemed as saints and/or doctors of the church. Wesley, on the other hand, remained much more selective as to whom he saw fit to reference with any degree of authority.

Regarding the authority of the church, Ávila kept this as a strong personal conviction. Molinos, on the other hand seemed to avoid the topic and remained more comfortable quoting from individuals than calling upon the corporate body of the Roman Catholic Church. Wesley maintained a love for the church universal and interpreted the Bible through those lenses, while opposing the authority of the Roman Catholic Church. Beyond these authoritative voices, these three authors also held a broader understanding of the means through which people arrive at knowledge.

2

Epistemology and Self-Knowledge

THE FAMOUS AUGUSTINE QUOTE referenced in the previous chapter, "Grant to me, O Lord, that I may know thee, and that I may know myself," places knowledge of the Divine and self-knowledge in parallel to one another. This basic idea, with some variations, permeated many Christian spiritual writings throughout the centuries. Ávila, Molinos, and Wesley were no exceptions. Each one saw self-knowledge as a means toward the greater end of knowing God. However, each one viewed knowledge of the self from slightly different angles.

Examining divine and self-knowledge brings to surface the broader question of how one arrives at knowledge in general. In many ways, each of these authors was a product of their times regarding their respective approaches to epistemology. However, the three also drew from many historical influences to inform their approach to the obtainment of knowledge. Although each of these spiritual writers drew from both *a priori* and *a posteriori* forms of divine knowledge, they all shared a strong *a posteriori* approach that remained dependent upon personal experience and direct encounter with God as a source of knowledge.

JUAN DE ÁVILA ON EPISTEMOLOGY AND SELF-KNOWLEDGE

As one who was instrumental in the formation of multiple universities, Ávila was committed to traditional forms of education and learning. In his *Audi Filia,* he urged his readers not to look down upon those with a high level of learning. He quoted Augustine at length to make a case for learning from teachers.[1] Although he was strong about his view that salvation is by faith, not knowledge, since the ways of God are higher than our reason, he did not see faith as contrary to reason, just "unattainable by reason."[2] That being said, he held that one "cannot be saved without knowing God," and this knowledge comes from divine revelation.[3] The distinction for Ávila is between *saber* and *conocimiento*.[4] The former, a possession of knowledge or act of knowing, is not sufficient for securing one's salvation. The latter, however, moves knowledge to a more personal and relational level, and it implies a first-hand knowledge or experience with the object.

This is also in keeping with Ávila's view on the role of experiential knowing. In addressing the motives for belief, he began with a description of soul-level experiences, and that which one feels in one's heart. With such experiences, he went on to explain, one need not look to books or the experience of others.[5] Ávila offered three cautions regarding or conditions to which this knowledge through experience ought to be attained. According to Ávila, such experiences may be trusted as long as they are accompanied by "profound humility."[6] He also held that belief must remain in unity with the church and not be based on individual opinion.[7] Thirdly, the pursuit of knowledge ought not to be based on mere curiosity. For this, it is worth including his direct words:

> Certainly, many people have heard God's words and have possessed excellent knowledge of subtle and lofty manners. But because they drew near to see, more through curiosity to see, than obediently to "incline" the ear of their reason, their seeing became blindness, and they stumbled about in the noonday light as if it were darkness.[8]

He went on to offer instructions on how one ought to incline the ear, which he equated with reason. In addition to these three cautions, he also urged his readers to apply their understanding. Using the word *saber* he distinguished between "knowing a truth and knowing how to use it properly"; the former without the latter, he believed to be harmful.[9] To summarize, Ávila

1. Ávila, *Audi, Filia* (Gormley),166.
2. Ávila, *Audi, Filia* (Gormley), 114, 145.
3. Ávila, *Audi, Filia* (Gormley), 117.
4. Ávila, *Audi Filia*—Spanish, capítulo 34, 45.
5. Ávila, *Audi, Filia* (Gormley), 125.
6. Ávila, *Audi, Filia* (Gormley), 163.
7. Ávila, *Audi, Filia* (Gormley), 167.
8. Ávila, *Audi, Filia* (Gormley), 146.
9. Ávila, *Audi, Filia* (Gormley), 261.

believed that experiential knowledge, *conocimiento,* of God is a necessary ingredient in salvation, and knowledge, *saber,* when it is applied knowledge, is beneficial to a life in service to God.

Self-Knowledge

In addition to the role of knowledge of God regarding salvation and spiritual development, Ávila wrote perhaps even more about the place of self-knowledge in one's spiritual well-being. His quoting of St. Augustine captures his desire well, "Lord, let me know you with loving knowledge, and let me know myself."[10] Ávila believed that self-knowledge serves as a means to knowledge of the Divine.[11] He held that self-knowledge comes from and exists as one of the first steps in salvation.[12] He believed that one's self-knowledge should be based on what God directs one to believe and feel about oneself, and that God is the source of accurate self-knowledge.[13]

There were three places in Ávila's *Audi Filia* where he described a process of understanding of oneself. This may be seen specifically in the sixty-fifth chapter where Ávila laid out a systematic process toward this self-knowledge. This process begins with an awareness that the goodness of being is a result of God's goodness in order to appreciate one's nothingness. Next, one ought to use great care to "remember when you lived in offense against God" in order to acknowledge one's "lowliness and vileness." Finally, he urged his readers to think about the mercy of God and how they have been made right through Jesus Christ.[14] He later summarized this process in chapter 93 in these three sentences:

> Look at what proceeds from you by looking at yourself within yourself; then look at yourself in God and in his grace. Consider in yourself, you are a great sum of debts, and however much you might do, not only will you not be able to merit eternal life, but you will not even pay what you owe. But in God and his grace, the very service you are obligated to render is received as merit for eternal life.[15]

10. Ávila, *Audi, Filia* (Gormley), 107.

11. Ávila, *Audi, Filia* (Gormley), 179.

12. Ávila, *Audi, Filia* (Gormley), 69, 79, 187.

13. Ávila, *Audi, Filia* (Gormley), 89, 185.

14. Ávila, *Audi, Filia* (Gormley), 192–94.

15. Ávila, *Audi, Filia* (Gormley), 265.

To Ávila, self-knowledge comes through a deep awareness of one's own faults and shortcomings. He exhorted his readers to examine "daily and very slowly what inclinations are in the depths of your heart, what passions are alive, into what faults you sometimes fall, and things of this sort."[16] He believed that through this daily *examen*, one would be able to spot one's faults easily after much practice and over the course of time.

There were a few key areas in which Ávila called for balance in one's pursuit of self-knowledge and in how one is perceived by others. In the opening chapters, he stated that "the noble heart should despise neither being esteemed nor being without esteem," and continued on to endorse virtue as a valuable pursuit apart from the affirmation of others.[17] As mentioned earlier, to Ávila, accurate self-knowledge comes from God, therefore, it ought not to be based on the high or low perception of others. As a tool offered by God, self-knowledge allows one to see the good in God without ascribing evil to God and allows one to see the wickedness in oneself without taking credit for the good.[18] This is not to say that Ávila didn't see any good in people. He actually wrote about the "glory of the 'being' that [humans] possess." His emphasis, however, was to acknowledge that this is a gift from God, not an attribute earned or developed by the person.[19] Consequently, he exhorted people to see themselves in the context of stewardship and caring for oneself as something which has been *entrusted*.[20]

Audi Filia serves as an insight into Ávila over time, as he developed it throughout his adult life, and as an insight into Ávila's thought on spiritual progression, as he developed it systematically from the early stages to higher levels of spirituality. Interestingly, his instructions on self-knowledge are found early on in the first section and carry throughout the book. He made his final statement about self-knowledge in the penultimate chapter with the instruction to "behold [Christ] in himself, and behold him within you. Behold him in himself so that you may see who you are; behold him in yourself in order to see who he is."[21] Given this high value for self-knowledge, Ávila also didn't want his readers to become stuck in an egocentricity. Rather, he urged his audience to examine oneself, then give little consideration to self. Instead, "first, look at yourself; then at God; and then at your neighbor."[22]

---

16. Ávila, *Audi, Filia* (Gormley), 223.

17. Ávila, *Audi, Filia* (Gormley), 44.

18. Ávila, *Audi, Filia* (Gormley), 79.

19. Ávila, *Audi, Filia* (Gormley), 192.

20. Ávila, *Audi, Filia* (Gormley), 186.

21. Ávila, *Audi, Filia* (Gormley), 313.

22. Ávila, *Audi, Filia* (Gormley), 175.

JOHN WESLEY'S EDITING OF ÁVILA ON EPISTEMOLOGY AND SELF-KNOWLEDGE

Wesley took seriously the doctrine of original sin and the fall. In his sermon "Original Sin," Wesley described the human condition "in his natural state, unassisted by the grace of God," as being in a state "that 'all the imaginations of the thoughts of his heart' are still 'evil, only evil', and that 'continually.'"[23] Given such strong statements about the sinfulness of humankind, it is interesting that Wesley edited out so many statements that dealt harshly with the sinful self as found in Ávila's works. In his third epistle, Ávila called for the removal of self-love. Wesley left in statements that called for people to love but eliminated the call to "apply the axe of diligence, to the roote of our owne selfe-love," and the call to "shed many teares" and to "groane out to God" when it is too easy.[24] In loving, Wesley would also consider a type of self-love as a virtue, not a vice.

In a later letter, the fifteenth, Ávila urged his reader to know himself in order to be known by God. Wesley preserved this portion. However, Ávila continued to instruct his reader to judge and condemn himself as a means to being absolved. Wesley preserved the idea of being absolved; he even allowed for the instruction to judge one's self as a means toward an end, but he removed the concept of self-condemnation as the means toward that goal.[25]

John Wesley also seemed to reject Ávila's perspective that sees dishonor as a virtue to be embraced. Wesley eliminated such statements as "how much wee are honoured, in being dishonored," and "he more desires dishonor for thy sake, than hee esteemes honour."[26] However, he preserved the words that preceded the former claim, which stated, "How great favour he doth us, by that which the world thinks to be disfavour."[27] Wesley kept this idea as it pertained to disfavor, but removed the connection pertaining to dishonor.

Wesley seemed to disagree with Ávila when it comes to self-care. In his thirty-ninth epistle, Ávila stated that "he who loves Christ our Lord, must abhorre himselfe." Wesley kept this statement, but eliminated what follows: "He who will not be cruell to Christ our Lord, lett him not be compassionate to himselfe. They who dandle themselves, shew unkindnes to Christ our Lord, and they who take soe much care of themselves cannot make God

23. Wesley, *Works* (Outler), 2:176.

24. Ávila, *Selected Epistles*, 21.

25. Ávila, *Selected Epistles*, 115; Wesley, *Christian Library* (Ávila), 46:290.

26. Ávila, *Selected Epistles*, 172, 176.

27. Ávila, *Selected Epistles*, 172.

their businesse."[28] As mentioned earlier, Wesley had a strong view on the depraved state of the human soul which may account for his preserving of the introductory statement to that which followed. However, Wesley also maintained a pragmatic view toward self-care. This can be seen in his medical publications, views on why he lived so long found in his journal, countless letters of health advice to friends, etc.

Perceptions of Self and Self-Condemnation

John Wesley maintained a perspective on the human condition as being deeply depraved. Given this perspective, it is interesting that Wesley removed a little less than twenty references to the human condition or God's dealing with the human soul in ways that are harsh or overly condemning. This may be observed in Ávila's treatment of suffering and his understanding of the sinful state and, consequently, how one ought to view oneself.

Ávila viewed suffering as means to a greater end, so much so that he often praised the desire to suffer as a virtue (this will be discussed more thoroughly in a later chapter but will be addressed briefly here as it pertains to self-condemnation). Specifically, he saw suffering as means to elimination of sin and growth into the likeness of Jesus.[29] Although Wesley saw a redeeming quality found within suffering, he removed any reference to a longing for or love of suffering. To Ávila, suffering was given from God for the greater good of the soul; however, in one place, he made the claim that "all bitter frosen afflictions procede but from distrust in God."[30] To Wesley, suffering has two sources—the world and/or one's sinful self as described in his sermons on "Heaviness" and the "Wilderness State." Therefore, Wesley removed references to suffering being from the hand of God and the claim that suffering comes from "distrust in God."

In his discourse on tribulations in letter 21, Ávila described how Saint Paul did not "murmure, nor complaine of God."[31] Wesley kept this portion. However, Ávila continued to describe how Saint Paul did not ask God to take away these tribulations and through implication stated that Saint Paul saw these as great favors from God. This latter portion, Wesley removed. As Ávila shifted beyond Saint Paul to describe the common suffering among God's people, he explained how God stretches out his "deare armes . . . towards us," which Wesley preserved in his version of the letter; yet, Wesley

28. Ávila, *Selected Epistles*, 304.

29. Ávila, *Selected Epistles*, 184.

30. Ávila, *Selected Epistles*, 344.

31. Ávila, *Selected Epistles*, 172.

removed Ávila's further description of how the wounds of tribulation "make sweete all that gall."[32] In a later letter, Wesley omitted Ávila's description of finding favor in suffering.[33]

From this same letter, Wesley also removed Ávila's statements that "hee whoe hath but little desire to suffer for thee" concerning those who do not know God with "perfect love."[34] He also eliminated a statement about growing "cleane by suffering."[35]

Where Ávila stated that suffering or tribulation were means to the removal of sin, toward Christ-likeness, and to seeing one's own misery, Wesley omitted such claims.[36] To Wesley, people could come to the realization of the removal of sin in this life and grow in Christ-likeness to the point of being perfected in love, so his issue with these claims of Ávila was not in the end but in the means toward that end. Suffering, to Wesley, is not the key ingredient to one's growth in holiness, nor is it to be desired for the sake of self-condemnation, nor is it a primary source for obtaining knowledge.

MIGUEL DE MOLINOS ON EPISTEMOLOGY AND SELF-KNOWLEDGE

To Molinos, knowledge is progressive. This progressive nature of knowledge is not relegated merely to individual experience, but to a broader realm of the whole of humankind. This may be seen in his praise for new publications. He even used the emphatic statement that "God needs these teachings." Molinos believed that "not everything has been said, nor has it been written, and so there must be writing always, until the end of the world."[37]

Molinos also acknowledged the progressive nature of divine knowledge for the individual who would progress along the spiritual, and especially the mystical, path. For such an ascent of knowledge, Molinos held relatively closely to the *via negativa* tradition, upholding the words of Pseudo-Dionysius asserting that, "we know God . . . more perfectly by negations than by affirmations." He continued with the words of the Pseudo-Aereopogite that describe a knowledge of God which comes through a realization of how transcendent above all reason God remains.[38]

32. Ávila, *Selected Epistles*, 173.
33. Ávila, *Selected Epistles*, 350.
34. Ávila, *Selected Epistles*, 176.
35. Ávila, *Selected Epistles*, 180.
36. Ávila, *Selected Epistles*, 184–86.
37. Molinos, *Spiritual Guide* (Baird and McGinn), 52.
38. Molinos, *Spiritual Guide* (Baird and McGinn), 57.

Due to this *via negativa* means toward obtaining knowledge of the Divine, according to Molinos, the senses are not sufficient vehicles for spiritual progression. Thus, he believed that for true spiritual ascent to occur, one must be purged of or mortify the senses. According to Molinos, this mortification of external senses begins with one's resolve, then progresses through external and internal acts of purgation done by God, then one may ascend "the high mountain of perfection and union with God."[39] However, in order to get to the point of resolve, one must gain a self-knowledge concerning one's "vileness, stench, and misery."[40] Molinos stated that "the less the soul enjoys this sensible love," it will enjoy God more and reach new levels of knowledge and understanding.[41]

Molinos equated knowledge through the senses with the scholastic practices. Thus, with his call for a purging and mortification of the sense, scholastic expressions of devotion only carry one so far. He believed that to arrive at "the most profound knowledge of divinity," one must embrace means that lead them to be "purely mystical and truly humble." This, he concluded is "hidden and closed to purely scholastic men."[42] Through the remainder of the third book, Molinos continued to praise the mystical way over the scholastic way. In the eighteenth chapter, he stated that "there are two paths that lead to the knowledge of God: the first is distant; the second is nearby. The first is called speculation, the second contemplation." The first, he equated to the Scholastic way, the second he attributed to the mystical way. The first, he believed will never lead to the second on its own, though the first does not make the second impossible.[43]

JOHN WESLEY'S EDITING OF MOLINOS ON EPISTEMOLOGY AND SELF-KNOWLEDGE

In a chapter on perseverance in prayer during a time of perceived deprivation, Molinos, following his *via negativa* approach, laid out the means through which one does *not* draw near to God before indicating the means through which one *does* draw near to God, the latter being "silent and humble resignation." Wesley preserved "humble resignation," but eliminated silence as a means toward the end. In that which does not serve to draw near to God, Wesley kept most of the modes presented by Molinos, but excluded

39. Molinos, *Spiritual Guide* (Baird and McGinn), 76.
40. Molinos, *Spiritual Guide* (Baird and McGinn), 161.
41. Molinos, *Spiritual Guide* (Baird and McGinn), 86.
42. Molinos, *Spiritual Guide* (Baird and McGinn), 172.
43. Molinos, *Spiritual Guide* (Baird and McGinn), 173, 174.

ratiocination as a way that fails to draw someone toward God.[44] This may be because Wesley did in fact see the use of reason as a viable vehicle through which one may move closer to God. This will further be explored later.

An editorial exclusion of this same word appears a few paragraphs later. Here, Molinos compared the soul to a seed in dormancy prior to growth as a plant. Wesley preserved the overall analogy but eliminated a statement asserting that God "deprives [the soul] of consideration and ratiocination" in this state.[45] Likewise, the first two paragraphs of the next chapter, which contained the word *ratiocination*, were taken out before Wesley released his version. In these paragraphs, Molinos held that not only does ratiocination not serve to draw one closer to God, but one "cannot attain to perfection and an union with God, by means of Meditation, and Ratiocination" as these are merely for beginners.[46]

Molinos concluded the aforementioned chapter with a series of exhortations in Pauline style urging his readers to persevere. Wesley reproduced this chapter mostly intact. He did, however, remove a phrase encouraging the readers to "walk as if thou wert blindfolded, without thinking or reasoning."[47]

Beyond the wording of ratiocination, Wesley seemed to remove or alter many statements pertaining to knowledge and reason. One example may be found in a chapter on purgation as a means to internal peace. In the closing paragraph, Molinos described that which results from God's purging work. He included in this description "thy soul to be whole hours-together in Prayer, dumb, resigned, and humble, without acting, knowing, or desiring to understand any thing." Wesley removed this entire paragraph.[48] Similarly, Wesley also removed a description of a pure and mature faith that was devoid of reasonings.[49]

When it comes to dealing with negative thoughts, Molinos presented two possible approaches. The first, which Molinos thought to be futile and counter-productive, is to resist the thoughts. Wesley eliminated this statement, likely because to Wesley resisting such harmful thoughts is beneficial. Wesley did, however, preserve the three-fold approach of despising the

44. Molinos, *Spiritual Guide*, 6; Wesley, *Christian Library* (Molinos), 38:252.

45. Molinos, *Spiritual Guide*, 7; Wesley, *Christian Library* (Molinos), 38:253.

46. Molinos, *Spiritual Guide*, 8.

47. Molinos, *Spiritual Guide*, 8; Wesley, *Christian Library* (Molinos), 38:253.

48. Molinos, *Spiritual Guide*, 23; Wesley, *Christian Library* (Molinos), 38:258.

49. Molinos, *Spiritual Guide*, 31; Wesley, *Christian Library* (Molinos), 38:263.

thoughts, acknowledging one's own sinfulness, and presenting an offering
to God.[50]

A couple paragraphs later, Molinos described "the fruit of true prayer."
Although lengthy, it is worth noting in its entirety to show the contrast with
Wesley's version. Molinos asserted that:

> The fruit of true Prayer consists not in enjoying the Light, nor in
> having Knowledge of spiritual things, since these may be found
> in a speculative Intellect, without true Virtue and Perfection;
> it only consists in enduring with Patience, and persevering in
> Faith and Silence, believing that thou art in the Lord's Pres-
> ence, turning to him thy Heart with tranquillity, and purity of
> Mind.[51]

Wesley maintained that the benefit of prayer is not in "enjoying the light,"
but removed the segment regarding knowledge of spiritual things, picking
up again at "it only consists in enduring patience," etc., while also keeping
the perseverance of faith, yet removing *silence* as an end product of prayer.[52]

The word *sensible* and its various forms, as used by Molinos, seem to
be another point of contention for Wesley. There are multiple places where
Wesley removed these words pertaining to the intellect and reason. For
example, in a chapter on recollection, Molinos described the "war" which
ensues as one enters into the state of recollection. This war, according to
Molinos, will not only "try, humble, and purge thee," but will also "deprive
thee of sensibility." The former, Wesley preserved; the latter, he removed.[53]
In the next chapter, which continued the same theme, Molinos talked about
those who enter into internal recollection only to abandon it when they
no longer feel the same consolations as they once experienced. One of the
results which he included in this lack of consolation is the loss of the "ability
to reason." Wesley also eliminated this statement.[54]

In the third book, Molinos described the process through which, upon
reaching the inward way, one's desires and shortcomings are removed and
replaced by virtue. To Molinos, this does not happen through conscious
effort, but occurs "without so much as thinking of the good which God . . .
prepared."[55] Wesley, however, removed this latter statement.[56] This move by

---

50. Molinos, *Spiritual Guide*, 31–32; Wesley, *Christian Library* (Molinos), 38:263.

51. Molinos, *Spiritual Guide*, 32.

52. Molinos, *Spiritual Guide*, 32; Wesley, *Christian Library* (Molinos), 38:263.

53. Molinos, *Spiritual Guide*, 32; Wesley, *Christian Library* (Molinos), 38:264.

54. Molinos, *Spiritual Guide*, 36; Wesley, *Christian Library* (Molinos), 38:265.

55. Molinos, *Spiritual Guide*, 119.

56. Wesley, *Christian Library* (Molinos), 38:271.

Wesley, perhaps, implies that one continues to think of the good prepared in advance by God.

In a later chapter, Molinos recounted the blessings found through being subdued, poor, despised, beaten down, and afflicted. All of these were preserved in Wesley's version. Interestingly, however, Wesley removed one statement from this list stating "what a credit of knowledge is it to be reputed ignorant."[57] Wesley's maintenance of the former items and elimination of the latter demonstrates the high value Wesley placed on knowledge and the contrasting perspective on ignorance.

Molinos perceived that divine purification impacts every faculty; included in this are the thoughts and desires, even those that are spiritual in nature. In the fourth chapter of his third book, Molinos included these among others of that which are purified by God. Wesley, however, kept his list while excluding the thoughts and desires "how spiritual soever" as something to be purified.[58] It was likely that Wesley was not opposed to the need for cleansing of one's thoughts and desires; his point of contention was likely that of needing spiritual thoughts and spiritual desires eliminated as these may serve toward the intended greater end.

This idea of purging of memory for Molinos does not merely involve a redirection toward more pure thoughts. Rather, for him, it is a removal of and reconstruction of one's mental faculties. So much so that even regarding one's own self denial "it doth not know whether it be alive or dead; lost or gained; whether it agrees or resists: this is the true resigned Life."[59] Wesley did not include this statement in his rendition. He maintained a different epistemological ideal, to be discussed later.

Later, in reflecting on true humility, Molinos described an attitude held by people in which they do not flinch at ill treatment and willingly accept what comes their way. In this description, Molinos stated that the humility comes through "the affection of the Will" and not "by the counsel of Reason."[60] Wesley extracted this latter claim.[61] Molinos continued to explain how through humility one endures trials "of God, and Men, and the Devil himself." Wesley preserved this claim while shedding the statement which followed, "above and reason and direction."[62] As can be seen, the Methodist was not as willing to jettison the role of reason as was the Quietist.

---

57. Molinos, *Spiritual Guide*, 123; Wesley, *Christian Library* (Molinos), 38:272.

58. Molinos, *Spiritual Guide*, 127–28; Wesley, *Christian Library* (Molinos), 38:275.

59. Molinos, *Spiritual Guide*, 139–40.

60. Molinos, *Spiritual Guide*, 149.

61. Wesley, *Christian Library* (Molinos), 38:283.

62. Molinos, *Spiritual Guide*, 150; Wesley, *Christian Library* (Molinos), 38:284.

Self-Knowledge

Wesley wrote much on the topic of self-knowledge. For him, self-knowledge was a means for understanding one's own sinful state and for the awareness of one's complete need for a savior. Although Molinos took a similar approach to self-knowledge in places, there were a few points where Wesley made some editorial changes, especially in the third book.

For example, Molinos saw the means toward humility as including "true contempt and knowledge of themselves."[63] This is somewhat different from a later statement where he claimed that humility comes through "the affection of the Will" and not "by the counsel of Reason."[64] Thus, there seems to exist a distinction in Molinos between self-knowledge and reason. Of interest here is that Wesley removed both sets of claims. With his value on reason and self-knowledge, the idea that humility may come through contempt and self-knowledge does not seem out of place for Wesley. Yet, he removed this assertion anyway. Perhaps, his removal had more to do with the idea of self-contempt than of self-knowledge.

Perhaps for the same reason, Wesley removed a later encouragement to maintain "a mean opinion of thy self" while reflecting on the pure love found in the cross of Jesus.[65] Likewise, Wesley cut an entire paragraph that spoke to self-knowledge as contempt for oneself. It is worth showing in its entirety here:

> He has no internal Humility who doth not abhor himself, with a mortal, but withal a peaceable and quiet hatred: But he will never come to possess this treasure, that has not a low and profound knowledge of his own vileness, rottenness and misery.[66]

As will be seen later, Wesley held to a strong perspective of depravity from original sin, though not a total depravity, yet seemed to oppose Molinos's strong wording of self-deprivation.

---

63. Molinos, *Spiritual Guide*, 120.
64. Molinos, *Spiritual Guide*, 149.
65. Molinos, *Spiritual Guide*, 138.
66. Molinos, *Spiritual Guide*, 153.

JOHN WESLEY ON EPISTEMOLOGY AND SELF-KNOWLEDGE

Wesley's Epistemology

Wesley's epistemology was multi-faceted. The starting point was reason, of which he held high value. To Wesley, knowledge may be obtained firstly through "natural reason"—a term which he applied to the understanding of the Chickasaw Native Americans. This, he believed, may be obtained apart from revelation.[67]

In his sermon "On the Discoveries of Faith and the Promise of Understanding," Wesley drew from Aristotle and Aquinas, quoting the Latin phrase "*Nihil est in intellectu quod non fuit prius in sensu*," which he translated, "there is nothing in the understanding which was not first perceived by some of the senses."[68] To Wesley, natural knowledge is obtained through the senses, which he continued to rank in order of epistemological importance with sight at the top, followed by hearing, then feeling, and lastly taste and smell.

From natural reason, one may add knowledge through the application of the tools of logic. In 1750, Wesley published a treatise titled *A Compendium of Logic*, to which he enlarged and, borrowing from Bishop Sanderson, added an appendix in 1756, then enlarged again at a later date.[69] This *Compendium* served to outline Aldrich's *Artis Logicae Compendium* for use in the Kingswood School.[70] This work highlights Wesley's understanding and training in classic logic and epistemology as he summarized the basic laws of deduction, syllogisms, logical fallacies, and logical methodology. For Wesley, knowledge is obtained through natural reason and logic; however, he did not hold these as the only source of knowledge.

In 1771, Wesley undertook a serious revision of his collected works. In his preface, he stated, "I present to serious and candid men my last and maturest thoughts, agreeable, I hope, to Scripture, reason, and Christian antiquity."[71] Here, another aspect of Wesley's epistemological approach is revealed. In addition to reason, he included Scripture and tradition. In this potent statement, Wesley bookended that which included deductive and inductive methodology with two forms of *conductive* epistemology—in other words, that which is passed on by means of others. As expressed elsewhere,

67. Wesley, *Works* (Ward and Heitzenrater), 18:185.

68. Wesley, *Works* (Outler), 4:29.

69. Wesley, *Works* (Jackson), 14:161–89.

70. Green, *Works of John and Charles*, 68.

71. Wesley, *Works* (Jackson), 1:iv.

to Wesley, ultimate knowledge was given through the divine revelation found in Scripture. He held to a near *sola scriptura* approach which is then enhanced through the application of reason in conversation with the traditional voice of the Christian church.

In his sermon "On the Discoveries of Faith and the Promise of Understanding," mentioned above, Wesley emphasized that the senses are limited to our engagement of the material world; he then articulated a source of knowledge which surpassed the senses and natural reason. He asserted that *faith* is the means through which spiritual knowledge may be obtained. In his words, "faith . . . is the 'evidence of things not seen', of the *invisible world*; of all those invisible things which are revealed in the oracles of God."[72]

This key component to Wesley's epistemological approach may be seen in the series of letter-correspondence with someone using the pseudonym "John Smith" from 1745 to 1747. In these letters, the term *perceptible inspiration* is applied to Wesley's understanding of the knowledge of God. At issue between Wesley and Smith was the *level to which* and the *means through which* faith is developed and God is revealed. To Wesley, a person can directly and tangibly experience God in a way that is *perceptible*. To Smith, spiritual progress occurs through interaction with the message of Scripture. Joseph W. Cunningham summarized Wesley's epistemological aspect of perceptible inspiration, stating, "Wesley viewed God as a relational Spirit-being, whose gracious witness to human beings enlightens our understanding, while moving the heart to happiness and holiness in Christ."[73] In other words, knowledge can be divinely and directly given. Wesley also held to the possibility of this divine inspiration being instantaneous or momentaneous. Smith, on the other hand, aligned with a more process-oriented development of faith. Cunningham summarized Smith's view as "faith is not given in a single moment, but is gradual trust in God that develops naturally and in accordance with the light of reason."[74] In Smith's own words in a letter dated May 1745, he argued that "such assent arises not momentaneously, but by the slow steps of ratiocination; by attending to the evidence, weighing the objections, and solving the difficulties."[75]

This quote is significant as it relates to Wesley's editing in his *Christian Library*. As Smith's letter was written four years prior to the publication of the first volumes of the *Library*, Wesley's editorial eye was likely influenced by his correspondence with Smith. As noted earlier, Wesley removed the

---

72. Wesley, *Works* (Outler), 4:30.

73. Cunningham, *Wesley's Pneumatology*, xii.

74. Cunningham, *Wesley's Pneumatology*, 8.

75. Wesley, *Works* (Baker), 26:141.

word *ratiocination* from Molinos's writings. Interestingly, Molinos believed that ratiocination does not help one to make spiritual progress toward the *telos*; Wesley's removal of the word may be an indication that a few years after his interaction with Smith, he allowed for ratiocination as a means toward spiritual growth. As mentioned above, Wesley's epistemology made room for natural reason; however, he also allowed for divine revelation. As his understanding of natural reason may be seen as a form of *intra-duction*, or internal knowledge, perceptible inspiration may be seen as another form of *intra-duction*, obtained not through natural means, but through divine revelation.

Wesley on Self-Knowledge

Wesley maintained the place of self-knowledge in high priority for spiritual progress. In his *Farther Appeal to Men of Reason and Religion*, he listed self-knowledge as accepted by the people among the virtues, which also include "gratitude and benevolence . . . modesty, mildness, temperance, patience, and generosity."[76] He especially wrote of the importance of self-knowledge as it relates to the early stages and process of salvation, or justification. He wrote of a three-fold component to self-knowledge including that which precedes and leads up to justification, that which accompanies justification and leads to salvation, and that which follows justification for the growth of believers.

In his sermon "The Way to the Kingdom," Wesley held self-knowledge as synonymous with repentance and as a precursor to faith, stating:

> This is the way: Walk ye in it. And, First, repent, that is, know yourselves. This is the first repentance, previous to faith, even conviction, or self-knowledge. Awake, then, thou that sleepest. Know thyself to be a sinner, and what manner of sinner thou art. Know that corruption of thy inmost nature, whereby thou art very far gone from original righteousness.[77]

Note that although there is an initial knowledge of oneself connected to initial repentance, he placed this first self-knowledge as prior to faith, conviction, and a second form of self-knowledge. In his sermon "Heaviness through Manifold Temptations," Wesley described this first level of self-knowledge as often "gradually increasing" leading up to and preceding justification. He went on to describe a self-knowledge that comes later as being

76. Wesley, *Works* (Cragg), 11:263.
77. Wesley, *Works* (Outler), 1:225.

"a far deeper, a far clearer and fuller knowledge of our inbred sin, of our total corruption by nature, after justification, than ever there was before it."[78]

This latter form of self-knowledge, or perhaps an intermediary form obtaining between the two, Wesley described as arriving in a "larger measure" in his sermon "On Working Out Our Own Salvation." He linked this expression of self-knowledge to *convincing grace* and *repentance*. He believed that it is through this form of self-knowledge and repentance, that one may experience "proper Christian salvation."[79]

A later form of self-knowledge is for those who are justified and saved. Wesley also linked this third version to repentance. However, in this case, it is applied to the ongoing repentance of believers. Wesley addressed this in his sermon "The Repentance of Believers" indicating that "repentance frequently means an inward change, a change of mind from sin to holiness." He continued, stating that this latter repentance is "one kind of self-knowledge—the knowing ourselves sinners, yea, guilty, helpless sinners, even though we know we are children of God."[80] Note that he associated this latter connection between self-knowledge and repentance as belonging to those who are already "children of God."

Wesley clearly linked self-knowledge to an internal awareness of sin, such that it leads to repentance. Interestingly, however, he affirmed that this awareness should be a positive experience. In a letter to Jane Catherine March, published as *To a Member of the Society*, dated March 4, 1760, he instructed the recipient that "there is no manner of necessity that this self-knowledge should make us miserable. Certainly the highest degree of it is well consistent both with peace and joy in the Holy Ghost."[81]

COMPARISON AND CONTRAST

Regarding Epistemology

Ávila, Molinos, and Wesley all exercised their own unique epistemological approach—that is, unique compared to one another. To Ávila, knowledge consists of the possession of information and understanding, and/or first-hand experience. He believed that knowledge is obtained through teachers, eye-witness interaction, and in unity with the church. He saw this attainment as incremental. Molinos, on the other hand, saw the obtaining of

78. Wesley, *Works* (Outler), 2:230–31.
79. Wesley, *Works* (Outler), 3:204.
80. Wesley, *Works* (Outler), 1:336.
81. Wesley, *Works* (Campbell), 27:185.

knowledge as progressive more than incremental. He believed that knowledge may be obtained through sensory interaction with the world, but this contains limits. He held that the attainment of ultimate knowledge comes not through reason and ratiocination, but through negations à la *via negativa*, contemplation, and the mystical way. Wesley, however, understood that knowledge comes through natural reason, ratiocination, classical logic, Scripture, tradition, and perceptible inspiration.

All three might agree that spiritual knowledge has a developmental aspect over time, but for Ávila this occurs incrementally, for Molinos it happens progressively, and for Wesley it can come about momentously. Each one among this trio allowed room for divine revelation, along with various forms of learning from external sources. Ávila and Wesley would stand together in their appreciation for the epistemological role of Scripture and tradition, though the latter may be interpreted differently, while Molinos stood alone in the level to which he elevated the role of negation in bringing about understanding.

Regarding Self-Knowledge

Ávila, Molinos, and Wesley all would agree that self-knowledge is necessary for spiritual progress and a means toward knowledge of the Divine. Each of them connected self-knowledge with the awareness of one's sinfulness and wickedness, while using different—though similar in intensity—terms to describe the human condition. However, Ávila and Wesley stand apart from Molinos in their allowance for a positive component to self-knowledge, as Ávila saw it as also including an awareness of one's own goodness as given from God, and Wesley saw it as being accompanied by peace and joy. Although Wesley took this even further than Ávila by seeing aspects of self-love and self-care, birthed out of self-knowledge, as virtues and not entirely as vices.

Ávila and Molinos affiliate around their placing a strongly epistemological value upon suffering. Wesley wrote on the progressive and systematic nature of self-knowledge as it occurs in stages, while Ávila and Molinos held to an ongoing practice of self-knowledge as keeping one's depravity ever in mind. In spite of these differences, all three, especially Wesley and Ávila, aligned closely in their understanding of self-knowledge as being associated with the economy of salvation in their respective soteriology.

3

Soteriology

THE REFORMATION AND THE Counter-Reformation of the sixteenth century brought to the surface debates of many kinds. Perhaps the most significant and long-lasting are the doctrinal distinctions which arose around the theme of soteriology. Discussion, debate, even arguments and fights ensued over issues of divine initiation, predestination, and free will, grace and works, and the role of faith in bringing one to salvation in relation to God. These issues, of course, were not new to the 1500s, as they were debated all the way back to Augustine of Hippo, Jerome, and Pelagius. Well before that, even the ancient philosophers differed on the role of fate and free will.

Unique to the doctrinal disputes of the sixteenth century, however, was the extent to which they divided the Christian church universal. The rise of Protestantism and its newly emerging camps forced people to decide and align with specific groups around a particular theological teaching. This period saw the rise of the Lutherans, the Calvinists, and a Roman Catholic Church more animately committed to their doctrinal distinctions, among others, with each systematically laying out their understanding of the order of salvation, or *ordo salutis*.

Although separated by three different centuries, Juan de Ávila, Miguel de Molinos, and John Wesley all represent distinct streams of thought which sprung from this time period. Ávila was heavily involved in the Counter Reformation and the Council of Trent, so he clearly represents the now traditional Roman Catholic views on soteriology. In the century following, Molinos perpetuated a distinctly Roman Catholic mystical approach to salvation. Wesley, though prone to borrow from many traditions, adhered to a more Lutheran understanding of justification.

JUAN DE ÁVILA ON SALVATION, FAITH, AND WORKS

Juan de Ávila published his *Audi Filia* twice during his lifetime. The first, he published in 1556 following the first two sessions of the Council of Trent. However, although it was published after the first session of Trent when many doctrines were defined in response to the Protestants, or perhaps *because* it was published following the first session, it fell under scrutiny by the Spanish Inquisition. Therefore, Ávila produced a second, revised edition of his work after the work of Trent was complete. Joan Frances Gormley pointed out that one of the issues of the first, among others, was the need to clarify his position on justification, where in the first edition, "some statements seemed to indicate that justifying grace was not inherent to the soul but merely a kind of external covering that left the person untransformed."[1] In spite of these editorial alterations on a few key points, Ávila maintained a strong Christology as connected to soteriology throughout both publications.

Ávila stated that Jesus is the only way of salvation, affirming that "there is no other path of salvation except him."[2] More specifically, it was the cross of Jesus through which "he overcame and destroyed our sins."[3] Ávila wrote and preached about the efficacy of Christ's death often. In his *Audi Filia*, he stated that "Christ's blood washed the heavens and the earth and the sea." He then continued to compare the cry for vengeance of Cain's one sin with the imagined *uproar* of all the sins of humankind, explaining that "however much they cry out, the blood of Christ cries out incomparably louder, begging pardon in the ears of divine mercy; it makes the voices of our sins inaudible, and they remain so low that God becomes deaf to them."[4] Elsewhere, he remarked that through Jesus' blood "our sins remain drowned in the sea of his mercy."[5] In a sermon on Pentecost Sunday, he specified that it was for *all* one's sins for which Jesus made amends.[6]

These statements would have received wide acceptance from his Catholic colleagues as well as the first Protestants contemporary to his time—though perhaps with some nuanced discussion on what the word *destroyed* entailed regarding sins. However, Ávila was also well aware of the different perspectives arising among the reformers. In the thirty-fourth chapter of his

---

1. Ávila, *Audi, Filia* (Gormley), 25.

2. Ávila, *Audi, Filia* (Gormley), 311.

3. Ávila, *Audi, Filia* (Gormley), 88.

4. Ávila, *Audi, Filia* (Gormley), 245.

5. Ávila, *Audi, Filia* (Gormley), 87.

6. Ávila, *Holy Spirit* (Dargan), 57.

Audi Filia, he wrote a paragraph that seems to address Calvin's perspectives published in his *Institutes of the Christian Religion* just twenty years before the first publication of Ávila's *Audi Filia*. He claimed that the knowledge of God necessary for salvation exists in the earth, this door is open, and the means to salvation are available.[7] This is opposed to Calvin's view that the means to salvation are only available to those to whom God makes them available. This was in keeping with Ávila's emphasis on free will as expressed especially in a sermon on Pentecost Monday.[8]

Sin, Temptation, the World, and the Flesh

In expressing his perspective on sin, Ávila offered a succinct summary in the twenty-first chapter of his *Audi Filia*. There, he attributed both justice and mercy to God. He began describing how God may look on human sin with justice and be provoked to wrath. Yet, through mercy God is driven "to compassion, and he does not regard them as an offense against him but as an evil for us."[9] Thus, God sees sin as a serious issue because it is damaging to people.

To Ávila, a person without the Spirit of God remains in a dismal state. With strong wording, Ávila expressed that "in so many defective, ugly, arid, and disordered things that you see, you should notice and recognize the corruption and disorder man has in his senses and works, without the Spirit of God."[10] Likewise, in one of his sermons he stated, "All that is good in man became depraved, his understanding dulled, his will weak, his flesh rebellious, rebellious in the extreme."[11] Although Ávila believed in a deep depravity within individuals apart from God, he again departed from his contemporary John Calvin on a key point. To Ávila this depravity, though extreme, is not total. As he described God as a watchful shepherd in *Audi Filia*, he stated:

> There are two things here for us. One is how much good we have
> in the body and soul that God made. The other is what we our-
> selves made, which is sin . . . We have made ugly and destroyed
> what the beautiful God had well constructed. But even our evil
> does not impede the surpassing goodness by which he desires

7. Ávila, *Audi, Filia* (Gormley), 118.

8. Ávila, *Holy Spirit* (Dargan), 112.

9. Ávila, *Audi, Filia* (Gormley), 85.

10. Ávila, *Audi, Filia* (Gormley), 194.

11. Ávila, *Holy Spirit* (Dargan), 52.

to save the good that he created and to destroy the evil that we committed.[12]

Here, we can observe that Ávila held to both a high degree of depravity along with a lofty adherence to the universal *imago Dei*, or image of God, which still resides in every person, though severely corrupted.

In keeping with the Roman Catholic tradition, Ávila made a distinction between mortal and venial sins; however, he was more apt to address the mortal sins. He urged his readers to avoid committing mortal sins if they desire to serve Jesus.[13] He also included among the mortal sins one's unwillingness to cast off a temptation which is known to be dangerous to one's spiritual well-being.[14]

A reason for Ávila's strong dealings with the resistance of temptation may be found in the opening paragraphs of part 3 in his *Audi Filia*. There, he described the stages of digression into sin beginning with a "disordered look," followed by a desire, then resulting in action, and climaxing with others becoming involved in the sin.[15] He went on to instruct his readers to deal with temptation at the initial look so that it does not escalate into sin. Earlier, he described a level of temptation that may even precede the look. He explained how one may have "foul imaginings" and face internal temptations within one's soul, he stated that it is better to war against such temptations than to concede and find oneself in even greater affliction.[16] When facing temptations, he urged his readers "immediately make the sign of the cross on your forehead and heart," then call upon the name of Jesus, and pray.[17]

Ávila attributed temptation to three primary sources, the world, the flesh, and Satan. The world, he said, deceives through "lies and false promises."[18] The flesh is the source of misguided appetite, the thinking, the will, and the heart that is inclined to evil.[19] Like the world, according to Ávila, the devil also uses deception, but his are both external and internal, using false sentiments, speeches, and light.[20]

12. Ávila, *Audi, Filia* (Gormley), 248.

13. Ávila, *Audi, Filia* (Gormley), 255.

14. Ávila, *Audi, Filia* (Gormley), 71.

15. Ávila, *Audi, Filia* (Gormley), 174.

16. Ávila, *Audi, Filia* (Gormley), 71–72.

17. Ávila, *Audi, Filia* (Gormley), 60.

18. Ávila, *Audi, Filia* (Gormley), 46.

19. Ávila, *Audi, Filia* (Gormley), 73, 121.

20. Ávila, *Audi, Filia* (Gormley), 77.

In dealing with sin, Ávila followed a multi-step process that involved God's reprimand, human confession, and repentance. There could possibly be another added to this; in a sermon he linked God's reprimand with God's desire to console and for people to amend their ways.[21] Thus, *consolation* may serve as an additional step in this progression.

In his *Audi Filia*, Ávila drew from the Lord's Prayer and from the Epistle of First John, specifically verse 1:8, to contend that people sin daily and therefore must acknowledge and confess these sins.[22] However, mere confession was not enough for Ávila; later, he called upon the authoritative voice of Saint Augustine to include penance and a turning away from sin, or repentance.[23] Thus, ultimately, this entire process of dealing with sin moves from God's reprimand, acknowledgment, confession, consolation, penance, and repentance—though the order may vary depending on the arrival of consolation. However, if these don't work and one finds oneself giving into temptations, Ávila referenced how some found freedom through ascetic practices. Though he maintained a degree of hesitancy and caution about reproducing such practices, he nonetheless wrote of pinching oneself, hitting oneself, self-flagellation, and other ascetic torture as possible remedies to sin and temptation when done in remembrance of and association with the sufferings of Jesus.[24]

To Ávila, this synergistic approach should stop at no less than the destruction of sin. He stated that it is God's desire to destroy (*destruir*) sin; however, people may impede (*impidiésemos*) God's work through their own love for sin.[25] He believed "that 'saving from sins' is not only removing punishment for them but giving interior purity and a heart and grace and spirit that suffice to make one keep God's commandments."[26] This is such that it may result in the complete removal of sin, which he saw as a necessary prerequisite for the Holy Spirit to remain with someone.[27]

21. Ávila, *Holy Spirit* (Dargan), 62.

22. Ávila, *Audi, Filia* (Gormley), 240.

23. Ávila, *Audi, Filia* (Gormley), 249.

24. Ávila, *Audi, Filia* (Gormley), 62.

25. Ávila, *Audi Filia*—Spanish, capítulo 86; Ávila, *Audi, Filia* (Gormley), 248.

26. Ávila, *Audi, Filia* (Gormley), 254.

27. Ávila, *Holy Spirit* (Dargan), 95; Ávila, *Audi, Filia* (Gormley), 258–59.

Justification and Faith

Ávila defined justification as "the resurrection of a soul that was dead in sin," and attributed it to "the cause of beauty."[28] As the Apostle of Andalusia, justification was an important doctrine in his preaching and his writing. When looking at the mechanics of justification in Ávila's writings, it is important to keep in mind his historical context. He was writing during the time of the Protestant reformation. In fact, his studies at the University of Salamanca came to a close the same year that Martin Luther published his *95 Theses*, and his studies at the University of Alcalá began only three years later. Thus, Ávila would have been quite aware of the debates ensuing over the issues of faith and works in justification. This was clearly reflected in his ensuing writings, especially in his *Audi Filia*.

In the introductory material of her edition of the *Audi Filia*, Joan Gormley pointed out that Ávila began writing this work early on, adding to it throughout his life.[29] That being the case, in this, his *magnum opus*, one may see Ávila's progression of theological development. Early on, there is a strong emphasis on the place of faith in salvation; it is only later that he spoke against the *sola fide*, or faith alone, argument of Luther. As a reformer himself—although from within—Ávila may have had an ear to Luther early on, only later to reject Luther as he was denounced by the Church.

For example, in the opening chapter Ávila asserted, *"porque como el principio de la vida espiritual sea la fe,"* or "the beginning of the spiritual life is faith."[30] He then reiterated this point nearly verbatim in the thirty-first chapter in the context of the "Catholic faith."[31] However, in the closing chapter of the first part, Ávila began to shift his focus; he still maintained that faith was the beginning of the spiritual life, but he started to speak out against Luther's *sola fide*. He explained how faith is given from God, but emphatically stated, "If anyone should say of this faith that through it alone justice is obtained and the pardon of sins, he will grievously err, as have those who have affirmed this."[32]

He continued to explain the role of acknowledging one's sin to God as a means for finding pardon; however, he again addressed the Lutheran perspective by stating that "whoever moved by this would say that sin is pardoned by the recognition of sin alone would commit no small error . . .

28. Ávila, *Confidence* (Benedictines), 127; Ávila, *Audi, Filia* (Gormley), 300.

29. Ávila, *Audi, Filia* (Gormley), 21.

30. Ávila, *Audi Filia*—Spanish, capítulo 1; Ávila, *Audi, Filia* (Gormley), 41.

31. Ávila, *Audi, Filia* (Gormley), 112.

32. Ávila, *Audi, Filia* (Gormley), 138.

it would be as baseless to say that it is obtained 'by faith alone' because in some passages of scripture it mentions nothing but faith."[33] Ávila then in a polemical statement, if not *ad hominem*, accused "those who attribute justification to faith alone, do it as a means of finding consolation for their mediocrity or for the wickedness of their lives."[34]

Interestingly, even amidst these strong condemnations of *sola fide*, Ávila maintained that it was right for the early church to place a strong emphasis on faith as the "first door to salvation." So, faith as the entry into salvation was not the issue for this Apostle of Andalusia; rather faith alone for salvation was his concern. He explained that "faith [is] formed by charity" and that "love 'is greater than faith and hope.'"[35] A few chapters later, he reiterated this by saying that "simple and humble believing [*is*] the principle of our salvation," and "if love is joined to it, we possess salvation in all its perfection."[36] Thus, to Ávila, it is charity, faith, and love that all play their part in moving one toward and into justification.

In the third part of his *Audi Filia*, Ávila laid out a brief *ordo salutis*, or order of salvation, in which he described the process of "judgment" where God "first shows us who we are," followed by a demonstration of love through the sending of "'a spirit of burning' that causes us pain," through which God "washes us, giving us his pardon and his grace."[37] Although epistemology and self-knowledge are discussed further in another chapter, it is worth noting their connection with salvation in Ávila's scheme of salvation. In this order, Ávila shows self-knowledge as the first step toward salvation, while earlier in his book, he stated that people must know God in order to be saved—which comes through God's self-discloser to the person.[38] Thus, it is self-knowledge and knowledge of the Divine which lead people to salvation. However, elsewhere he made a seemingly contradictory statement where he asserted that due to the deficiencies of human knowledge, "God arranged to save us through faith and not through our knowledge."[39] Here, his original Spanish proves helpful. The word he used for knowledge of God, *conocimiento*, connotes a broader knowledge, awareness, or consciousness; whereas the word he used in contrast to being saved through faith, *saber*,

33. Ávila, *Audi, Filia* (Gormley), 139.

34. Ávila, *Audi, Filia* (Gormley), 141.

35. Ávila, *Audi, Filia* (Gormley), 139–40.

36. Ávila, *Audi, Filia* (Gormley), 156.

37. Ávila, *Audi, Filia* (Gormley), 187.

38. Ávila, *Audi, Filia* (Gormley), 117.

39. Ávila, *Audi, Filia* (Gormley), 145.

indicates a possession of information.[40] Therefore, salvation comes through awareness and encounter of God and oneself, and a response of faith, not through mere facts and data according to Ávila.

Merit and Works

In Ávila's writings on the place of merit, there emerges a similar tension as expressed in his writings on the place of faith as discussed above. In his writing of the *Audi Filia*, a progression of thought may be seen as he nearly denounced the place of merit in salvation early on, then affirmed the place of merit later as he condemned Luther's *sola fide*. For example, in chapter 40, he asserted that Jesus' death, which made friends out of his enemies, done by love "did not come about from their merit but from his supreme goodness."[41] A few chapters later, he spoke of salvation as a gift, referencing the apostle Paul's letter to the Ephesians. He wrote concerning this salvation, "it is not inherited or merited or achieved by human strength."[42] However, in the next chapter he continued by railing against *sola fida* and affirming the link between faith and charity (*fe* and *caridad*), the necessity of love, and the place of penance as requisite to justification.[43] The distinction seems to be between his use of the words *mereciesen* and *caridad*, or merit and charity, where *mereciesen* refers to something earned based on one's deserving and *caridad* refers to kind acts of love. To Ávila, the former is not involved in salvation or justification, but the latter is required through its inseparable connection to faith.

Many places may be found in the writings of Ávila where he maintained this position that merit is not a factor in salvation, or even in other aspects of one's relationship with God. For example, in one sermon, he described times when a person may have a strong desire to connect with God and they only experience a small degree of this connection, yet at other times the heart and soul are set aflame, in his words, with a "tremendous fire of love." The latter of which is not based on merit, nor is the former for that matter.[44] In fact, to Ávila, receiving consolations of various kinds are also not merit-based.[45] In addition, the coming of the Holy Spirit, he stated, is

---

40. Ávila, *Audi Filia*—Spanish, capítulo 34, 35.

41. Ávila, *Audi, Filia* (Gormley), 128.

42. Ávila, *Audi, Filia* (Gormley), 135.

43. Ávila, *Audi, Filia* (Gormley), 138–39.

44. Ávila, *Holy Spirit* (Dargan), 114.

45. Ávila, *Confidence* (Benedictines), 5–6.

based on the merits of Jesus, not the merit of the recipient.[46] That being said, there seem to be other places that add a bit of confusion as to where Ávila stood on the role of merit. Elsewhere, he made a seemingly contradictory statement as he concluded that asking and desire are not enough for the Holy Spirit to come, "unless your actions merit His coming to you."[47]

Although the place of merit was mostly downplayed in Ávila's writings, there are numerous times when Ávila expressed a high value for charity and acts of service. To Ávila, even the simplest of acts may serve to accomplish great good. For example, in a letter to Don Diego de Gusman and Dr. Loarte about their joining the Society of Jesus, he exhorted them to see their acts of service, even the washing of dishes, as a meaningful contribution to the overall mission of the Jesuits in bringing about the salvation of souls.[48] Elsewhere, in a sermon he urged his listeners to "remember the poor . . . feed the hungry! Give a gown to the naked; give a shirt to him who needs it! Release prisoners from prison!" He went on to encourage those who could not afford to give to "forgive injuries! Pray to God for those who persecute you, comfort those in sorrow, suffer with the downfallen, make the troubles of others your own." Such giving, he believed, should be done because of God's giving of himself to people.[49]

As Ávila held faith and works in close tension, he also held motive and action in a similar tension. He believed that motive contains greater value than the quantity of works, especially when the motive is a deep love.[50] He even went so far as to say that "whatever has not been inspired by the fire of the love of God, will not be received by Him"; although he stopped just shy of expounding upon the theological debate on the merit of works in themselves.[51] However, he also stressed that mere intention is not enough, but must express itself in action.[52]

Forgiveness

To Ávila, the extent to which God forgives people is immense and effectual and necessary for salvation. In his own words, he exclaimed that "the accomplished redemption is so abundant that the fact that God pardons

46. Ávila, *Holy Spirit* (Dargan), 102.

47. Ávila, *Holy Spirit* (Dargan), 75.

48. Ávila, *Confidence* (Benedictines), 10.

49. Ávila, *Holy Spirit* (Dargan), 44.

50. Ávila, *Confidence* (Benedictines), 119.

51. Ávila, *Holy Spirit* (Dargan), 34.

52. Ávila, *Holy Spirit* (Dargan), 62.

the offenses that man commits against him is a gift beyond all human calculation."[53] He believed that God took more joy in giving salvation and forgiveness than the one who was seeking it.[54] He held that because God's forgiveness is boundless, then people too ought to extend a limitless forgiveness to others.[55]

To Ávila there are two primary means through which one receives the grace of forgiveness—confession and penance. Regarding confession, he referenced Augustine, stating that the remedy for having God not to look at one's sins is "you look at them."[56] In other words, acknowledgment of one's own sins will move God to set the sins aside. However, he also included penance in this process both here and elsewhere. Earlier in his *Audi Filia*, he asserted that "grace and justice are given by means of this sacrament"— that is, the sacrament of penance. However, he went on to include all seven sacraments of the Roman Catholic Church as means to the grace.[57] Not only did Ávila believe that God's forgiveness is immense and effectual, but he also understood this extension of grace to be immediate at the time of one's crying out to God.[58]

Assurance and Backsliding

Ávila believed that people may live in a state of certainty about their salvation. However, this certainty is not based on merit. Rather, the certainty is given by divine revelation.[59] In a sermon "Within the Octave of the Ascension," Ávila called upon the authoritative voice of Athanasius to explain assurance, in this case not just assurance of salvation, but assurance of the presence and working of the Holy Spirit. Quoting the saint of old, he said that assurance does not come through baptism, but through feeling the presence of the Holy Spirit within, the way that a pregnant woman feels a baby within her. When pressed further, Athanasius described it like this: "you will feel your heart burning with the fire of charity and the unwavering love of God . . . and you will feel this flame of love leaping within you."[60] In another sermon, Ávila explained this assurance as an inner and "profound

53. Ávila, *Audi, Filia* (Gormley), 82.

54. Ávila, *Audi, Filia* (Gormley), 248.

55. Ávila, *Audi, Filia* (Gormley), 93.

56. Ávila, *Audi, Filia* (Gormley), 249.

57. Ávila, *Audi, Filia* (Gormley), 140.

58. Ávila, *Audi, Filia* (Gormley), 238.

59. Ávila, *Audi, Filia* (Gormley), 105.

60. Ávila, *Holy Spirit* (Dargan), 14.

peace and tranquility of soul" and through a feeling of consolation and confidence.[61]

Although Ávila maintained the possibility of assurance, he did not believe that salvation was necessarily secure. He maintained that God is the principal agent at work in those who are justified, and that God gently aligns one's free will to cooperate with his will. Yet, even with this emphasis on free will, he did not shy away from the application of the term predestination "by which [God] determined 'from eternity' to save you."[62] However, he also held that people could fall away from God by embracing heresy.[63] In addition, he believed, though not as severe, that people could also fall away from sanctifying grace, while preserving the state of justification.[64] He held that this falling away may happen through neglect, error, and through the passions.[65] Therefore, there exists a need for ongoing repentance.[66]

JOHN WESLEY'S EDITING OF ÁVILA ON SALVATION, FAITH, AND WORKS

Works Righteousness

Although there are clear statements of the high place of works and merit for Ávila, he also placed a strong emphasis on God's part in salvation. To Ávila, it is not merely works, but works in conjunction with faith that brings about entrance into the kingdom of God. In fact, in his earlier works, Ávila seemed somewhat influenced by his contemporary Martin Luther as he, like Luther, elevated the place of faith. Later, however, it is clear that Ávila felt that Luther went too far and again wrote on the role of works in salvation. In other words, to Ávila the place of faith and works in salvation is a *both/ and* not an *either/or* scenario.

Wesley's self-proclaimed alignment with the Arminian tradition and, consequently, his emphasis on human free will over divine predestination did not in any way minimize Wesley's perspective on a sovereign God who remains active in the world and in human lives. In his diligent editing, Wesley showed great care in removing any phrase that even remotely hinted at a works based salvation or righteousness. He even went so far as to remove

---

61. Ávila, *Holy Spirit* (Dargan), 39.

62. Ávila, *Audi, Filia* (Gormley), 195–96.

63. Ávila, *Audi, Filia* (Gormley), 120, 152.

64. Ávila, *Audi, Filia* (Gormley), 120; Ávila, *Holy Spirit* (Dargan), 83.

65. Ávila, *Holy Spirit* (Dargan), 56.

66. Ávila, *Confidence* (Benedictines), 130.

phrases and wording that placed human spiritual progression in an active voice.

Ávila, in speaking of friendship with God as having "more value than all the rest of things," stated that it is "obteyned by the exercise of virtue."[67] The language of friendship with God and its accompanying high value resonated well with Wesley's theological framework. However, Wesley removed the latter phrase that highlights virtue as the means toward such friendship with God. For Wesley, virtue is a result of such friendship, not the cause.

A similar example also appears elsewhere in Ávila's first letter where Wesley removed a lengthy couple of paragraphs about obedience being the means to entering God's kingdom.[68] Here, Wesley made no attempt at editing, but completely eliminated the entire section. Like Wesley's view of virtue, it could be said his view of obedience would be more of a result than a cause to entering God's kingdom.

Ávila stated that "it is he [God] who secures us, but, upon condition that wee relye on him."[69] Wesley also removed this entire sentence. There could be a couple possible reasons for this removal. (1) It is possible that Wesley was uncomfortable with the wording of security, perhaps implying an eternal security held by his more Calvinistic contemporaries, since the context of Ávila's statement is in regard to salvation. Or, (2) it is possible that Wesley's issue with this statement resided in the word *condition*. To place God's securing of human beings as conditional upon human reliance seems to shift the role of activity from the Divine to the human. Given Wesley's careful editing and removal of other such statements further supports the latter. Or, (3) it is possible that it is a combination of the two which Wesley opposed.

In his fifteenth letter, Ávila wrote, "If wee be changeable, and weake, in working let us looke upon this author of our faith, and see how he is nayled to that Crosse."[70] Although Wesley kept this sentence and that which followed, in addition to contemporizing the spelling he intentionally removed the words "in working."

If the preceding examples demonstrate some of the more overt statements of works, Wesley also removed the subtler statements that alluded to human action in various aspects of relationship to God. For example, Wesley eliminated a number of statements that began with the words *let us*; for example, "let us apply the axe," "let us entertain good thoughts," "let us

---

67. Ávila, *Selected Epistles*, 3.

68. Ávila, *Selected Epistles*, 9–10.

69. Ávila, *Selected Epistles*, 118.

70. Ávila, *Selected Epistles*, 124.

place ourselves," "let us cover it with the ashes," "let us renew ourselves," "let us search hearts," "let us keep him close imbraced by us."[71] With the consistency he used with his removal of such phrases, it could be concluded that their elimination was due to a perspective held by Wesley that these things are not up to *us* to execute; rather, these are things left to divine action.

There are also many other examples where Wesley removed Ávila's active language as it pertains to human action. Statements like "for as much as remains in our power," "you may well prepare yourself," "the just man pays for sins," and "laid up with diligence" found their way out of Wesley's edition.[72]

Penance and Repentance

In Ávila's letters which Wesley included, Ávila used the word *penance* five times. Of these five times, Wesley omitted the word altogether four times and changed the word *penance* to the word *repentance* once. The latter appears in a list of that which should be loved after one should "cast all that out of your hart, which is not God," the list of that which should be loved includes "teares, solitude, humilitie, and penance."[73]

Wesley eliminated two references to penance in a letter Ávila wrote to a friend who had "grown cold in the way of virtue." The first includes a means toward the end of leading a new life, the means being "procuring to appease the Lord, by penance, and consession, for that which is pait."[74] In the second reference, Wesley eliminated the words "exercise of penance" from a list of things that ought not be neglected. Wesley did leave in the list "prayer, the reading of spiritual books, the Sacraments."[75]

The final two omissions of penance are found in Wesley's editing of Ávila's thirty-third letter. In both places, Ávila connected the love of God with contempt for oneself or self-knowledge and the doing of penance or the love of penance.[76] In both places, Wesley kept the connection between the love of God and contempt for oneself in the first occasion and self-knowledge in the second occasion but eliminated the doing and love of penance in this connection.

71. Ávila, *Selected Epistles*, 21–23, 61, 306.

72. Ávila, *Selected Epistles*, 96, 121, 189, 306–7.

73. Ávila, *Selected Epistles*, 54.

74. Ávila, *Selected Epistles*, 97.

75. Wesley, *Christian Library* (Ávila), 46:286.

76. Ávila, *Selected Epistles*, 266–77.

MIGUEL DE MOLINOS ON SALVATION, FAITH, AND WORKS

Faith and Works

In the sixteenth century, Martin Luther's influence reached broadly. Before his full break from Rome, Luther's emphasis on faith was gaining some influence among the learned, religious and lay alike. For example, John of the Cross wrote that entrance into the spiritual life is by faith. Likewise, Juan de Ávila stressed the role of faith in spiritual initiation. However, by the seventeenth century, the Protestant and Catholic divide was solidified. Influenced by the Council of Trent, the post–Counter-Reformation Roman Catholic Church upheld a salvation that requires both faith and works over and against the *sola fide*, or faith alone, of Luther. Miguel de Molinos existed in this post-Trent Catholicism. Interestingly, however, Molinos veered away from writing about works as prerequisite to salvation and tended to show good deeds as an expression of one's commitment to God.

For example, in the fifth chapter of his first book, Molinos stated that "the essential devotion is the spirit's quickness for doing good, so that it may carry out the commandments of God and do all things in his service."[77] Here, Molinos praised good deeds as the higher display of devotion over and above a devotion based on the affect and senses. Similarly, in chapter 17, Molinos made the pointed assertion that "good works, not good words, show love."[78]

To Molinos, other expressions of love and devotion fall short of proper deeds. In his second book, he continued this idea by cautioning his readers not to use the reading of books as a substitute for sound spiritual direction. He especially warned of highly speculative mystical books that "do not have a practical cast."[79] He believed that such pragmatic application is necessary throughout one's spiritual development, not just relegated for the early stages (this is somewhat contrary to the accusations made by his critics and contrary to later practitioners of the Quietist movement). Molinos encouraged his readers as they grow and develop spiritually "not to quit the exterior practices of its occupation."[80]

This being said, Molinos did not hold outward works as the highest goal of the spiritual life. He cautioned his readers to consider if God would have them do certain acts, no matter how great an achievement these may

77. Molinos, *Spiritual Guide* (Baird and McGinn), 73.

78. Molinos, *Spiritual Guide* (Baird and McGinn), 99.

79. Molinos, *Spiritual Guide* (Baird and McGinn), 104.

80. Molinos, *Spiritual Guide* (Baird and McGinn), 115.

accomplish. In other words, obedience to the will of God transcends the deeds themselves.[81]

JOHN WESLEY'S EDITING OF MOLINOS ON SALVATION, FAITH, AND WORKS

Works

In a paragraph pertaining to the receiving of "Divine Operations" through consent and toward purification, Molinos began with the phrase "with new efforts thou't," which Wesley eliminated.[82] This is seemingly a minor alteration, but it does carry significant implications. While Wesley preserved the language of *consent, receiving,* and even the word *exercise* as "the only Means whereby thou wilt be purged," he excluded the wording of *effort.*

In a paragraph on the value of prayer over pilgrimage, Wesley kept the initial premise of Molinos, but removed his more detailed particularization of the matter. The premise stated that God is happier with "quiet and devote Prayer for the Space of an hour, than to go on great Pilgrimages."[83] The portion left out by Wesley included a brief description of the benefits of prayer including those for self, others, God, and the way in which prayer "merits a high degree of glory." The reason for Wesley's editing may be that of motive. To Wesley, prayer is not to be entered into because of what one gets out of it. The latter phrase specifically may have been removed due to his view on merit.

Though Protestant in his loyalties, Wesley did not totally shy away from the language of works. This can be seen in his preservation of the words of Molinos in his chapter on internal recollection, urging readers to "exercise thyself outwardly in the external Works of thy Calling" as an act of doing God's will.[84] However, Wesley was also quick to offer cautions concerning the role of works. This cautionary counsel may be seen a bit later, where he kept the wording of being "raised also from outward actions to the Love of Humanity and Divinity."[85] Here, we see an appreciation for, if not approval of, seeing love as the ultimate end, exceeding the importance of works. Similarly, Wesley also removed Molinos's exhortation to avoid loving

81. Molinos, *Spiritual Guide* (Baird and McGinn), 109.
82. Molinos, *Spiritual Guide,* 23; Wesley, *Christian Library* (Molinos), 38:258.
83. Molinos, *Spiritual Guide,* 37; Wesley, *Christian Library* (Molinos), 38:265.
84. Molinos, *Spiritual Guide,* 39; Wesley, *Christian Library* (Molinos), 38:266.
85. Molinos, *Spiritual Guide,* 118; Wesley, *Christian Library* (Molinos), 38:270.

activity as an end to itself.[86] In so doing, Wesley communicated that perhaps loving activity is actually an end to itself.

In a chapter on *internal and mystical silence*, Wesley preserved a statement arguing that perfection is not found in speaking or thinking a lot about God, but "in loving him sufficiently."[87] Later, we will see how Wesley affirmed this perspective. Interestingly, however, he removed the Scriptural text of John 3:18 that Molinos used to support this claim encouraging the readers to express love through good deeds and not merely words.

Salvation

In a chapter on internal recollection, Molinos included a few paragraphs pertaining to salvation and the initial entering into that which leads to eternal life. Wesley left these paragraphs relatively intact, while removing the lengthy descriptions of the shift from meditation to contemplation interspersed within the explanations on salvation. The lines written by Molinos and kept by Wesley on the topic at hand affirm that "our Lord Christ is the Guide, the Door, and the Way," that he is "the only Door," the essential need for one's entry into a relationship with God "to be washed with the precious Blood of a Redeemer," the dependence on both the divinity and the humanity of Jesus, and the need for a "simple Act of Faith."[88]

JOHN WESLEY ON SALVATION, FAITH, AND WORKS[89]

John Wesley saw the spiritual life as an ongoing progression toward an end with multiple stages and seasons. Influenced by the works of Martin Luther, especially in connection with John's Aldersgate experience, Wesley saw the means of this spiritual progression as beginning with God's grace while becoming functional through faith. For Wesley, God's grace and human faith remain *the* means of Christian advancement; however, in his sermons Wesley also described various other secondary means which contribute to this spiritual progression. These include self-knowledge (primarily as an awareness of sin, as addressed in the previous chapter) and self-denial. He also placed a strong emphasis on an active spirituality through human response.

86. Molinos, *Spiritual Guide*, 161; Wesley, *Christian Library* (Molinos), 38:289.

87. Molinos, *Spiritual Guide*, 57; Wesley, *Christian Library* (Molinos), 38:131.

88. Molinos, *Spiritual Guide*, 52–55; Wesley, *Christian Library* (Molinos), 38:267.

89. This section includes a portion that has been edited and expanded upon from this author's DMin dissertation, "Stages of Spiritual Growth: A Comparative Study of Pseudo-Dionysius, John of the Cross, Teresa of Avila, and John Wesley," 119–31.

For example, although he was a strong proponent for *sola fide*, faith alone, for salvation, Wesley held works in close relationship to faith; he also emphasized the role of prayer, fasting, and abstinence, stressed the need for spiritual diligence, and used language like "stir up," "agonize continually," and "earnestly strive" pertaining to one's spiritual pursuit.[90]

However, Wesley remained careful not to stress human activity at the expense of God's initiation of grace extended to the soul as prompted by the Holy Spirit. He held strongly to the role of God's initiative, not human effort, to bring about the ends of holiness, righteousness, perfection, and entire sanctification within the souls of people. As a further example of God's role in human spirituality, Wesley stated that the witness of the Spirit is necessary to know God's pardoning love, and that righteousness maintains both an active and a passive nature toward forgiveness and acceptance by God.[91]

The Pre-Christian State

Wesley's views of the pre-Christian state existed in a tension of stark contrast. On the one hand, he saw God's work of creation saturated with God's grace as humanity existed and continues to exist with the stamp of the image of God upon their souls.[92] On the other hand, which Wesley emphasized far more frequently, humanity contains the deep stains of depravity forever marked by sin. Throughout his sermons, Wesley described the person trapped in this pre-Christian state as maintaining a heart that "is altogether corrupt," "separated from God," corrupt in soul and body, bound for "death eternal," "in bondage and fear," in whom "'dwelleth no good thing;' but whatsoever is evil and abominable," full of pride, idolatry, ungodliness, and the image of the devil, while possessing no knowledge of God.[93] In a journal entry dated Monday, August 27, 1739, Wesley claimed that "no

90. See sermons "Salvation by Faith" and "Justification by Faith," Wesley, *Works* (Outler), 1:125, 192–93; "Upon the Lord's Sermon on the Mount: III," Wesley, *Works* (Outler), 1:511–12; "Satan's Devices," Wesley, *Works* (Outler), 2:151; "Wilderness State," Wesley, *Works* (Outler), 2:211.

91. See sermons "Witness of the Spirit: I," Wesley, *Works* (Outler), 1:274–75; "Lord Our Righteousness," Wesley, *Works* (Outler), 1:458.

92. See sermon "Salvation by Faith," Wesley, *Works* (Outler), 1:117.

93. See sermons "Salvation by Faith," Wesley, *Works* (Outler), 1:118; "Justification by Faith," Wesley, *Works* (Outler), 1:185; "Spirit of Bondage and of Adoption," Wesley, *Works* (Outler), 1:258; "Upon the Lord's Sermon on the Mount: I," Wesley, *Works* (Outler), 1:477; "Original Sin," Wesley, *Works* (Outler), 2:179, 182; "Witness of the Spirit: II," Wesley, *Works* (Outler), 1:291; "New Birth," Wesley, *Works* (Outler), 2:190, 192.

good works can be done before justification."[94] Jason Vickers described Wesley's theological perspective on this state as "a complete impairment of the spiritual senses" where "one's spiritual senses are so 'locked up' that they are 'in the same condition as if [one] had them not.'"[95]

Even amidst such a dismal description of the fallen state of humanity, Wesley saw the potential of such people to make movement toward God. However, Vickers stressed that such movement cannot take place on one's own apart from the working of the Holy Spirit, according to Wesley's soteriology.[96] In other words, Wesley was not Pelagian. This also highlights that Wesley's soteriology and pneumatology remain inseparable. On July 25, 1741 at St. Mary's, Oxford, Wesley preached a message titled "The Almost Christian." Here, he described the person who, by God's grace, is beginning to make the transition away from the natural, depraved state toward salvation. Wesley gave three characteristics of such a person. First, an *almost Christian* possesses "heathen honesty," in other words, a person who is beginning to understand a sense of right and wrong. The second characteristic held by an *almost Christian* includes a form of godliness. This will be a person who has a form of religiousness, yet apart from true salvation. Finally, an *almost Christian* will maintain sincerity. Sincerity exists as the beginnings of a desire to know, serve, and please God. All this, Wesley would categorize as an act of God's *prevenient grace* leading to salvation.[97]

In a theme that began early in Wesley's ministry, but wasn't fleshed out until later, Wesley wrote about the *faith of a servant* as opposed to the *faith of a child*. In an article titled "Real Christianity as Integrating Theme in Wesley's Soteriology: The Critique of a Modern Myth," Kenneth Collins tracked the development of Wesley's teaching on the faith of a servant along with his doctrine of assurance as they relate to Wesley's understanding of *real Christianity*. According to Collins, Wesley first made the distinction between a servant of God and a child of God at the Methodist Conference of 1746, stating that the former serves God out of fear and the latter out of love.[98] Wesley saw the servant of God as someone who was not quite a Christian, or to use the language above, an *almost Christian*. Collins pointed out that, in his 1754 *Explanatory Notes on the New Testament*, Wesley linked the servant to the "spirit of bondage."[99] For the most part, Collins saw Wes-

94. Wesley, *Works* (Ward and Heitzenrater), 19:89.

95. Maddox and Vickers, *Cambridge Companion to Wesley*, 200.

96. Maddox and Vickers, *Cambridge Companion to Wesley*, 200.

97. Wesley, *Works* (Outler), 1:131, 132, 134.

98. Collins, "Real Christianity," 18.

99. Collins, "Real Christianity," 23.

ley's use of the phrase *servant of God* as an intermediate state between the pre-Christian "child of the devil" and a "child of God."[100]

However, this interpretation of Wesley is not without its opposing views. Collins separated Wesley's teaching on the *faith of a servant* into the broad and narrow sense, with the former inclusive of justification and the latter serving as a pre-cursor to salvation.[101] Collins pointed out that Randy Maddox and Scott Kisker were more apt to view Wesley's understanding of a servant as one who is justified. Kisker made a separation between justification and regeneration, and Maddox reads a process approach in Wesley in order to account for these differences.[102]

Related to, yet distinct from, assurance in evaluating Wesley's pre-Aldersgate state, elsewhere, Kenneth Collins argued that the fear of death also serves as a precursor to salvation in Wesleyan theology.[103] Although this may not necessarily come directly from Wesley's standard sermons in such distinct terms, Wesley's experience clearly reflects this fear prior to Aldersgate and the subsequent release of fear after Aldersgate. Drawing from such a profound experience, Wesley later spoke about the freeing from such fear in a sermon entitled "Sermon against the Fear of Death."[104]

Salvation

For centuries, the debate between predestination and free will continues to ensue, even predating the most famous respective champions of the causes John Calvin (1509–64) and Jacobus Arminius (1560–1609). John Wesley, by his own admission, found himself in the latter camp, seeing salvation as a gift from God available for all who by his/her free will would receive this gift. However, Wesley was not completely opposed to the concept of predestination per se. In his journal entry dated Wednesday, August 24, 1743, Wesley addressed George Whitefield's understanding of predestination by first affirming the possibility, if not the probability of God unconditionally electing "certain persons to do certain works . . . some nations to receive peculiar privileges . . . some nations to hear the Gospel . . . some persons to many peculiar advantages, both with regard to temporal and spiritual things . . . [and] some persons to eternal glory."[105] Where Wesley had contention

100. Collins, "Real Christianity," 31.
101. Collins, "Real Christianity," 34.
102. Collins, "Real Christianity," 26–27.
103. Collins and Tyson, *Conversations*, 56–58.
104. Collins and Tyson, *Conversations*, 67.
105. Wesley, *Works* (Ward and Heitzenrater), 19:331–32.

with Whitefield includes the idea that those not elected would face eternal punishment and that there would be anyone who did not have the opportunity to escape eternal damnation.

That being said, Wesley continued to preach a message of unlimited atonement. In an article titled "A Change of Heart in Bristol? John Wesley's Doctrine of Election in Perspective, 1739–1768," Joel Houston pointed out that Wesley attributed the vast and intense response of the people in Bristol to his proclamation that God's grace is available to all.[106] Houston also pointed out how Wesley may have retracted his previously held view of the possibility of God predestining some as expressed in a letter to his brother Charles dated August 8, 1752, but later softened back to an ecumenicism in the mid- to late 1760s.[107] However, Albert Outler pointed out that in 1778 Wesley amped up his apologetic for doctrines opposing Calvinism with the release of his *Arminian Magazine*.[108]

Even when emphasizing a universal offer of salvation and a free-will response, Wesley used strong wording to express the divine initiative in bringing a person to salvation. In his sermon "The Spirit of Bondage and of Adoption" Wesley stated:

> By some awful providence, or by his Word applied with the demonstration of his Spirit, God touches the heart of him that lay asleep in darkness and in the shadow of death. He is terribly shaken out of his sleep, and awakes into a consciousness of his danger. Perhaps in a moment, perhaps by degrees, the eyes of his understanding are opened.[109]

From here, he began to unfold the process of transition from the natural state toward the spiritual state, crossing over through the point of salvation. Wesley saw this process as beginning with an awareness of God and his nature; next emerges a greater self-awareness that moves beyond the outward actions toward an inner awareness of the soul's need.[110] After this, self-knowledge makes known the depravity within, driving the person to confession of sin.[111] According to Wesley, the depravity still remains at this point, until finally, the person has "found grace" and salvation comes.[112]

106. Houston, "Change of Heart," 69.

107. Houston, "Change of Heart," 75.

108. Wesley, *John Wesley* (Outler), 425.

109. Wesley, *Works* (Outler), 1:255.

110. Wesley, *Works* (Outler), 1:255.

111. Wesley, *Works* (Outler), 1:256.

112. Wesley, *Works* (Outler), 1:258, 260.

These stages in Wesley's *ordo salutis*, or order of salvation, ought to be seen as human responses, not human initiative. Wesley held that God's grace was necessary at every stage as the initiator of spiritual progression. As Jerry L. Mercer summarized it, "since, according to Wesley, we are naturally hindered in grasping the overwhelming reality of divine grace, God helpfully enables us to both understand (at least its elemental features) and appropriate it."[113]

Faith and Salvation

The writings of Martin Luther clearly shaped the direction of Wesley's life beginning at his Aldersgate experience. Due to this encounter, the fingerprints of Luther's theology remain imprinted upon the text of Wesley's sermons. This may be seen primarily through Wesley's emphasis upon faith as it relates to salvation. For Wesley, faith does not consist of an abstract mindset or state of being. Rather, faith remains connected to the object upon which (or upon *whom* as the case may be) one trusts and believes.[114] This object is the person of Jesus Christ with his work on the cross at the center.[115]

Wesley often held the role of faith and works in high tension. As examined at length in a previous chapter, like Luther, it was the idea of salvation by faith *and* works with which Wesley took issue with many Roman Catholics. Although the Lutheran influence remained high upon Wesley, unlike Luther, Wesley refused to compartmentalize faith from works. Wesley even went so far as to say, "To preach salvation or justification by faith only is to preach against holiness and good works."[116] He continued to describe how faith remains as "necessarily productive of all good works, and all holiness."[117] Although Wesley never wavered from this strong connection between faith and works, he did hold to the perspective that belief precedes good works as a means for salvation.[118]

113. Mercer, "Centrality of Grace," 225-20.

114. See sermon "Salvation by Faith," Wesley, *Works* (Outler), 1:120.

115. See sermons "Justification by Faith" and "Means of Grace"; Wesley, *Works* (Outler), 1:186, 382.

116. See sermon "Salvation by Faith"; Wesley, *Works* (Outler), 1:125.

117. Wesley, *Works* (Outler), 1:125.

118. See sermon "Righteousness of Faith"; Wesley, *Works* (Outler), 1:214. See also Sugden's footnote 3.1 in Wesley and Sugden, *Works*, (*Standard Sermons*), 1:46.

Saved from Sin

In his sermon "Salvation by Faith," Wesley summarized what one is saved from by using a single word, *sin*.[119] He continued to describe the types of sin from which one is saved including "original and actual, past and present sin, 'of the flesh and of the spirit' . . . from the guilt and from the power of it."[120] In other words, Wesley maintained a strongly all-encompassing view of the sins from which one is saved.

Wesley continued to name and describe specifically some of these sins, including (but not limited to) guilt and fear, specifically fear of punishment and God's wrath, as well as purification from "pride, anger, desire, 'from all unrighteousness,' 'from all filthiness of flesh and spirit.'"[121] It is important to note that Wesley did not see this salvation as merely an issue of forgiveness (although forgiveness remains a major component of salvation); rather he carried the concept further, stating that one is saved from the power of sin and from the continuation of habitual sin, though not from the potential to fall away.[122] Further still, he saw the word *habitually* as an inappropriate addition to the words of Scripture, "doth not commit sin."[123] To Wesley, this salvation from sin affects one's outward actions; however, the change in outward action emerges primarily as the result of an inward change.[124] Once one passes through this point of salvation, Wesley described such a person as an *altogether Christian*. He characterized this person as one who possesses "the love of God," the love of neighbor, and a deep desire for and delight in God.[125]

Initial Repentance, Justification, New Birth, and Initial Sanctification

There are many words that may be applied to the process and experience of salvation. John Wesley certainly had his preferred terminology. Marlon D. De Blasio noted that Wesley rarely used the term *conversion* because of

119. Wesley, *Works* (Outler), 1:121.

120. Wesley, *Works* (Outler), 1:122.

121. Wesley, *Works* (Outler), 1:122–23; see also sermon "Almost Christian"; Wesley, *Works* (Outler), 1:139.

122. Wesley, *Works* (Outler), 1:123–24.

123. See sermon "Marks of the New Birth"; Wesley, *Works* (Outler), 1:420.

124. See sermon "Upon the Lord's Sermon on the Mount: XI"; Wesley, *Works* (Outler), 1:66.

125. See sermon "Almost Christian"; Wesley, *Works* (Outler), 1:137, 140–41.

its infrequent use in the New Testament. However, De Blasio continued to affirm that Wesley "developed a theology of conversion that began with an initial repentance and an inward experience of grace, and then onward with a gradual transformation of life in Christ."[126] Although De Blasio's summary does capture some of the key aspects in Wesley's theology, there are four important words that Wesley used to capture the major components of salvation. These four wordings maintain a strong interconnectedness *with* mixed with a clear distinction *from* one another. These components consist of initial repentance, justification, new birth, and initial sanctification. As salvation comes by God's grace, through faith, expressed in but not merited in works, Wesley held that each of the above features of salvation remain dependent upon God's grace, faith in Christ, and his work to bring them to fruition.[127]

Initial Repentance

With Wesley's strong emphasis upon the depravity of humanity prior to salvation, it remains logical that he would also place such strong emphasis upon the role of repentance both for salvation and, as will be discussed later, for ongoing spiritual growth. However, Wesley stated clearly that repentance is not necessary in the same way as faith for salvation.[128] According to Wesley, two main components lead toward this repentance. First, the process begins with the goodness of God as that which leads people to this repentance.[129] Secondly, self-knowledge serves to bring an awareness of one's sin, thus displaying the necessity for repentance.[130] Countless Christian authors have written about self-knowledge as a means toward spiritual progress, yet Wesley seemed to keep self-knowledge limited to the awareness of sin and depravity as the way of knowing the need for repentance and growth. In other words, as one becomes aware of the goodness of God, one sees oneself as sinful, needing to repent of the old ways and progress toward the holiness of God.

This initial repentance must not be confused with an ongoing repentance in Wesley's theology. Initial repentance leads to salvation, maintaining a two-fold relationship with justification. First, this repentance comes

126. De Blasio, "Conversion, Justification, Experience," 23.

127. See sermon "Scripture Way of Salvation," Wesley, *Works* (Outler), 2:162, 163–64, 167.

128. Wesley, *Works* (Outler), 2:167.

129. See sermon "Salvation by Faith"; Wesley, *Works* (Outler), 1:126.

130. See sermon "Way to the Kingdom"; Wesley, *Works* (Outler), 1:225.

prior to justification in association with the initial awareness of God and self-awareness with sin. As preceding justification, this repentance is a turning away from the sinful depravity toward God. Secondly, this repentance comes consequent upon justification.[131] Where the first relationship between initial repentance and justification turns a person away from the sinful, in this latter sense, initial repentance starts a person on the path toward good works.

Justification

In an article titled "The New Birth in the Early Wesley," Mark K. Olson laid out Wesley's understanding of justification and the new birth before 1738. There, he noted that Wesley's initial doctrine was largely shaped by the teachings of the Church of England. Thus, Wesley saw two aspects to justification—initial and final. Initial justification, according to the early Wesley, would begin with baptism and reach its fulfillment at death and entrance into eternal glory.[132] Therefore, justification is ultimately a destination, not a beginning point.

However, Wesley's understanding of justification that would carry throughout his ministry was strongly shaped by a few other sources. Joseph W. Cunningham argued a strong case for the influence of Richard Baxter's *Aphorisms of Justification* upon Wesley's *ordo salutis*, order of salvation, in an article titled "'Justification by Faith': Richard Baxter's Influence upon John Wesley." There, Cunningham asserted that Wesley's 1738 sermon "Justification by Faith," which he described as "one of John Wesley's most soteriologically mature sermons," was directly impacted by Baxter's writings.[133] Cunningham pointed out the similarities between the two concerning themes like *sola fide*, their respective views on the fallenness of humankind, the attack on Calvinism and the accompanying antinomianism of their respective times, forgiveness, God's free and unmerited offer of grace, and Christ's sacrifice.[134] Some of this, however, was not unique to Baxter, but was shared among Protestants, non-conformists, and/or Puritans.

In addition to Baxter, Wesley's soteriology also took shape through conversations with the Moravians Peter Bohler and Count Zinzendorf. In the time leading up to his Aldersgate experience on May 24, 1738, when his

---

131. See sermon "Scripture Way of Salvation," Wesley, *Works* (Outler), 2:164.

132. Olson, "New Birth," 82, 83, 98.

133. Cunningham, "Justification by Faith," 8.

134. Cunningham, "Justification by Faith," 12–13.

heart was strangely warmed, following a conversation with Bohler, Wesley recounted in his journal that he had resolved to seek justification:

> 1. By absolutely renouncing all dependence, in whole or in part, upon *my own* works or righteousness; on which I had really grounded my hope of salvation though I knew it not, from my youth up. 2. By adding to the constant use of all the other means of grace, continual prayer for this very thing, justifying, saving faith, a full reliance on the blood of Christ shed for *me*; a trust in Him, as *my* Christ, as *my* sole justification, sanctification, and redemption.[135]

It was later that evening when Wesley's heart was strangely warmed upon hearing read the introductory words from Martin Luther's commentary on the book of Romans.

Later that year, on Wednesday, July 12, Wesley heard Zinzendorf respond to questions on justification with the following points:

1. Justification is the forgiveness of sins.

2. The moment a man flies to Christ he is justified;

3. And has peace with God; but not always joy:

4. Nor perhaps may he know he is justified, till long after.

5. For the assurance of it is distinct from justification itself.

6. But others may know he is justified by his power over sin, by his seriousness, his love of the brethren, and his "hunger and thirst after righteousness," which alone prove the spiritual life to be begun.

7. To be justified is the same thing, as to be born of God. (Not so.)

8. When a man is awakened, he is begotten of God, and his fear and sorrow, and sense of the wrath of God, are the pangs of the new birth.[136]

From there, he continued to recount very similar points made by Bohler in a previous conversation. The blend of Luther, Bohler, and the count influenced Wesley's soteriology for years to come. From there, he went on to question and investigate the teachings of the Church of England on justification both in their official doctrines and in the contemporary preaching of his colleagues.[137] His conclusions continued to stir controversy

---

135. Wesley, *Works* (Ward and Heitzenrater), 18:248–49.

136. Wesley, *Works* (Ward and Heitzenrater), 18:261.

137. See Wesley's journal entry for Sunday, November 12, 1738 in Wesley, *Works* (Ward and Heitzenrater), 19:21.

especially over the next couple of years to follow and periodically throughout his ministry.

Wesley used the word *justification* to summarize the salvation previously described.[138] Due to this connection with salvation, justification exists
as the entrance point into the spiritual life with faith being the "condition
of justification" not only the condition, but the "only condition."[139] As noted
at length in a previous chapter, it was the issue of faith alone as opposed
to faith and works as conditions for salvation that set Wesley apart from
his Roman Catholic contemporaries. When accused of being a papist, he
touted that his preaching of justification by faith alone "is overturning Popery from the foundation."[140] Although faith may be viewed as the human
response and in Wesley's words the "only condition," it remains important
to understand Wesley's stress on the divine initiative through the working of
the Holy Spirit in order to bring someone to the point of salvation.[141]

Wesley defined the purpose of justification as remitting "the punishment due to our sins, to reinstate us in His favour, and to restore our dead
souls to spiritual life, as the earnest of life eternal."[142] Although Wesley often
emphasized the need no longer to commit sin and to strive toward Christian perfection, he did acknowledge that "sin remains (at least for a time)
in all that are justified."[143] Yet justification is forgiveness so that there is no
longer any condemnation.[144] Although sin remains, justification marks the
beginnings of the changes that are to come, brought about through self-
denial.[145] These changes begin with the emergence of peace, joy, and love
given through the Holy Spirit.[146]

As these changes begin, Wesley observed that truly good works follow justification because the works are now done by faith in Jesus Christ.[147]
These works also accompany justification because they are the expression

138. See sermon "Salvation by Faith," Wesley, *Works* (Outler), 1:124.

139. See sermon "Justification by Faith," Wesley, *Works* (Outler), 1:195; and journal
for December 13, 1739, Wesley, *Works* (Ward and Heitzenrater), 19:128; see also sermon "Scripture Way of Salvation," Wesley, *Works* (Outler), 2:162.

140. See Wesley's journal entry for August 27, 1739 in Wesley and Jackson, *Works*,
1:246.

141. See sermon "Witness of the Spirit: I," Wesley, *Works* (Outler), 1:275.

142. See sermon "Justification by Faith," Wesley, *Works* (Outler), 1:186.

143. See sermon "On Sin in Believers," Wesley, *Works* (Outler), 1:331.

144. See sermon "Scripture Way of Salvation," Wesley, *Works* (Outler), 2:157.

145. See sermon "On Sin in Believers," Wesley, *Works* (Outler), 1:326–27; see sermon "Self-Denial," Wesley, *Works* (Outler), 2:238.

146. See sermon "Scriptural Christianity," Wesley, *Works* (Outler), 1:162.

147. See sermon "Justification by Faith," Wesley, *Works* (Outler), 1:192.

of faith and the presence of God's grace.[148] John Wesley used three terms to describe those who have been justified: the *regenerate* refers to the actual inward change, the *justified* refers to the relative change (relative to one's relationship to God), and finally, *believers* refers to the means through which the others occur.[149]

In an article titled "Justification, the New Birth, and the Confusing Soteriological Passages in John Wesley's Writings," Scott Kisker pointed out that there is "considerable scholarly disagreement concerning the development of Wesley's soteriology" based on Wesley's "seemingly contradictory statements." However, Kisker argued that a way to account for these apparent inconsistencies is to see a difference in Wesley's thought between the processes related to justifying faith and being justified.[150]

Kisker concluded that processes related to justifying, and in parallel to sanctifying, "proceed by degrees but cross certain markers, when a person is said to 'be' what she has been becoming."[151] He went on to state that a person is justified after God's grace has been doing the justifying work. He argued the same process for God's convincing grace leading to conviction and God's sanctifying grace leading to sanctification. His argument makes sense of some of the aspects of the tension found in Wesley between the process of spiritual development and the instantaneous nature of the phases of spirituality that Wesley seems to have promoted. However, the three-fold approach to Wesley's economy of spirituality may be a bit oversimplified, leaving out some other key aspects of spiritual progression in Wesley, as will be discussed in later chapters.

New Birth

In tracking the pre-Aldersgate development of Wesley's perspective, Mark K. Olson noted the influence of the Church of England on the younger Wesley in shaping his understanding of the new birth in addition to justification. According to Olson, like justification, the early Wesley believed that the new birth begins with baptism, has a progressive nature, and reaches its climax upon the transition from death to eternal life.[152] However, Olson observed that the influence of the Anglican holy living tradition upon Wesley began to shape his view of the necessary moment of crisis and consequent decision

---

148. See sermon "Salvation by Faith," Wesley, *Works* (Outler), 1:125.

149. See sermon "On Sin in Believers," Wesley, *Works* (Outler), 1:319–20.

150. Kisker, "Confusing Soteriological Passages," 47.

151. Kisker, "Confusing Soteriological Passages," 62.

152. Olson, "New Birth," 80–82, 86.

point, such that by mid-1734 Wesley called his hearers to make a critical decision regarding their salvation in his sermon "The One Thing Needful."[153]

Post-Aldersgate—though developing before 1738—Wesley viewed the new birth as something distinct from justification, though occurring simultaneously. He defined justification as a relative change and the new birth as providing an actual change.[154] The former being something "God does for us," and the latter being that which "God does in us."[155] This actual change that God does within the person, according to Wesley, is possible due to the giving and receiving of the Holy Spirit at this point—the Holy Spirit being the one who renders this change.[156] Although different from justification, the link between the two remains inseparable and both maintain the same foundation of faith as the means through which they are received and actualized.[157]

In an article titled "Conflicting Views of New Birth between John and Charles Wesley," Laurence Wood pointed out that this link between justification and the new birth developed in varied perspectives for Wesley over time. Wood showed how Wesley initially connected justification with sanctification through a merging of William Law's understanding of perfection with Peter Bohler's emphasis on faith alone.[158] However, after his visit to Herrnhut, Germany, in 1738, Wesley began to make a clearer distinction between justifying faith and sanctifying grace following his interactions with Christian David.[159] Even so, Wood asserted that John Wesley was more apt to link the new birth with initial justification, whereas his brother Charles held the new birth in connection with the climactic state of Christian perfection—the latter of which will be discussed in a later chapter.[160] However, according to Wood, John Wesley also distinguished between a lower and a higher form of new birth—in other words, two distinct *new births*—with the former being linked to justification and the latter married to the state of Christian perfection.[161]

153. Olson, "New Birth," 87, 91.

154. See sermon "Great Privilege of Those That Are Born of God," Wesley, *Works* (Outler), 1:431.

155. See sermon "New Birth," Wesley, *Works* (Outler), 2:187.

156. See sermon "Marks of the New Birth," Wesley, *Works* (Outler), 1:423–24.

157. See sermon "Marks of the New Birth," Wesley, *Works* (Outler), 1:417.

158. Wood, "Conflicting Views," 44.

159. Wood, "Conflicting Views," 48, 51.

160. Wood, "Conflicting Views," 57.

161. Wood, "Conflicting Views," 64.

Wesley emphasized the role of faith, hope, and love as evidence of this new birth, with love being the most important. He saw this triad of virtues as something obtained consequent upon justification but linked more directly with the new birth, and especially in the higher and more perfect sense of new birth as mentioned above.[162] In addition to these three virtues, Wesley also identified many other characteristics of those who have experienced this new birth. These characteristics include enjoying the peace of God, good conscience, the witness of the Spirit, a soul sensible to God, a greater understanding of God, a recognition of the voice of God, a love for others, "mercies, kindness, gentleness, long-suffering," holiness, and even happiness.[163]

Following the new birth, Wesley spoke of a belief in God that leads to committing no sin; however, this does not mean one remains completely immune to temptation.[164] In his sermon "The Great Privilege of Those That Are Born of God," Wesley described the process of falling into sin after experiencing the new birth as a possible and common reality.[165]

Initial Sanctification

Wesley saw justification and the new birth as the point of entrance into sanctification, while maintaining a distinction among the three.[166] Justification is not the actual making of a person to be just and righteous; Wesley reserved this for sanctification.[167] The distinction between justification and sanctification Wesley described, saying that justification implies "what God *does for us* through His Son; [sanctification] what He *works in us* by his Spirit."[168] For Wesley, the new birth occurs in a moment, with sanctification occurring as a process over time.[169] Like justification and the new birth, sanctification also occurs by faith.[170]

162. See sermon "Marks of the New Birth," Wesley, *Works* (Outler), 1:417, 422, 425.

163. See sermon "Marks of the New Birth," Wesley, *Works* (Outler), 1:427–28; sermon "Great Privilege of Those That Are Born of God," Wesley, *Works* (Outler), 1:434; sermon "New Birth," Wesley, *Works* (Outler), 2:194–95.

164. See sermon *Marks of the New Birth*, Wesley, *Works* (Outler), 1:427–28.

165. Wesley and Outler, *Works*, 1:440.

166. See sermons "Scripture Way of Salvation" and "New Birth," Wesley, *Works* (Outler), 2:158, 198.

167. See sermon "Justification by Faith," Wesley, *Works* (Outler), 1:187.

168. See sermon "Justification by Faith," Wesley, *Works* (Outler), 1:187.

169. See sermon "New Birth," Wesley, *Works* (Outler), 2:198.

170. See "Scripture Way of Salvation," Wesley, *Works* (Outler), 2:163.

As related to the new birth, Wesley emphasized the product of love as the result of the sanctification process.[171] Although sanctification occurs by faith, it expresses itself through works of piety. These include prayer (consisting of public, family, and private prayer), receiving communion, studying Scripture, fasting, and works of mercy.[172]

Although Wesley maintained a clear distinction among initial repentance, justification, the new birth, and initial sanctification, he viewed these as aspects of the salvation experience. These all hold their respective places of involvement in bringing one to the moment of saving faith in Christ. However, Wesley maintained a clear adherence to his perspective of spiritual maturity being a process toward the ultimate goal. In other words, there exists more beyond this initial stage. Kisker summarized this process as including God's preventing or convincing grace leading toward the moment of conviction and initial repentance, then God's justifying grace leads to the point of justification and the new birth, and finally, God's sanctifying grace leads to the threshold of entire sanctification and perfect love—the latter of which will be addressed in a later chapter.[173]

Assurance

For Wesley, the doctrine of assurance played a significant role in his Arminian-leaning soteriology. In fact, Jason Vickers attributed the rise of Arminianism in England to its offering of "an alternative solution for the problem of assurance."[174] Wesley recorded that his experience of assurance arrived in conjunction with his Aldersgate experience.[175] However, his doctrine of assurance developed over time.

Wesley's perspective on assurance began when he heard Count Zinzendorf teach on justification. One of the points made by the count which struck Wesley was that "the assurance of [justification] is distinct from justification itself."[176] In his journal, reflecting on his conversations with Christian David while in Hernhuth, Wesley took note of David's statement that "'being justified' is widely different from . . . having the 'full

171. See "Scripture Way of Salvation," Wesley, *Works* (Outler), 2:158.

172. See "Scripture Way of Salvation," Wesley, *Works* (Outler), 2:166.

173. Kisker, "Confusing Soteriological Passages," 55.

174. Maddox and Vickers, *Cambridge Companion to Wesley*, 201.

175. Wesley, *Works* (Ward and Heitzenrater), 18:249–50.

176. Wesley, *Works* (Ward and Heitzenrater), 18:260–61.

assurance of faith.'"[177] Assurance became a prevalent theme in Wesley's journal from that time through 1745 and beyond.

In conjunction with Wesley's perspective on *real Christianity*, Kenneth J. Collins tracked the development of the Wesleyan understanding of assurance throughout his life, beginning with his encounter with the Moravians. Collins noted that as early as 1740 or sooner, Wesley began to speak on degrees of faith and assurance.[178] Collins identified a few key dates in the development of the place of assurance for Wesley. He noted that in 1745 Wesley emphasized the importance of assurance as a part of *true Christianity* in a letter to John Smith.[179] In that letter, Wesley connected assurance with the working of the Holy Spirit. Thus, here and in many other aspects, one cannot separate Wesley's soteriology from his pneumatology. This is further observed in Wesley's sermon "The Marks of the New Birth" in which he proclaimed that part of the fruit of the new birth includes a "full assurance of faith" and a "full assurance of hope." He then immediately linked these expressions of assurance to the inner witness of the Spirit.[180]

Collins noted that in a letter to Richard Thompson dated February 18, 1756, Wesley began to express the possibility of one being justified without having a full assurance and, in a letter to Dr. Rutherford in 1768, he detailed out the exceptions to assurance with justification as possibly including one's own ignorance.[181] A few years later, Wesley made the distinction between initial and full assurance. Collins stated it this way:

> By 1771, Wesley had distinguished full assurance, which excludes doubt and fear, from initial assurance which does not; he had come to a greater appreciation of the faith of a servant and its degree of acceptance; and he had realized that in exceptional cases one may even be justified and yet lack assurance due to either ignorance of the gospel promises or due to bodily disorder.[182]

Collins was then quick to note that, even so, Wesley continued to hold a high value for the role of assurance in one's salvation story.

177. Wesley, *Works* (Ward and Heitzenrater), 18:274.

178. Collins, "Real Christianity," 19.

179. Collins, "Real Christianity," 20.

180. Wesley, *Works* (Outler), 1:423.

181. Collins, "Real Christianity," 24–25.

182. Collins, "Real Christianity," 33.

COMPARISON AND CONTRAST

Although Ávila, Molinos, and Wesley lived in their respectively different centuries, were separated geographically, and maintained relatively different theological traditions, they still held to many points of commonality. Within their soteriological understanding, all three preserved a strong Christology and Pneumatology. Each of these authors placed Jesus as *the* way to salvation with Ávila and Wesley especially emphasizing the centrality of the cross. All held to a strong view of moral depravity in the natural state (though, perhaps not going as far as the total depravity explained by John Calvin), and all perceived the need and the possibility through the inner working of God to be freed from the sinful state. The entirety of this trio also emphasized the place of human free will in one's justification and formation of a relationship with God. Each one also stressed the need for faith and works, although this is where they also significantly differed.

Early on, Ávila stressed the role of faith in one's salvation; however, as Lutheranism took hold, he increasingly denounced the doctrine of *sola fide*, or faith alone, promoted by Luther. Rather, Ávila taught the post-Tridentine marriage of faith and works as necessary for justification. Molinos, on the other hand, kept this marriage of the two but held the union a bit more loosely than Ávila. Molinos understood works to be more of an expression of faith and the highest expression of devotion. Yet he also included a great deal of human effort in his teachings on spiritual entry and development. It could be said that Molinos remained somewhere in between Ávila and Wesley on this issue. Wesley held strongly to the *sola fide* of Luther, emphatically proclaiming God's grace along with faith as the human response as the *only* means to salvation made possible by the efficacy of the cross of Jesus. It is important to stress here that Wesley saw faith as the human response, not human initiative. However, Wesley was also quick to state that works closely follow faith and the two should remain inseparable. To summarize, if the teachings of these aforementioned were placed on a continuum from the necessity of faith and works together on one end to faith alone on the other, it would follow in this respective order: Ávila to Molinos to Wesley to Luther.

In addition to the relationship between faith and works, these three maintained other points of theological contention regarding their soteriology. Wesley would tend to find a friend in Ávila on many points of doctrine, while Ávila and Molinos would hold fellowship through many aspects of their catholicity. The two Catholics perpetuated the teachings of penance and confession to a confessor as key aspects of repentance, while Ávila also saw a place for ascetic practices, although not without his cautionary counsel. They also made the distinction between venial and mortal sins. These are doctrines which Wesley did not teach and, in many cases, edited out of his *Christian Library*.

Ávila and Wesley promoted an understanding that salvation is available to any and all who would receive it by faith as an act of free will (and works for Ávila). Both included a high value on assurance, though Wesley took this further. Both stressed the sources of temptation as coming from the world, the flesh, and the devil, thus the need for ongoing repentance and the need to be saved from sin. Notably, each had relatively well-developed understandings of the *ordo salutis*, with some variations, whereas Molinos concerned himself more with the processes of development after one's connection with God begins.

Ávila wrote that the starting point of divine encounter arrives through God's reprimand trailed by confession. Following confession, one participates in penance and the willful act of repentance. Throughout this process, a God-given consolation may follow confession at any time. Then, on the heels of consolation comes assurance.

Wesley parsed this process out in more detail. He held that the initial work of the Divine comes through God's prevenient grace extended to all persons. Then, God touches the human heart through conviction. Following this, one comes to an awareness of God and a self-awareness of one's own sin. If one moves forward on this work of God, then one will initially repent, at which point through a response of faith, one is then justified while initial repentance continues. Following justification, the new birth begins, initial assurance is granted, and the first expression of sanctification is then given. The process of spiritual growth then continues through one's self-denial, ongoing repentance, and the accompanying development of faith, hope, love, peace, and joy in the Holy Spirit. If this growth continues, one should arrive at the *telos*, or end, of the Christian life, as will be addressed in a later chapter. In other words, to Wesley, as well as Ávila and Molinos, entrance into a relationship with God is just the beginning toward an ever-growing, ever-deepening spiritual experience and spiritual life.

4

Spiritual Growth

As the *ordo salutis* traditionally became a topic approached systematically with great hair-splitting precision, the overall process of spiritual growth from beginning toward the end goal, or *telos*, has likewise resulted in countless methodical writings and debate. Although each tradition may have particular leanings on this point, the topic has not resulted in the same level of divide as that produced by the doctrines of soteriology. Strong distinctions do exist, however.

This topic may be examined at two main points: the stages of spiritual growth and the means through which one advances spiritually. Issues of debate around the stages of spiritual growth may include the question of whether distinct stages even exist, ponderings over the possibility of full arrival at a spiritual destination, and process verses crisis points, to name a few. Regarding the means of growth, one may consider the role of human activity versus divine action and how much rests upon either side.

John Wesley used the term "means of grace" to refer to the practices in which people participate in placing themselves in a posture of receiving the grace of God or connecting in some way with God. These also serve as means through which people grow in relationship with God and toward a spiritual maturity, or even toward a spiritual *telos*. This terminology and usage certainly were not unique to Wesley, nor were they necessarily used in the same way by Ávila or Molinos. Nonetheless, "means of grace" as Wesley understood them will serve as the way the phrase will be used here.

JUAN DE ÁVILA ON SPIRITUAL GROWTH

The Means of Grace

Juan de Ávila identified a number of means of grace, though he did not use that term per se; rather, he was more apt to use the term *ejercicios devotos*, or "devout exercises."[1] In his treatise *On the Priesthood*, he identified learning, study, the reading of Scripture, and understanding of historical theology as some of these exercises necessary for priests, so that they may impart them to the laity.[2] In his *Audi Filia*, he expanded on a couple of these themes. For reading theological books, he recommended, first of all, assuring that they contain sound doctrine. Then, he encouraged the combined practices of reading and prayer. He instructed his audience to read, then to pause and prayerfully reflect on an insight that came from the reading.[3] He recommended reading as a way of reflection upon a particular aspect of the passion of Jesus after one concludes spending time in prayer. Specific recommendations which he gave include "the *Meditations* of Saint Augustine in Latin, those of Father Luis de Granada in Spanish, and the Carthusian who writes on all the gospels."[4]

Ávila promoted structure and intentionality in carrying out these devout exercises. He encouraged relegating them to a particular place of quiet and setting aside two times a day for such reflection—the morning for reflecting on the passion of Jesus and the evening for exercises of self-knowledge.[5] The spiritual exercise which Ávila addressed most frequently was contemplative prayer. His definition, however, may have slightly varied from some of his contemporaries. Whereas John of the Cross described contemplation as an emptying of oneself in order to remain passively silent before God (the concept later picked up upon by Miguel de Molinos), Ávila described contemplation as an active intellectual exercise of reflection. In his *Audi Filia*, he presented a four-fold prayerful approach to contemplation including contemplating one's being, contemplating one's dependence upon God, contemplating God's presence, and contemplating God in others.[6]

1. Ávila, *Audi Filia*—Spanish, capítulo 64; Ávila, *Audi, Filia* (Gormley), 190.
2. Ávila and Fernández-Fígares, *Love of God, Priesthood*, 85.
3. Ávila, *Audi, Filia* (Gormley), 181.
4. Ávila, *Audi, Filia* (Gormley), 214.
5. Ávila, *Audi, Filia* (Gormley), 181.
6. Ávila, *Audi, Filia* (Gormley), 190–92.

God's Part and Human Part

Though Juan de Ávila was a contemporary of John Calvin, it was not until after Ávila's death in 1569 that the debates of Calvinism developed further. It was nearly twenty years after Ávila's passing that his fellow Spaniard, Luis de Molina, published a four-volume set titled *De liberi arbitrii cum gratiae donis, divina praescientia, praedestinatione et reprobatione concordia*, addressing God's infinite foreknowledge. The free-will teachings of Jacobus Arminius didn't appear in public debate until a few years later in the 1590s. Thus, placing Ávila in a particular category on the issues of free will, predestination, and divine foreknowledge remains difficult.

That being said, it is clear that Ávila held to a high level of divine action in human salvation and spiritual maturation. However, he was not a monergist. Rather, he believed strongly in human free will and human participation in divine involvement. It may, however, be observed that Ávila's thought did progress over time. As noted earlier, his *Audi Filia* was written over the course of many years from beginning to end; though some editing took place for a second edition to appease the Inquisition, Joan Gormley observed that the first edition remained intact with only additions for clarification or quotes from saints for authoritative support added.[7] Therefore, there are many points at which clear development of thought may be seen in the progression of the text. The issues of God's work and free will are some of those cases. Earlier on in his *Audi Filia*, Ávila emphasized the working of God. Where he mentioned the role of belief or faith, even these he attributed to the hand of God. He didn't mention the role of free will until the second half of the book. Initially, he continued to stress God's initiation in free will, then placed God's part as primary and human action as secondary, and by the end of part 3 he took a more synergistic approach to the divine and human interactions.[8] This is likely to set himself apart from the then growing awareness and broader embrace of Calvin's teachings.

In looking at this progression of thought regarding the divine working and the human response, early on Ávila stated that "everything has already been given on the part of God: pardon, grace, and heaven."[9] Here, he alluded to human response, but maintained strict focus on the divine action. Toward the beginning of his *Audi Filia*, he stressed and reiterated a couple of times that Jesus' death and salvation are gifts based on God's goodness,

---

7. Ávila, *Audi, Filia* (Gormley), 24.

8. Ávila, *Audi, Filia* (Gormley), 195, 198, 260.

9. Ávila, *Audi, Filia* (Gormley), 82.

not on merit.[10] He did the same with the claim that belief and faith are enabled by God.[11] Here again, he referenced human response, but maintained a strong emphasis on God's role.

In the earlier parts of his *Audi Filia*, he did not relegate the divine action to salvation only but stressed the working of God in Christian virtue as well. For example, in writing about the virtues exhibited by Christians in a way that stands out against that of others, he credited this to the doctrine that "God dwells in us."[12] Stated another way, "the good comes from God and not from ourselves, and by his power we do the good."[13]

It was around the sixty-sixth chapter that he began to place stronger emphasis on the human action as noted above, beginning with discourse on human free will and God's initiation, shifting the primary work of God and secondary work of the person, and ultimately describing God's part and the human part working synergistically together.[14] It appears that in his letters and sermons, those means of communication that were less public than his treatise *Audi Filia*, he exhibited more freedom in presenting a synergistic approach. For example, in a letter to a wealthy lady, he urged her to do her part in drawing near to God and out of faithfulness God would reciprocate the divine response.[15] Similarly, in a sermon on Pentecost Monday, Ávila exhorted his listeners to yearn and desire for God and "he will do the rest."[16] That being said, even within the final chapters of his *Audi Filia*, he still preserved his emphasis on the working of the hand of God throughout the whole of spiritual progression from rising out of sin to sustaining a certain level of goodness.[17] Thus, it may be summarized that Ávila presented a synergist approach with primary action credited to the Divine.

Imagination and Desire

For Ávila, the imagination was a strong means through which one could encounter God and grow in that communion. In his *Audi Filia*, Ávila encouraged his readers to think about the life and death of Jesus and to

10. Ávila, *Audi, Filia* (Gormley), 128, 135.
11. Ávila, *Audi, Filia* (Gormley), 134, 136, 137–38.
12. Ávila, *Audi, Filia* (Gormley), 119.
13. Ávila, *Audi, Filia* (Gormley), 177.
14. Ávila, *Audi, Filia* (Gormley), 195, 198, 260.
15. Ávila, *Confidence* (Benedictines), 81.
16. Ávila, *Holy Spirit* (Dargan), 101.
17. Ávila, *Audi, Filia* (Gormley), 197.

contemplate about him as a source of nurture for the soul.[18] However, he did caution them to use balance in considering the image of Jesus.[19]

More than imagination, Ávila held desire in high esteem as a part of the spiritual maturation process. Arguably, desire may be considered one of the key components of human action in Ávila's synergistic approach to spirituality. In a homily "Within the Octave of the Ascension," Ávila linked desire with the coming of the Holy Spirit to a person. He followed this with the assertion that "your desires for God will bring God to you."[20] In one of his Pentecost sermons, he stated that "he who loves Jesus Christ and desires Jesus Christ will in return receive the Holy Spirit."[21] In another message, he contrasted the desire which men have for pretty women with the lack of desire people have for the Holy Spirit, then proclaimed in a conditional statement that if longing and desire are present, then God works in the human.[22]

Exterior/Interior

Teresa of Ávila, a contemporary of Juan de Ávila, wrote her *Interior Castle* to describe progression of spiritual growth as a movement from the exterior to the interior of a person. As was relatively common for this era, tradition, and region, Juan de Ávila also made a similar distinction between the external and internal workings of God in the life of a person. One distinction he made included the difference between the *words* and *hearing*. Words come from God exteriorly, but hearing is attained interiorly from God. However, he also saw something as more important than these external and internal exchanges—seeing. This seeing, he defined as both the exterior seeing of God's creation and the interior seeing of Godself, which he described as "happier and more helpful."[23]

Unlike some of the mystics before him and contemporary to him, Ávila did not view spirituality as a movement away from the exterior in order to embrace the interior. Rather, he saw the exterior as necessary for enlightening the interior.[24] In other words, external acts of devotion are necessary for interior development. He also made the connection between outward

18. Ávila, *Audi, Filia* (Gormley), 213, 215.
19. Ávila, *Audi, Filia* (Gormley), 216.
20. Ávila, *Holy Spirit* (Dargan), 7.
21. Ávila, *Holy Spirit* (Dargan), 59.
22. Ávila, *Holy Spirit* (Dargan), 100–101.
23. Ávila, *Audi, Filia* (Gormley), 173.
24. Ávila, *Audi, Filia* (Gormley), 218.

character and inward desire, where desire prompts action.[25] Elsewhere, he credited outward virtue to the inner working of the Holy Spirit.[26] Thus, according to Ávila, the outer and inner work together with great importance placed on both.

The Stages

In his book *Audi Filia*, Juan de Ávila described a three-step process for drawing near to God. The first step is penance for sins involving a withdrawal from distractions, careful self-reflection, and confession. The second step follows with an expression of gratitude to God. The third step in this process engages the thoughts and imagination to reflect upon the death of Jesus.[27] According to Ávila, as these stages help assist a person with entering into God's presence in the moment, he also followed a similar pattern of progression for one to live more fully in the presence of God over the long-term. In a letter to a student, he summarized the process of getting a new heart from God as including an amendment of one's deeds, a lament over one's faults, and an honest self-accusation of sins.[28]

This progression, to Ávila, has no easy or quick methods for arrival. Rather, referencing the apostle Paul in Gal 5:24, Ávila asserted that crucifying the flesh though "said in only one word is accomplished in many years."[29] It is worth noting that Paul used the aorist form of the word for crucify, εσταυρωσαν, a form that connotes undefined timing. This would leave room for the possibility of a lengthy process, though not necessarily. Ávila continued, stating that "this relationship is completely personal, secret, and kept for those whom the Lord wants to give it, after they have labored many years and with much love."[30] Worded differently, Ávila further stressed the role of process by referencing Bernard of Clairvaux when he described growth toward perfection as something that happens by walking, not flying.[31]

In addition to emphasizing the place of process in one's spiritual progression, Ávila also emphatically described the uniqueness of individual experience in spiritual growth. In fact, he stressed this relatively early on

25. Ávila, *Holy Spirit* (Dargan), 111.
26. Ávila, *Holy Spirit* (Dargan), 150.
27. Ávila, *Audi, Filia* (Gormley), 210, 211, 213.
28. Ávila, *Confidence* (Benedictines), 99.
29. Ávila, *Audi Filia*—Spanish, capítulo 77; Ávila, *Audi, Filia* (Gormley), 224.
30. Ávila, *Audi Filia*—Spanish, capítulo 98; Ávila, *Audi, Filia* (Gormley), 225.
31. Ávila, *Audi Filia*—Spanish, capítulo 99; Ávila, *Audi, Filia* (Gormley), 98.

in his treatise *Audi Filia*. He asserted that God works in people in various measures, and through various means. The measures, he claimed, include the gift of chastity to particular persons, and freedom from certain, if not all, temptations for some, while others struggle against temptation. The means involve natural tendencies for some and grace and election for others.[32]

Early Stages

Ávila's view of the spiritual life, as that which requires growth and maturation, placed the bulk of this work on divine action. He believed that God would develop that which he started. He summarized this by stating, "because of the good will that he [*God*] has given them [*persons whom God has enlightened*], they can be confident that he is and will be their friend, increasing the good that he planted and perfecting what he began."[33] In Gormley's translation, it appears as though Ávila held a view that initiation does not necessitate maturation. Note his use of the word *may* in his claim "it may be that this relationship, having begun thus, continues to go forward."[34] However, in his original Spanish, Ávila claimed that "*y si este trato así comenzado pasa adelante,*" or more literally translated "and if this deal begins, it goes forward."[35] In Gormley's translation, the statement implies other contingencies to growth; in Ávila's direct statement the sole contingency to maturation is initiation.

That being said, Ávila continued to lay out certain contingencies for those who continue to make spiritual progress. The primary means to growth in the early stages involve a high level of self-denial and suffering.[36] Though he would not fall completely into the asceticism movement per se, Ávila did hold to an ascetic expression of faith for these early stages. In his *Audi Filia*, he counseled his readers who found themselves assaulted by temptations or those who have offended God to "deal severely with their flesh by cutting down on food and sleep, by using a hard bed and the hair shirt, and by other helpful means of this kind"; he then continued on to encourage readers to love chastity, temperance, and discipline of the flesh.[37] However, Ávila was also quick to caution against extremes. In a later

---

32. Ávila, *Audi Filia*—Spanish, capítulos 15–16; Ávila, *Audi, Filia* (Gormley), 70, 72.

33. Ávila, *Audi Filia*—Spanish, capítulo 23; Ávila, *Audi, Filia* (Gormley), 90.

34. Ávila, *Audi, Filia* (Gormley), 122.

35. Ávila, *Audi Filia*—Spanish, capítulo 36.

36. Ávila, *Confidence* (Benedictines), 40.

37. Ávila, *Audi Filia*—Spanish, capítulo 5; Ávila, *Audi, Filia* (Gormley), 50.

chapter, he recounted many examples from past saints and their respective ascetic practices; he then cautioned his readers not to imitate some of these practices, seeing them as unique to that individual person. Rather, he urged others to learn from their dedication to preserve their souls and to confront sin.[38] It is also clear that Ávila promoted ascetic actions not as an end to themselves, and not as punishments from a vengeful God, but as means to repentance for the sake of a loving God. He summarized this well in a letter to a devout friend, "looking within his soul, the Christian sees cause only for repentance, and so lifts his eyes to his Creator, in whose loving kindness he can trust without fear of being forsaken."[39]

Although Ávila encouraged an active approach to dealing with one's sinfulness, he did not view this process as merely dependent upon one's herculean efforts. His approach to spiritual progression, like his approach to justification, was more synergistic. In a later part of his *Audi Filia*, he encouraged those who were not seeing quick results not to lose heart, but to "sigh more and beg the Lord with greater humility that his mercy may not permit you to remain infirm."[40] Thus, a person humbly pleads to God, but it is ultimately God's work to see this work through to completion, from Ávila's standpoint. He saw this especially as coming from the working of the Holy Spirit.[41]

To Ávila, however, navigating through these early stages is not enough. In a letter to a friend about charity, he asserted that "the feeling of tender devotion toward God which beginners call charity, although holy, is not of so high a degree of purity as that which unites souls with their Beloved."[42] To Ávila, these early stages are just that—early stages. He saw the need to move beyond that which carried people to a certain point.

Next Steps in Growth

As just mentioned, Ávila placed high value on the role of the Holy Spirit in moving a soul forward toward spiritual maturity. In some of his sermons, he laid out the prerequisites for such Holy Spirit–guided growth. In one of his sermons given on a "Sunday within the Octave of the Ascension," Ávila recounted these qualifications. They include an awareness of the Holy Spirit's power and a trust in the Spirit's ability to "accomplish marvels." The second

38. Ávila, *Audi Filia*—Spanish, capítulo 10; Ávila, *Audi, Filia* (Gormley), 62.

39. Ávila, *Confidence* (Benedictines), 130.

40. Ávila, *Audi Filia*—Spanish, capítulo 77; Ávila, *Audi, Filia* (Gormley), 224.

41. Ávila, *Audi Filia*—Spanish, capítulo 50; Ávila, *Audi, Filia* (Gormley), 159.

42. Ávila, *Confidence* (Benedictines), 106.

requirement "is to have the will to receive Him as our guest, sincerely and anxiously to desire His coming." Later in the sermon, he urged his hearers toward a deep dedication that refused to rest until one had arrived at this connection with the Holy Spirit.[43]

This awareness, trust, will, and dedication generally occur after the initial stages of spiritual progression are experienced. In the same sermon, he affirmed a need for initial cleansing of the thoughts, words, and deeds from evil, along with a presence of virtue in order to create a pure environment in which the Holy Spirit may dwell.[44] To Ávila, this transformation from the early stages to higher stages are quite drastic as guided by the Holy Spirit. In a sermon on Pentecost Sunday, he gave a lengthy and potent description of this change. Due to its thoroughness, it is worth noting in its entirety:

> Has it never happened that your soul has felt dry, lacking in fervor, discontented, full of fear, sorrowful, disillusioned, so that nothing can satisfy you; and while you are in distress, and perhaps distraught in mind, a breath of holiness comes to you, a feeling of relief revives you, strengthens, encourages you, and makes you yourself again; gives you fresh aspirations, ardent love, great and holy peace, and makes you speak words and accomplish deeds that astonish you yourself. That is the Holy Spirit.[45]

He went on to describe this change in word, actions, and desires, accompanied by a renewed vigor. He saw it as a move from annoyance to a zest for life and learning.[46] Yet he also believed that fear and distress precede the counsel of God; therefore suffering plays a significant role in one's spiritual advancement.[47]

Self-Abandon

Ávila saw detachment as a crucial part of the process of spiritual growth. He often called his readers to no less than a complete abandonment and surrender of the self *to* and *for* God. For Ávila, it is almost, though not literally, a spatial relationship where oneself and the Holy Spirit cannot occupy

43. Ávila, *Holy Spirit* (Dargan), 3, 4, 12.

44. Ávila, *Holy Spirit* (Dargan), 11.

45. Ávila, *Holy Spirit* (Dargan), 84.

46. Ávila, *Holy Spirit* (Dargan), 85.

47. Ávila, *Holy Spirit* (Dargan), 36.

the same dwelling without one being the more dominant. For example, in a letter to a friend at the time of Pentecost, he wrote:

> Let us invite the Paraclete, then, by heart and voice, to dwell within us, and let us be sure we have some feast to offer Him when He comes. To please Him, we must destroy our fleshly passions, for He detests them; we must mortify our own judgment, so that we can be taught by Him, for two people cannot govern a house well unless the wiser take control.[48]

He continued instructing the reader to renounce the will, to cleanse the "consciences by confession and penance," and to get rid of anything that may offend him.

To highlight this abandonment in an apophatic style, Ávila wrote in his *Audi Filia* that "if you want him to remember you, 'forget your people.' If you want him to love you, do not love yourself in a disorderly fashion. If you want him to care for you, do not confide yourself to your own care."[49] He continued in similar fashion stressing that pleasing God comes through abandoning pleasure in oneself, and finding God comes through losing everything. He took a similar approach in a letter "to an invalid" in which he stated, "If you desire Him to dwell in your heart, empty it of yourself and of all creatures," thus stressing that such an emptying is the means to the end of having Christ dwell in the heart.[50]

The level of abandonment which Ávila called for is an all-encompassing extreme. He encouraged a grieving mother to "keep back nothing for yourself . . . abandoning yourself entirely to Him."[51] In a letter to a young lady, he prayed that he would surrender *all* luxuries and that he would be *all* God's.[52] To a friend, he urged to offer the self "wholly, as a perpetual sacrifice to Him."[53] To another devout friend, he stated that "even if you purchased Him with your life, so small a price should count as nothing."[54] The examples continue. Ávila saw Christ's act of sacrifice on behalf of humankind as deserving nothing less than a full and complete offering of the self to him. Throughout his writings, Ávila called for the surrender of the

---

48. Ávila, *Confidence* (Benedictines), 136.

49. Ávila, *Audi, Filia* (Gormley), 278.

50. Ávila, *Confidence* (Benedictines), 40.

51. Ávila, *Confidence* (Benedictines), 66.

52. Ávila, *Confidence* (Benedictines), 114–15.

53. Ávila, *Confidence* (Benedictines), 117.

54. Ávila, *Confidence* (Benedictines), 131.

will, a denial of self interests, even on a small scale, a fasting from consolation, and a detachment, to a degree, from others.[55]

JOHN WESLEY'S EDITING OF ÁVILA ON SPIRITUAL GROWTH

Means of Grace

Sacraments

John Wesley embraced the Protestant definition of sacraments, applying
the term to baptism and the Eucharist, but not the entire seven sacraments
of Roman Catholicism. Wesley maintained a high view of the sacraments
and, although not applying the term *sacrament* beyond the two, wrote much
about many other "means of grace." Wesley often decried the Quietists who
willingly and very vocally threw off the sacraments and the other means of
grace in order merely to be quiet before God.

In the letters of Juan de Ávila which Wesley included, Ávila did not
make much mention of the sacraments. However, where he did, Wesley
took great care to edit out Roman Catholic perspectives, such that there
no longer remained any reference to the sacraments in Wesley's edition.
This, possibly, was to avoid conflicting or controversial language about such
matters.

For example, in Ávila's fifteenth epistle, Wesley omitted Ávila's statement "who receive . . . the holy Sacraments of the Church, that soe they
may be cured and saved."[56] Here, Ávila linked the sacraments very closely
to salvation and being "cured." Wesley viewed the sacraments as means to
grace, and grace as the means through which people are saved. However,
Wesley would not have declared the sacraments as means to salvation as this
would be eliminating the key element of grace.

Later in the same letter, Ávila described the act of falling into sin, at
times repeated sin, and feeling the grief of committing such sin. Ávila emphasized a greater weight of grief when such sin is committed in close proximity of time to "receiving the body of our Lord Jesus Christ," and harboring
"his precious body in our bosomes." When such sin happens, according to
Ávila, "we drive his grace out of our soules."[57] In Wesley's edited version,

55. Ávila, *Confidence* (Benedictines), 90; Ávila, *Audi, Filia* (Gormley), 278, 286, 287.

56. Ávila, *Selected Epistles*, 110.

57. Ávila, *Selected Epistles*, 112.

Wesley included the description of the grief that comes with committing sin. In fact, Wesley wrote, preached, and published an entire sermon about this theme, which he titled "The Wilderness State," on this very topic. However, Wesley eliminated the portion which connects the timing to the grief of this sin to that of receiving the Eucharist. He also left out the portion about driving the grace of God out of the soul.

There are a couple possible reasons for Wesley's omissions. Wesley may have omitted the Eucharistic reference because, to Wesley, the committing of such sin and the ensuing grief which one feels is irrelevant to the timing of when one has last received the Eucharist. This can be seen in his "Wilderness State" sermon. Another possibility may be that perhaps Wesley eliminated this reference because the language alludes to a transubstantiation perspective of the sacrament.

With Wesley's strong emphasis on grace throughout his ministry, it is not surprising that he eliminated the statement about God's grace being driven from the soul. Although Wesley viewed the sacraments as means to grace and would find himself in agreement with Ávila on that point, Wesley also taught about a prevenient grace that works on the soul before one even realizes it, this will be explored later.

In Ávila's thirty-third epistle, he described various consolations which one may receive from God, instructing his readers not to give too much attention and adoration to such things. He warned that "the enemy may mingle somewhat with them" and that sanctity is found not in these things, "but in the humble love of God, and your neighbor." He urged his readers only to "adore Christ our Lord in heaven or in the Sacrament."[58] Wesley preserved all the above, except for the phrase "in heaven or in the Sacrament"; thus he placed the emphasis on the adoration of Christ alone without referencing a place or means to such adoration.

Desire, Heart, and the Imagination

Desire

In keeping with the affective tradition, Ávila often used the language of desire and saw the heart as the seat of such desire. Wesley, however, being a product of early modernity, was more apt to speak of the mind, thoughts, and belief over the heart and desire. Eight times, Wesley removed or altered the wording of desire and eliminated or changed Ávila's references to the heart an additional seven times.

58. Ávila, *Selected Epistles*, 266–77.

Ávila saw the possibility of a pure desire that placed its yearnings toward the love of God. In questioning the process of the beginnings of one's movement toward God, Ávila asked of God, "When shall wee beginn, I say not to love thee, but at least to desire to love thee? When I say shall we conceive a desire of thee."[59] In this, Ávila showed that a desire to love precedes love itself. Wesley, however, changed the wording here to ask, "when shall we begin to love Thee? When, I say, shall we conceive a Desire of Thee," leaving out the question that separates *love* from a *desire to love*.[60] Perhaps, Wesley merely removed the redundancy. Or, more likely, Wesley would not have viewed a desire to love God as the starting point for a love of God. Instead, Wesley stressed that a love for God begins with God's love for people. In other words, love originates with God, not with human desire. This can be seen elsewhere in Wesley's writings, as will be explored later.

In the opening paragraph of Ávila's ninth epistle, he used the word *desire* five times. Wesley removed three of these uses, keeping only two. Ávila spoke of the insufficiency of a mere desire for true repose without knowing how to seek the means through which to obtain it. Wesley trimmed this portion to emphasize the knowing of "the means of true repose" rather than knowing how to seek and desire such means. In this, Wesley drew a more direct connection between the means of such rest with the recipient, removing the intermediaries of *seeking* and *desiring*.[61] Wesley also had issue with the idea of repose in general. In his journal dated Wednesday, July 17, 1782, he wrote that "repose is not for me in this world."

As Ávila opened his fifteenth letter, he began with a description of the two things which Augustine desired, that he may know God so that he may know himself. Wesley kept this quote from Augustine as well as Ávila's connection to desire. He even preserved the strong statement that "these two are things which we must all desire." However, Wesley removed the next mention of desire that Ávila linked to the absence of salvation. Ávila stated that all must desire to know God and know self, "unless with all he desire to be found without salvation."[62] Wesley kept the connection of desiring to know God and self as the preservation against being found without salvation yet removed the statement "with all he desire." Perhaps this was due to a perspective that desiring other things does not necessarily negate salvation.

The thirty-ninth letter of Ávila saw the removal of the word *desire* twice by Wesley. The first, similar to the above, may have been removed to

---

59. Ávila, *Selected Epistles*, 18.

60. Wesley, *Christian Library* (Ávila), 46:260.

61. Ávila, *Selected Epistles*, 63; Wesley, *Christian Library* (Ávila), 46:272.

62. Ávila, *Selected Epistles*, 107.

connect the person more directly to the experience without an intermediary of desire. In describing how those who love God are not as deeply impacted by the suffering they endure, Ávila urged his reader to "be taken with a great desire of goeing to see this vision," then allegorically connects the burning bush which did not get consumed to the idea of suffering without being affected.[63] Wesley shortened this statement to simply, let us "go and see this vision."[64] In so doing, Wesley's version invited a direct participatory response from the reader beyond merely desiring it.

Later in this same letter, Wesley removed the sentence "A life, which is spirituall & holy, admits to weare noe shoes, that is to say noe desires of selflove."[65] Just prior to this sentence, Wesley included a similar reference to the removal of shoes; therefore, the removal of this sentence was not done as a way of eliminating all reference to the discalced Carmelite friars, but perhaps for the sake of redundancy. Or, the removal of this statement may have had more to do with its statement about the desire of selflove. If this is the case, it may be, according to Wesley, that a spiritual and holy life is not completely free from a desire of selflove but may be free from the act of selflove.

The Heart

Ávila's first epistle recounts a life of worldly pleasures contrasted with true repose. In describing the former, one of the symptoms Ávila described includes those "who grow angry at the hart."[66] Wesley discarded "at the hart" leaving the statement to read those "who grow angry."[67] Although this may seem like a benign or inconsequential rendering, this is not the only place where Wesley removed the reference to heart.

In Ávila's third letter, he described how Christ enters into people and works in them to "remove all impediments." He then followed this up with the statement "And if we cannot soe soone make our harts as subject to us as we would, lett us yet endure it with patience."[68] Wesley removed this portion. Wesley's editing here may be one of two things, or perhaps both. As Wesley frequently removed the word *heart* from Ávila's writings, he could be taking issue with this use here as well. Or, perhaps, Wesley may

---

63. Ávila, *Selected Epistles*, 303.

64. Wesley, *Christian Library* (Ávila), 46:318.

65. Ávila, *Selected Epistles*, 304.

66. Ávila, *Selected Epistles*, 5.

67. Wesley, *Christian Library* (Ávila), 46:255.

68. Ávila, *Selected Epistles*, 24.

have removed this statement because of the active voice used with the word *make*. With Wesley's strong emphasis on the working of God, it may be that he rejected the idea here of one *making* one's own heart subject to oneself. This to Wesley is something reserved for the working of God.

In Ávila's eighth letter, he linked belief with the heart, stating "that you would beleeve with a faithfull hart" regarding the source of true repose being found in God.[69] Wesley removed "with a faithfull hart."[70] For Wesley, belief was more than merely an affection of the heart, but also strongly involved the mind and the will, as will be shown later.

In describing those who desire to sin more, Ávila described how they "come little by little, towards a hardness of hart; and to dry themselves up."[71] Wesley kept the first portion alluding to a gradual progression (or digression as the case may be) toward this state. He also preserved the latter outcome of dryness. However, he eliminated the middle phrase of "towards a hardness of hart."

In Ávila's forty-fifth epistle, he urged his reader "you must therefore procure to have a strong heart towards God."[72] Wesley altered this statement in three ways: he removed "you must" and "procure to," and changed *heart* to *confidence*. Thus, Wesley's version read, "therefore have strong confidence towards God."[73] The first alteration seems to soften the language from imperative demand to a somewhat gentler urging. The second elimination reduces the active voice by removing the act of procuring. The latter change may reflect Wesley's early modernity with its shift away from affect toward a more cognitive approach or act of the will.

Later in the same letter, Wesley changed "humble your hart" to "humble yourself."[74] Again, this may be a demonstration of the influence of modernity on Wesley. Or, perhaps, Wesley may have been calling for a more holistic approach to humility—one that includes intellectual consent, an act of the will, and behavioral expression.

The Imagination

There are two places where Wesley removed references to the imagination in Ávila's letters; both appear in Ávila's thirty-third letter. The first is found

69. Ávila, *Selected Epistles*, 55.

70. Wesley, *Christian Library* (Ávila), 46:268.

71. Ávila, *Selected Epistles*, 94.

72. Ávila, *Selected Epistles*, 349.

73. Wesley, *Christian Library* (Ávila), 46:326.

74. Ávila, *Selected Epistles*, 353; Wesley, *Christian Library* (Ávila), 46:328.

in connection with the distinction between exterior and interior means through which God teaches the soul.[75] As will be shown later, Wesley removed a lot of the language that made such distinctions between exterior and interior. Given the broader context, the first alteration concerning the imagination may be more due to the exterior/interior language than to the imagination itself.

The latter changes that Wesley made to the letter regarding the imagination may offer a little more insight into Wesley's perspective on this topic. Ávila wrote about the place of visions. He cautioned against loving the visions rather than loving God and others. He exhorted his reader to turn her heart toward heaven and toward "that which is represented in your imagination" if and when such visions come.[76] It is not completely clear why Wesley removed this portion. Perhaps, it is an issue with connecting the visions with mere imagination when earlier Ávila stated that these were visions from God. It could be that in Wesley's modernity, the imagination was looked down upon as unreasonable and unreliable.

Interior and Exterior Distinctions

In general, mystical theology places a great deal of emphasis on the distinction between exterior and interior means of connection with the Divine. The emphasis is often placed on the interior as the highest form of experience. The mystics often claimed that true union with God is experienced in the most interior parts of one's soul.

Wesley altered five occasions of Ávila's mention of this distinction in his compilation. The first is found in a letter that discusses the contrast between external and internal consolations with temporal and exterior pleasures. In the opening paragraphs, Wesley preserved the distinctions between eternal and temporal, but eliminated the wording of interior and exterior experience. The following sentence did not make it into Wesley's version: "What an ill exchange doth hee make, who Looses that which may be interiourly possessed, and which indeede is the true fruite; for that which is exteriour, and which is noe better then the shell, or crust."[77] The idea of losing consolations or even salvation by turning away from God was not foreign to Wesley, so that is likely not the reason for his removal of this statement. It is possible, however, that Wesley may have taken issue with the connection of the "true fruite" with that which is interior because, to Wesley,

75. Ávila, *Selected Epistles*, 262.

76. Ávila, *Selected Epistles*, 267.

77. Ávila, *Selected Epistles*, 1–2.

the interior working of God is exhibited in outward fruit. Given this, it is most likely that Wesley removed this statement because the distinction between interior and exterior are blurred due to the nature of the influence of the interior upon the exterior.

Another issue Wesley may have had with the emphasis on interior spirituality was the demarcation of levels of interiority. This can be found in his editing of Ávila's third epistle. In this letter, Ávila offered a prayer beginning with the words "O God, o Lord, o thou the true repose of the most interior part of our soules."[78] Wesley kept this opening, but eliminated the words "the most interior part," thus making it read, "the true repose of our souls."[79] To Wesley the soul exists as a single entity without distinction of levels or aspects.

Later in the same letter, Ávila urged his reader to grow "in knowledge and love of Christ our Lord," stressing that this is obtained outside of the soul.[80] In other words, it remains an exterior to interior movement. Wesley maintained the exhortation to grow in knowledge and love but eliminated Ávila's description of the process through which this moves from without to within one's soul.

In Ávila's seventh epistle, he offered counsel to those beginning their spiritual pursuit. One point of counsel he provided was that beginners should not show too many exterior signs of sanctity. He felt that this could result in more hurt than help. Wesley eliminated these three sentences of instruction. Again, this was likely due to the strong conviction Wesley maintained for demonstrating one's faith through works.

The last place where Wesley removed the language of the exterior/interior dichotomy can be found in Ávila's eighth epistle. Wesley removed a lengthy explanation of how people value the exterior over the interior along with the temporal over the eternal.[81]

MIGUEL DE MOLINOS ON SPIRITUAL GROWTH

Purgation

Miguel de Molinos, in more general themes, adhered relatively closely to the Pseudo-Dionysian three-fold way of Purgation, Illumination, and Enlightenment, though the wording somewhat differed. This is especially seen in

78. Ávila, *Selected Epistles*, 18.
79. Wesley, *Christian Library* (Ávila), 46:260.
80. Ávila, *Selected Epistles*, 23–24.
81. Ávila, *Selected Epistles*, 59.

his view of the early stages which include the process of purgation. To both the Pseudo-Dionysius and Molinos, purgation is closely linked to suffering, pain, and a sense of divine withdrawal. Molinos often drew upon the harsh sounding words of *annihilation* and *mortification* to express the inner workings during such seasons of spiritual growth. To both spiritual writers, however, purgation is not an end to itself, but contains the means through which one progresses toward the *telos*.

To Molinos, there exists both an act or state of purgation and an ongoing effort of what may be called purgation maintenance. Molinos started his treatise with a reasoning for the former while offering a brief description of the latter. It is worth noting in its entirety here:

> Know that your soul is the center, the residence, and the kingdom of God. But in order for the great King to rest on that throne of your soul, you must try to keep it clean, quiet, empty, and peaceful: clean of sins and defects; quiet of fears; empty of affects, desires, and thoughts; and peaceful in temptations and tribulations.[82]

Molinos believed that purgation happens both externally and internally, and through both active and passive means. He viewed external purgation as something that is actively executed from the standpoint of the person, while the internal purging is received passively by the person as coming from the work of God. To Molinos, the movement of purgation transitions from external to internal; he asserted that "as soon as you firmly resolve to mortify your exterior senses so as to climb to the high mountain of perfection and union with God, his Majesty will take your hand to purge your . . . hidden vices you do not know about."[83] The latter, though passive, does require an active response, however. The passive work begins when consent is given.[84]

The breadth of this purging is extensive according to Molinos. It includes the removal of "evil inclinations, disordered appetites, vain complacency, self-esteem . . . affects and attachments of natural and temporal goods . . . [and] supernatural goods," which also include "the internal communications, raptures, interior ecstasies."[85] This idea of being purged not only of the vices but also of the "supernatural goods" is in keeping with the long-standing mystical tradition that views spiritual progression as a move from external to internal experiences. Whereas in the earlier stages

82. Molinos, *Spiritual Guide* (Baird and McGinn), 64.
83. Molinos, *Spiritual Guide* (Baird and McGinn), 76.
84. Molinos, *Spiritual Guide* (Baird and McGinn), 77.
85. Molinos, *Spiritual Guide* (Baird and McGinn), 76.

one experiences God through the senses (the sights, sounds, feeling, etc.), in the higher stages one experiences God in the inner depth of the soul. Therefore, to Molinos and others in this stream, one must also be purged of sense experience in order to arrive at the interior state. Molinos stated that "God will deprive your senses in order to test you, humble you, and purge you."[86]

According to Molinos, purgation comes in two forms. One is relegated to the early stages of spiritual progression and arrives through suffering and difficulty. The second, which is associated with higher spiritual states, arrives through "the burning fire of inflamed, impatient, and ravenous love."[87] In keeping with the former, one of the primary means through which this purgation comes is by way of temptation. In the ninth chapter of the first book, he described these as "the dull file of temptation," yet in the chapter immediately following, his adjectives intensify to "the fire of horrible and painful temptation."[88] Both of these are used by God for the sake of purging and purifying the soul. Although such temptations are used by God, Molinos pointed to a different source, stating that "all these temptations are occasioned by the devil and at the same time prescribed by the divine hand for their gain and spiritual profit."[89]

Just as Molinos's descriptions of temptation intensified from one chapter to the next, his wording concerning this general state of purgation also intensified from his first book to the second. Part of this is due to the shifting from external to internal and from a more active to a passive state. In the former, he remained consistent with the wording of *purgation* and its various forms. In the latter, he opted to shift toward the wording of *mortification* and *annihilation*. To Molinos, annihilation is both an ongoing process and a point of arrival closely linked to purgation.

As an arrival point, Molinos described a state that is not obtained by everyone, "but only to the detached, the resigned, and those who pass through perfect annihilation by way of terrible tribulations and passive purgation."[90] Thus, the tribulations and purgation he described here serve as means to the end of *perfect annihilation*. However, arrival at this end does not mean the annihilation comes to a close. In the nineteenth chapter of the third book, he described this state of *perfect annihilation* as arriving with "many gifts of light and divine affects," but he continued to assert that those who have been annihilated "will strip itself of all of them if it does not

86. Molinos, *Spiritual Guide* (Baird and McGinn), 83.

87. Molinos, *Spiritual Guide* (Baird and McGinn), 144.

88. Molinos, *Spiritual Guide* (Baird and McGinn), 79–80.

89. Molinos, *Spiritual Guide* (Baird and McGinn), 79.

90. Molinos, *Spiritual Guide* (Baird and McGinn), 110.

want them to be an impediment on its way to deification."[91] In other words, when one arrives at annihilation, the process of annihilation continues. He reinforced this by stating that when a soul arrives at this state, "the knowledge that it always has further and further to go in order to purify itself to be annihilated is important." He believed that the annihilation ought to be all encompassing and is not complete until it occurs in one's judgment, will, affections, inclinations, desires, thoughts, self, wanting, desiring, obtaining, understanding, and thinking.[92]

To Molinos, mortification is the shedding that takes place both exteriorly and interiorly.[93] The latter begins with a mortification of the passions.[94] He believed that the exterior form did not lead to perfection, but the interior type, in a sense, serves as the initiatory work which leads into annihilation.[95] Without this interior mortification, one "will never arrive at this state" of union with God.[96]

This process of purgation through exterior and interior mortification and leading to annihilation reaps many benefits according to this Quietist. These include entering into an *interior solitude* in which the soul is emptied, then becomes filled with the divine spirit according to the degree to which it is emptied.[97] Likewise, as the soul is purged of various vices, it will be filled with virtues.[98] As he neared the close of his treatise, Molinos referenced St. Thomas in describing the indicating signs of one who has been purged as including diligence, severity, and benignity.[99]

Surrender and Self-Denial

Molinos saw spiritual progression in both active and passive forms. One area where he relatively maintained an active expression was in the area of surrender of the will. He held that one must actively surrender one's will in order for the passive reception of the work of God to begin. This, he believed, to be a one-time act in which one need only to continue.[100] Such a

91. Molinos, *Spiritual Guide* (Baird and McGinn), 176.
92. Molinos, *Spiritual Guide* (Baird and McGinn), 177.
93. Molinos, *Spiritual Guide* (Baird and McGinn), 132, 138.
94. Molinos, *Spiritual Guide* (Baird and McGinn), 177.
95. Molinos, *Spiritual Guide* (Baird and McGinn), 138.
96. Molinos, *Spiritual Guide* (Baird and McGinn), 155.
97. Molinos, *Spiritual Guide* (Baird and McGinn), 163.
98. Molinos, *Spiritual Guide* (Baird and McGinn), 167.
99. Molinos, *Spiritual Guide* (Baird and McGinn), 170.
100. Molinos, *Spiritual Guide* (Baird and McGinn), 87, 92.

surrender is only necessary once because he saw it as complete and total, or a surrender "with perfect resignation" as a "pure act of faith."[101]

Although Molinos viewed the *surrender* of one's will as a one-time act, he believed that the *subduing* of one's will was an ongoing need until one might subdue the will to a point of its complete annihilation.[102] Such a complete surrender, perfect resignation, and annihilation of the will results in a detachment from other things.[103] In his third book, Molinos listed the things from which one ought to become detached—they include "created things . . . temporal things . . . gifts of the Holy Spirit . . . himself . . . and . . . God himself."[104] This detachment and annihilation then in turn lead one on the path toward perfection, resulting in peace, joy, and happiness.[105]

Stages

Molinos understood the spiritual life to be that of progression through many stages. It was examined earlier the way that he saw the shift from meditation to contemplation, from active to passive, from exterior to interior, and from senses to affect. However, he also named other stages through which one passes in order to arrive at the higher states. Some of these stages are merely a rewording for the same level, while others describe a passage through a different aspect of spiritual advancement.

Prayer is one of the aspects within which Molinos identified different states. In his first book, he indicated the differences between two stages of prayer, labeling the first *animal life* and the second *human life*. This aligns with his descriptions of the shift from senses to affect in the ways in which a person relates to God. The first, he asserted, "God usually gives to beginners," while the second is for those who "reach perfection."[106] Similarly, the Quietist indicated the need for two types of martyrdom. These are related to, but not synonymous with the two levels of prayer. The first martyrdom, he described, is part of the purging process toward arriving at an interior expression of spiritual growth. The second is reserved for those who already have a degree of perfection. Molinos reserved two chapters in his third book offering instructions on these two stages.[107]

101. Molinos, *Spiritual Guide* (Baird and McGinn), 90.
102. Molinos, *Spiritual Guide* (Baird and McGinn), 118.
103. Molinos, *Spiritual Guide* (Baird and McGinn), 139.
104. Molinos, *Spiritual Guide* (Baird and McGinn), 175.
105. Molinos, *Spiritual Guide* (Baird and McGinn), 176–77, 181.
106. Molinos, *Spiritual Guide* (Baird and McGinn), 70–71.
107. Molinos, *Spiritual Guide* (Baird and McGinn), 147–51.

Molinos held that the highest state of being involves a perpetual existence in quiet contemplation. He also divided this climax into various stages. For example, he classified three types of silence: "the first is the silence of words; the second, the silence of desires; the third, the silence of thoughts," or the silence of *palabras*, *deseos*, and *pensamientos*. He ascertained that these are a movement from perfection to *more perfect* to the *most perfect*.[108] Regarding the aspect of contemplation at these higher levels, Molinos ascribed three levels to *infused contemplation*, and six other stages of contemplation, along with an additional twelve as found in the fifteenth chapter of the third book. The first three he marked as a movement from satiety and hatred of worldly things, followed by intoxication, and climaxed with security and a removal of fear. He went on to describe the other six grades as including "fire, unction, elevation, illumination, enjoyment, and rest." He concluded the chapter by listing "many other grades of contemplation: ecstasies, raptures, liquefaction, dereliction, jubilation, the kiss, the embrace, exultation, union, transformation, betrothal, and matrimony." To these, he did not give further description.[109] In relation to these higher levels, Molinos asserted that few souls arrive or even desire to arrive.[110]

There are a few other places where Molinos laid out what may appear to be more stages. However, these spoke less about the stages per se, and more about the maturation process. For example, in the opening chapter of the third book he elaborated upon the progression through which people have traversed who have arrived at a certain degree of internal peace and knowledge of the Divine. These souls, he explained, have endured *interior mortification*, purgation through many trials, an intense denial of oneself, and have arrived at a state of light, knowledge, and inner rest.[111] Later in chapter 8, he described the movement of beginners to those progressing to perfection as involving a shift from doing (*hacer*) to suffering with desire (*padecer con deseo*) to dying to oneself (*morir siempre en sí mismos*), though few attain this development.[112] The reason that this process is necessary, according to Molinos, is because people come to a point when that which carried a person to a certain level loses its efficacy and new means are needed to continue progress. One of the examples he offered was in the reading of books. He stated that such reading, "even if they are holy, will not console

108. Molinos, *Guia Espiritual*, 24; Molinos, *Spiritual Guide* (Baird and McGinn), 98.

109. Molinos, *Spiritual Guide* (Baird and McGinn), 167–69.

110. Molinos, *Spiritual Guide* (Baird and McGinn), 183.

111. Molinos, *Spiritual Guide* (Baird and McGinn), 139.

112. Molinos, *Guia Espiritual*, 47; Molinos, *Spiritual Guide* (Baird and McGinn), 155.

you as they did before."[113] Though reading still has its place at higher stages, he believed that progress is made through "time, prayer, and counsel."[114]

A few chapters later, he reiterated this procedure as passing through a "stripping of oneself," then an "attachment to contemplation," followed by a "total and absolute submission" to God and God's will.[115] The word that Molinos used, *desnudez*, translated by Baird as *stripping*, refers more to the state of nakedness than the process of stripping.[116] Thus, as a noun, Molinos saw it as a distinct state of being as opposed to a means toward an end. Likewise, he also used the noun form for attachment, *apego*, and submission, *entrega*, which also place these into states of being, whereas the verbal forms, *desnudar*, *apegarse*, and *entregar* would place these as action steps and not distinct stages.

Active to Passive

Right from the beginning in the *Proem*, Molinos identified spiritual development as a progression from active to passive. This involves a shift from the efforts of an individual to the sole working of God within a soul. As mentioned earlier, he described the earlier phases of meditation as more active and the latter and higher stages of contemplation as more passive.[117] The degrees of activity verses passivity were further emphasized when Molinos stated that meditation "gathers fruit through labor, while contemplation gathers greater fruit . . . without labor."

Though, for the most part, Molinos held to the movement from meditation to contemplation as a movement from active to passive, he also explained how both meditation and contemplation have their counter-voice. The person in the early stages finds themselves in a season of intense purgation along with the development within meditation. Though he held that meditation involves *trabajo*, he also believed that much of the purgation is passive, with the primary action being that of consent, or *consentimiento*.[118] He stressed the importance of active consent again in his third book as he spoke of the passive working that takes place through "the fire of tribulation

113. Molinos, *Spiritual Guide* (Baird and McGinn), 148.

114. Molinos, *Spiritual Guide* (Baird and McGinn), 103.

115. Molinos, *Spiritual Guide* (Baird and McGinn), 166.

116. Molinos, *Guia Espiritual*, 52.

117. Molinos, *Spiritual Guide* (Baird and McGinn), 55.

118. Molinos, *Guia Espiritual*, 14; Molinos, *Spiritual Guide* (Baird and McGinn), 77.

and interior torment."[119] He also identified both active and passive forms of contemplation with the former being reserved for the early stages and the latter for the more mature stages.[120]

This move to a more passive spirituality does not negate good deeds and activity to Molinos. He encouraged his readers to continue to participate in the daily routines of life and ministry as they too are God's will, while at the same time finding peace in the internal presence and working of God.[121] He found that the activities of those who "work more *passively* than *actively* are undertaken with prudence, measure, gravity, and means."[122]

Exterior to Interior

Just as the movement from meditation to contemplation is a progression from active to passive, for Molinos, this spiritual trajectory travels from the exterior to a more interior experience. In the *Proem*, he quoted from the *Mystical Theology* of Pseudo-Dionysius to offer support to this point of view. Both the Pseudo-Areopagite and the Quietist counseled their readers to leave off, or *dejar* as used by the latter, all that pertains to the external—both to the affect and to the cognition—in order to reach mystical union with God.[123] The intensity and level to which one experiences this detachment may be found in the strong wording that Molinos used in the second chapter of his third book. He stated that when one finds oneself in the interior state, "virtue is established, attachments are uprooted, imperfections are destroyed, and passions are extirpated."[124] The three Spanish verbs he used here, *desarraigan*, *destruyen*, and *arrancan*, all allude to a complete eradication or annihilation of their respective objects.[125]

The distinction between the exterior and interior spirituality were stark enough to Molinos that he indicated that "there are two kinds of spiritual people: interior and exterior." He went on to describe exterior people as those who strive toward virtue through "discursive prayer, imagination, and consideration," and make strong use of the practice of penance. The interior people, he explained, are those who have been through the process

---

119. Molinos, *Spiritual Guide* (Baird and McGinn), 146.

120. Molinos, *Spiritual Guide* (Baird and McGinn), 59.

121. Molinos, *Spiritual Guide* (Baird and McGinn), 93.

122. Molinos, *Spiritual Guide* (Baird and McGinn), 172.

123. Molinos, *Guia Espiritual*, 6; Molinos, *Spiritual Guide* (Baird and McGinn), 58.

124. Molinos, *Spiritual Guide* (Baird and McGinn), 140.

125. Molinos, *Guia Espiritual*, 41.

of stripping away the exterior and remain "recollected in the interior of their souls."[126]

In the seventh chapter of the third book, Molinos offered a summary of benefits wrought by this interior state. Molinos asserted:

> The foundation of our souls is the seat of our happiness. There the Lord shows us divine wonders. There we are lost, engulfed in the immense sea of his infinite goodness, in which we nevertheless remain stable and immobile. There is the ineffable delight of our soul and eminent and loving quietude. The humble and resigned soul that comes to this foundation looks for nothing but the pure pleasure of God, and the divine and loving Spirit teaches it all things with a gentle and vivifying unction.[127]

A few chapters later, he continued to describe this blissful state, or *interior center*, as a place of renewal, change, and filling accompanied by happiness, peace, delight, and serenity.[128]

Molinos spoke of this transition from exterior to interior as a process of growth, even giving four signs to help recognize this transition.[129] However, he also asserted that this could happen instantaneously by the hand of God.[130] Though such a high and lofty state may be accessible to many, if not all, he alleged that few truly arrive at this state.[131]

Senses and the Affect

As Molinos believed that spiritual progression involves a movement from active to passive and from exterior to interior, he also saw it as a movement from the senses (*sentidos*) to the affect (*afecto*). In the early stages, he believed, one's senses are beneficial for spiritual growth as one learns, reads, prays, and connects with God. However, he believed that these senses only carry one so far and it is necessary for mortification of the senses and the purging of the soul from this form of spiritual connection in order to make way for higher experiences.[132]

126. Molinos, *Spiritual Guide* (Baird and McGinn), 138.

127. Molinos, *Spiritual Guide* (Baird and McGinn), 152.

128. Molinos, *Spiritual Guide* (Baird and McGinn), 163–64.

129. Molinos, *Spiritual Guide* (Baird and McGinn), 169.

130. Molinos, *Spiritual Guide* (Baird and McGinn), 153.

131. Molinos, *Spiritual Guide* (Baird and McGinn), 153.

132. Molinos, *Spiritual Guide* (Baird and McGinn), 76, 83.

He held that the learning that comes through science is reasoned at the level of the senses. Thus, he argued that "God is more pleased by an affect of the heart than by the effect of worldly science."[133] That being said, Molinos also made a distinction between two types of affect—the *sensible affects* and the affect of the soul which connects with the Divine above and beyond all senses. He strongly cautioned against a devotion based on the sensible affects but praised the latter. To him, feelings and reason were not enough to carry the soul to the deeper expressions and experiences of spiritual progression.[134]

JOHN WESLEY'S EDITING OF MOLINOS ON SPIRITUAL GROWTH

Purgation, Mortification, and Annihilation

Based on the number of times in which Wesley removed the word *mortification* and its various forms, he clearly took issue with at least some aspects of Molinos's teaching on the subject. However, Wesley did not eliminate every usage of this word altogether. Therefore, it may be concluded that he did not maintain a completely oppositional stance on the concept of mortification.

Molinos wrote about mortification both in a positive sense and with cautionary counsel. For example, in his first book, he wrote about people tiring themselves with "external acts of mortification and resignation," stressing the value of God doing the purging in one's soul. Wesley kept this word of warning about mortification while excluding "and resignation."[135]

An example of Molinos attributing value to mortification which Wesley edited out may be found at the end of the first book. Molinos described a love for God that was demonstrated "in Tongue and not in Deed." He explained that the evidence of such love may found when one proclaims a love for God above all other things, but at the slightest difficulty one does not "resign thyself, nor are mortified for the love of [God]."[136] Wesley left alone the phrase concerning resignation but eliminated that on mortification.

In his third book, Molinos described those who were "truly spiritual" as those who had passed through "interior Mortification" and a cleansing "with the Fire of Tribulation."[137] Here, Molinos alluded to the idea of mor-

---

133. Molinos, *Spiritual Guide* (Baird and McGinn), 175.

134. Molinos, *Spiritual Guide* (Baird and McGinn), 73.

135. Molinos, *Spiritual Guide*, 21; Wesley, *Christian Library* (Molinos), 38:257.

136. Molinos, *Spiritual Guide*, 58.

137. Molinos, *Spiritual Guide*, 116–17.

tification functioning as a distinct stage of spiritual development. Wesley altered this to read as a cleansing by God through tribulation, while eliminating the portion on mortification, and reducing it from a distinct stage to an experience endured.[138]

Molinos tended to use the various forms of the word *annihilation* in close connection with the concept of *mortification*, if not synonymously. Thus, Wesley's keeping of the former word at times and his removal of it at other times follows very closely with his treatment of mortification. For example, at the end of the second chapter of the third book, Molinos lamented that "few there be that are willing so to Die and be Annihilated" regarding the death of the senses and an overall mortification. Wesley removed the word *annihilated*, while preserving the overall concept of the elimination or death of the senses and purification of one's soul.[139]

Interestingly, in the next chapter, Wesley preserved Molinos's assertion that few attain to the level of mortification and annihilation described— keeping both terms intact. It is worth noting these descriptions. Molinos stated that few are able to "mortifie continually all inward passions, to annihilate ones self in all respects, to follow always that which is contrary to ones own will, appetite and judgement," though many teach these things.[140] It is possible that Wesley preserved this paragraph to emphasize the number of people proclaiming such a state of mortification and annihilation without living up to it, as opposed to keeping it for instructional purposes as a how-to guide of mortifying and annihilating one's senses and passions, as he also frequently referred to people in his time who claimed a higher spiritual state than that which they had actually reached.

In a description on the benefits of tribulation in removing vice and producing virtue, much of the lengthy list made its way into Wesley rendition. However, Wesley did remove three main themes. The first was the claim that tribulation "blots out Sins," the second that such trials annihilate, and the third that suffering deifies people. The former and latter are addressed elsewhere, but the middle item is worth looking at here. Molinos connected this annihilation with a refining and perfecting work. Keeping the latter two, Wesley only eliminated the word *annihilation*.[141]

Later, in that same chapter, Molinos continued the connection between annihilation and perfection. Wesley had no problem with the wording of *perfection*, as will be examined in a later chapter, but he did take issue

138. Wesley, *Christian Library* (Molinos), 38:270.

139. Molinos, *Spiritual Guide*, 120–21; Wesley, *Christian Library* (Molinos), 38:271.

140. Molinos, *Spiritual Guide*, 123.

141. Molinos, *Spiritual Guide*, 126; Wesley, *Christian Library* (Molinos), 38:275.

with Molinos's understanding of the means toward arriving at perfection. Molinos believed that the soul, in order to fully receive the "Divine Lord into it," ought to be "disposed, naked, denied, [and] annihilated."[142] Wesley preserved *naked* and *denied*, while removing *disposed* and *annihilated*.[143]

There are places where Wesley removed the wording of annihilation or mortification, but the issue may not necessarily have been with these terms or concepts. For example, in the seventh chapter of the third book, Wesley removed Molinos's statement "Thou wilt find impatience and bitterness of heart to grow from the depth of sensible, empty and mortified love."[144] Here the issue may not have existed with "mortified love," but with the connection made among impatience, bitterness, and spiritual growth. To Wesley, impatience and bitterness were a hindrance to growth, a product of sin, and would actually hinder spiritual growth, not serve as a by-product of maturing.

Similarly, a couple sentences later, Wesley removed an entire paragraph pertaining to prayer and its outcome of mortification. Here too, Wesley was likely not taking issue with mortification per se, but with the idea of mortification serving as the intended end to prayer. To Wesley, prayer was much more than that, as will be explained later.

As another example where Wesley demonstrated an acceptance, at least to some degree, of the concept of mortification may be found in the paragraph following the aforementioned statements. Molinos described how "the recreation of the senses is a sort of death" to "the simple and the mortified."[145] Here, interestingly, Wesley kept *the mortified*, yet eliminated *the simple*.[146] Thus, in some way he acknowledged, perhaps, that there are indeed people who have progressed through a state of mortification.

In the next chapter, eight, which also addresses mortification, Wesley continued the practice of keeping some statements on mortification, while eliminating others. He preserved the imperative statement to "mortifie thy self in all things and at all hours, and by this means thou wilt get free from many imperfections" and to "mortifie thy self in not judging ill of any body at any time." Yet, shortly after, he eliminated the statement about people who "exercise Prayer" as being "always imperfect and full of self-love" because "they are not mortified.[147] This may be because to Wesley, perhaps,

---

142. Molinos, *Spiritual Guide*, 128.

143. Wesley, *Christian Library* (Molinos), 38:275.

144. Molinos, *Spiritual Guide*, 138; Wesley, *Christian Library* (Molinos), 38:279.

145. Molinos, *Spiritual Guide*, 138.

146. Wesley, *Christian Library* (Molinos), 38:280.

147. Molinos, *Spiritual Guide*, 144–45.

mortification may serve as *a* means to purification, but not necessarily *the* only means to perfection. In other words, one may experience a degree of purity by progressing through a state of mortification, but they may also arrive at a deeper level of purity by other means and may not require a state of mortification to get to that end.

Another example where Wesley preserved Molinos's description of mortification may be found in the opening paragraph of the thirteenth chapter. To show the impact of these changes, the complete paragraph is added here with the words which Wesley cut in italics:

> *You must know, that* when once the Soul is *habituated to internal Recollection, and acquired Contemplation, that we have spoken of; when once* 'tis mortified, and desires wholly to be denied its Appetites; when once it efficaciously embraces internal and external Mortification, and is willing to dye heartily to its passions and its own ways, then God uses to take it alone by it self, and raise it *more then it knows*, to a compleat repose, where he sweetly and inwardly infuses *in it* his Light, his Love and his Strength, *inkindling and* inflaming it with a true disposition to all *manner of* Vertue.[148]

Molinos laid out the paragraph in a cause and effect relationship among recollection, contemplation, and mortification as the causes to the effect of repose, and an infusion of light, love, strength, and virtue. Wesley edited out the causes of recollection and contemplation, preserved the causes of outward and inward mortification, and left the effects relatively intact.

Although Wesley kept, at times, and removed, at times, the wording of both *mortification* and *annihilation*, he tended to remove the concept of annihilation more frequently. Perhaps the most notable example of this may be found in the third book where Wesley completely removed chapters 19 and 20 in their entirety—the former covering the topic of annihilation and the latter addressing the *via negativa* path toward purity and contemplation.

Wesley included the twenty-first chapter about the outcome of internal peace, but he did remove the language of annihilation found throughout the chapter. He removed the opening sentence which asserted that a soul in peace and "perfect Union of love" arrives there after having been "once annihilated and renewed with perfect nakedness."[149] He removed a similar statement a couple paragraphs later that likewise proclaimed the means toward this peace as including "the steps of annihilation."[150] Finally, the link

---

148. Molinos, *Spiritual Guide*, 158; Wesley, *Christian Library* (Molinos), 38:288.

149. Molinos, *Spiritual Guide*, 185; Wesley, *Christian Library* (Molinos), 38:291.

150. Molinos, *Spiritual Guide*, 185–86; Wesley, *Christian Library* (Molinos), 38:291.

between annihilation and humility was removed from the chapter's closing paragraphs.[151]

Stages of Progression

It is rather clear that Molinos viewed the spiritual life as a progression through various stages which lead one toward a climactic state of being. To Wesley, following Jesus involves various seasons of life and a movement toward, if not arrival at, a *telos*. However, the latter would be less likely to emphasize a series of stages that serve as steps of ascent. The following highlight a few examples where the two parted ways in this regard.

In the sixth chapter of Molinos's third book, and the corresponding editorial rendition by Wesley, we may see how the two were in agreement on the idea of spiritual progress yet differed in the logistics. Molinos spoke of a martyrdom which occurs "in Souls already advanced in perfection and deep contemplation."[152] Wesley maintained the phrasing of advancement while eliminating the latter portion which specified "in perfection and deep contemplation."[153]

Later, Molinos laid out three distinct stages as they relate to inward mortification. Though Wesley preserved much of the chapter at hand, he removed the two paragraphs which addressed these stages. These levels include beginners, proficients, and the accomplished and perfect. Molinos assigned *doing* to the first level, "suffering with desire" to the second, and "dying always in themselves" to the highest level.[154]

It may also be found that these two writers differed on the means of progress. In the eleventh chapter of the same book, Molinos linked humility and suffering to one who "makes great way in a little time." Wesley kept the link between humility and progress yet removed the aspect of suffering as a component to speeding up movement toward the spiritual heights.[155] Earlier, Molinos described some of the things that carry the soul along in the early stages yet fail to do so later. These include the spiritual counsel, reading books, and crying out to God for aid.[156] Wesley, however, removed this entire paragraph, perhaps demonstrating his belief that these things do assist the soul at all levels.

151. Molinos, *Spiritual Guide*, 187; Wesley, *Christian Library* (Molinos), 38:292.

152. Molinos, *Spiritual Guide*, 135.

153. Wesley, *Christian Library* (Molinos), 38:278.

154. Molinos, *Spiritual Guide*, 143.

155. Molinos, *Spiritual Guide*, 152; Wesley, *Christian Library* (Molinos), 38:285.

156. Molinos, *Spiritual Guide*, 132.

Finally, another telling display of diverging perspectives on theories of spiritual stages may be found in Wesley's complete removal of the fifteenth chapter of the final book. In this chapter, Molinos identified six stages through which one ascends toward contemplation. Molinos also concluded the chapter indicating that this list was not exhaustive, but there exist many other such stages.

Desire

Like Molinos's positive and negative perspectives on pleasure and delight, he maintained a similar treatment of desires. Whereas desires, rightly directed, may serve to move one closer toward the spiritual climax, wrongly directed desires may result in spiritual hindrances. In addition, also like his own treatment of pleasure and delight, Wesley was more apt to avoid the usage of desire as either a virtuous means toward the intended end or a vice-filled obstacle to spiritual growth.

These respective treatments of the role of desires may be found in Molinos's opening paragraph and Wesley's edited version of the same. In these opening lines, Molinos stressed the value of the soul in relation to God's habitation of it and the importance of protecting it in cleanness, quiet, and peace. In this list of protections, Molinos included keeping the soul "void of affections, desires, and thoughts."[157] Thus, here, Molinos expressed the hazards of desires on the soul. Wesley, however, removed this phrase while maintaining most of the remainder of the list.[158]

In a positive treatment of desire, Molinos included a relatively lengthy quote by St. Austin regarding his wandering away from God and his ensuing *longing* and *breathing* after God as he sought to find him.[159] These aptly directed desires, though initially exercised in vain, were removed from Wesley's rendition.[160] Similarly, in that same chapter, Molinos described wrong decisions done with proper motives. Included in this proper motive were "a good Will, good Desires, and pure Intentions."[161] Wesley kept this statement yet removed the words "good Desires."[162] In that same paragraph, Molinos used the analogy of young birds in relationship to the older ones as he described people opening "their mouths to Heaven, declaring their wants"

157. Molinos, *Spiritual Guide*, 2.
158. Wesley, *Christian Library* (Molinos), 38:249.
159. Molinos, *Spiritual Guide*, 9.
160. Wesley, *Christian Library* (Molinos), 38:253.
161. Molinos, *Spiritual Guide*, 11.
162. Wesley, *Christian Library* (Molinos), 38:254.

and the ensuing provisions of God that follow.[163] Wesley, however, removed the description of the ravens, kept the imagery and the hope of answered prayer, yet removed the phrase "declaring their wants."[164] This is yet another example of Molinos's positive use of wants or desires and Wesley's avoidance of such terms.

In his third book, Molinos went back to the negative side of desire when he stated that one will "never arrive at this happy State . . . till it become purified from the disordered Passions of Concupiscence, Self-esteem Desire and Thoughts, how spiritual soever, and many other Interests and secret Vices."[165] Interestingly, Wesley preserved this portion while eliminating the "Desire and Thoughts, how spiritual soever," as well as the word *interests*.[166] Perhaps to Wesley, there is not a need for the obliteration of desires, thoughts, and interests necessarily.

In the chapter that follows, Wesley removed an entire paragraph where Molinos described the spiritual hindrance of even the positive side of desire. This includes "an inordinate desire of sublime Gifts" and an "appetite of feeling spiritual Consolation."[167] However, just a few chapters later, Molinos wrote about the desire for mortification as being a means toward knowing "true love."[168] Wesley kept this paragraph, but excluded the word *desires*.[169] However, in the same chapter, Molinos also warned of a desire for suffering that went too far—a paragraph which Wesley completely eliminated.[170] Yet, Molinos later affirmed the role of maintaining a "desire to be despised" as necessary to move toward humility.[171] Wesley also edited out this phrase.[172]

As referenced in the chapter addressing pleasures, the most notable editorial alteration Wesley made concerning desire was the elimination of chapter 15 in its entirety from the third book. In this chapter, Molinos described two means toward contemplation as including "the Pleasure, and the Desires of it."[173] This chapter emphasized the high value Molinos placed on the role of positive desire in making movement toward one's spiritual

163. Molinos, *Spiritual Guide*, 11.

164. Wesley, *Christian Library* (Molinos), 38:254.

165. Molinos, *Spiritual Guide*, 127–28.

166. Wesley, *Christian Library* (Molinos), 38:275.

167. Molinos, *Spiritual Guide*, 128.

168. Molinos, *Spiritual Guide*, 138.

169. Wesley, *Christian Library* (Molinos), 38:280.

170. Molinos, *Spiritual Guide*, 140; Wesley, *Christian Library* (Molinos), 38:280.

171. Molinos, *Spiritual Guide*, 149.

172. Wesley, *Christian Library* (Molinos), 38:283.

173. Molinos, *Spiritual Guide*, 163.

telos. Thus we see Molinos describing desire as rightly directed as well as wrongly directed, and as both a virtue and a vice, while Wesley seemed to remove most references to desire altogether.

Interior/Internal

Miguel de Molinos opened his *Spiritual Guide* with the words "thou art to know that thy Soul is the Center, Habitation, and Kingdom of God. That therefore, to the end the Sovereign King may rest on that Throne of thy Soul."[174] With these initial words, Molinos laid out his thesis which stressed the importance of interior spirituality, the theme that he would then develop throughout his work. Wesley preserved these words with the exception of stating that the soul is "the Center."[175] This was the first of many places where Wesley editorially removed certain references to the inward spiritual way laid out by Molinos.

In his opening chapter, Molinos urged his readers to "pacifie that Throne of thy Heart, that the Supreme King may rest therein." He continued by describing the means of pacification as entering "into thy self by means of internal recollection."[176] The end was preserved by Wesley, but the means removed.[177] Wesley did, however, keep the next points of instruction on prayer and recollection as one's protection. Thus, it does not appear to be recollection with which Wesley took issue, but the withdrawal into oneself and the emphasis, or over-emphasis, on the internal nature.

In the second chapter of Molinos's first book, he began by saying, "thou'lt find thy self, as all other Souls that are called by the Lord to the inward way, full of confusion and doubts."[178] Here, Wesley allowed for the description of this state of confusion and doubts as Molinos continued. However, he selectively removed the statement "as all other Souls that are called by the Lord to the inward way." Though it is not immediately clear as to why Wesley removed this statement, there are a few possibilities. Perhaps Wesley believed that: (1) the *inward way* is not a unique calling, but a calling to all; (2) no one is called to this concept of *inward way*; or (3) the state of doubt described is not unique to those called to the *inward way.*

As Molinos continued the theme of internal recollection in his eleventh chapter, he described a spiritual battle which takes place as people give

174. Molinos, *Spiritual Guide*, 1.
175. Wesley, *Christian Library* (Molinos), 38:249.
176. Molinos, *Spiritual Guide*, 2–3.
177. Wesley, *Christian Library* (Molinos), 38:250.
178. Molinos, *Spiritual Guide*, 4.

themselves "up to thy Lord in this inward Way." He continued to describe in strong terms that "all Hell will conspire against thee" and how greater war is waged against "one single Soul inwardly retired . . . than a thousand others that walk externally."[179] Wesley's editorial move here is likely due to his emphasis on the efficacy of good works, as will be evaluated later.

Interestingly, in chapter 12 of book 1, Wesley went contrary to his tendency to remove references to Catholic saints by preserving a lengthy description of prayer by Francesca Lopez of Valenza. He did, however, remove the title of "venerable Mother" and the reference to her connection with the "third Order of St. Francis." Relevant to the topic at hand, however, he removed the words pertaining to a soul "to be internal" in a description of constant prayer as the means to keeping one's "Heart always right toward God" and the instructions to "act with the affection of the Will, than the toyl of the Intellect."[180]

Molinos placed love as the greatest of means toward perfection over and above speaking and thinking about God. The means toward this love, however, he identified as "perfect Resignation and internal Silence," which "all consists in Works."[181] Wesley maintained the declaration of love serving as the greatest of the means toward perfection and kept *perfect resignation* as the means toward love. However, Wesley did not reserve a place for *internal silence* or *works* in his publication of Molinos's economy of perfection.[182]

It is fair to say that in most books, the opening paragraphs generally lay out the overarching theme, if not the thesis, of the text at hand. In Molinos's third book, this is the approach he took. He began in an apophatic way describing the *interior way* by first describing its contrasting counterpart, the *external way*. These first two paragraphs serve as summaries and the framework for what follows in book 3. However, Wesley removed the first paragraph, which describes the *external way*, in its entirety and nearly half of the second paragraph, which explains the *interior way*. Wesley valued external works, so it is likely not because of the emphasis on an outward way that Wesley removed these portions. It is likely due to one or both of two possible reasons for this editorial move: (1) the type of works described by Molinos represent a different set of values than the type of works praised by Wesley, and/or (2) Wesley did not see the *interior way* as superior to the *external way* as described by Molinos.

179. Molinos, *Spiritual Guide*, 31.

180. Molinos, *Spiritual Guide*, 37; Wesley, *Christian Library* (Molinos), 38:265.

181. Molinos, *Spiritual Guide*, 57.

182. Wesley, *Christian Library* (Molinos), 38:130.

At the conclusion of the opening chapter of book 3, Molinos described a state of existence in the internal way that leaves a person "disinterested" not in a *laissez-faire* way, but in a state of holy contentment. Molinos stated that "there is no News that chears 'em; no Success that makes them sad; Tribulation never disturb them; nor interiour, continual and divine Communication make 'em vain and conceited."[183] Though preserving most of these words, in addition to a couple word alterations, Wesley removed the words *interiour* and *continual* regarding the "divine Communication."

As the third book continues, Wesley again removed an opening paragraph, this time in the second chapter. Again, the opening paragraph gave a summary of the *external way*. He also removed the closing paragraph to the chapter which may serve to shine a bit more light on the reasoning for such a removal. The closing paragraph does not state anything of great substance or detail, rather it reinforces that one "will know the great difference which is between the outward and inward Man."[184] Thus, Wesley may have removed the mention of the *outward man*, or *external way* because he did not see such a bifurcation between external and internal. Rather, to Wesley, such interior recollection and communion will necessarily result in an external expression (this will be examined later under the section on Wesley's view of these matters). This may be further seen in his elimination of the word *inwardly/internal* to describe the sense of content/peace which a spiritual person may exhibit in the face of adversity and the expulsion of the word *interiour* pertaining to *true humility*.[185] In other words, this content and humility, though felt internally, will display itself externally.

The idea of internal spirituality, though not completely abandoned by Wesley's editorial eye, was selectively reduced. Another aspect of this reduction may be found in Wesley's removal of the concepts of going into oneself and internal solitude. This may be observed in his removal of this wording in the context of going into oneself for a deep spiritual change, regarding the process of disrobing and being "cloathed with God," and regarding the spiritual *telos*.[186]

---

183. Molinos, *Spiritual Guide*, 118.

184. Molinos, *Spiritual Guide*, 121.

185. Molinos, *Spiritual Guide*, 140, 149, 152; Wesley, *Christian Library* (Molinos), 38:280, 283, 285.

186. Molinos, *Spiritual Guide*, 137, 157.

Senses and Affections

John Wesley demonstrated his departure from Molinos regarding the place of senses in one's spiritual progress by removing words, sentences, and a paragraph pertaining to the senses. One notable statement made by Molinos which Wesley eliminated includes the proclamation that "senses are not capable of divine blessings."[187] Interestingly, however, Wesley did preserve the assertion that one may "advance towards . . . union with God" after being resolved "to mortify thy external senses."[188]

In a chapter on "Declaring the Nature of internal Recollection," Molinos urged his readers to arrive at a point where they no longer reflect upon themselves or their perfection. He continued to encourage them to "shut up the Senses, trusting God with all the care of thy Welfare."[189] Wesley, however, extracted this portion, perhaps because of his encouragement toward self-examine.

For Molinos, the senses were connected to early forms of prayer. In the chapter following the chapter mentioned above, Molinos described a state at which the soul enters where the "prayer of the senses" is removed from the soul and one no longer should use verbal prayer, but remain in quiet.[190] This larger, nearly paragraph-length, description was excluded in Wesley's version. Wesley did, in time, value extemporaneous prayer over written prayers, but did not promote giving up of vocal prayer.

Wesley preserved an assertion by Molinos that praying for fifteen minutes does more good than many harsh ascetic practices. Molinos, however, specified that this is prayer done "with recollection of the senses and faculties, with resignation and humility." Wesley kept the latter two modes, while eliminating the former—recollection of the senses and faculties.[191]

In a chapter on the effects of contemplation, Molinos laid out a profound description of a soul united to God where the soul is ruled by "the pure Spirit, who is God." Wesley removed a few words of great significance here. Although keeping the concept of the soul being *united to* God, he removed the mystical word *union* as a description of this state early in the paragraph but kept it at the end. Regarding the senses, he maintained that this is "above all human understanding," but intentionally removed the words *sense and* which initially appeared after the word *above*. Thus, in Wesley's version, this

187. Molinos, *Spiritual Guide*, 7.

188. Molinos, *Spiritual Guide*, 21; Wesley, *Christian Library* (Molinos), 38:257.

189. Molinos, *Spiritual Guide*, 30–31.

190. Molinos, *Spiritual Guide*, 35.

191. Molinos, *Spiritual Guide*, 36; Wesley, *Christian Library* (Molinos), 38:265.

state is above understanding, but not necessarily above sense. He also removed from this paragraph the strong assertion that "the purity of the Soul being uncapable of sensible things."[192]

Hiddenness and Forgetfulness

Molinos believed that the deeper inner workings of God were so deep that they were beyond one's awareness. He penned words like *secret, hidden, forgetfulness*, and *not knowing* to describe the cognizance one possesses during such phases of spiritual maturation. Wesley, however, removed such words in favor of a spirituality of knowledge and understanding of the divine action within.

One example of this may be found in Molinos's fourth chapter of the first book. There, he described how dryness produces humility, yet through dryness, one "may not know what he is working in us."[193] Wesley removed this phrase yet preserved the following implication that too much knowledge and awareness of the divine working may lead to presumption.[194]

A few chapters later, Molinos praised the greatness of the wisdom of God "who can pry into the depth of the secret and extraordinary means, and the hidden paths whereby he guides the soul."[195] Wesley, however, removed the language of "secret and extraordinary" and "the hidden paths."[196] Likewise, in the fourth chapter of Molinos's third book, Wesley removed the words "secret virtue" as a description of the strength which God gives to resist the temptation of pride in souls which have advanced through the spiritual martyrdoms.[197]

Wesley's issue with unknowing may also be found in his removal of the word *forgetfulness* in descriptions that nearly bookend Molinos's first book. In the opening paragraphs, Molinos presented a list of nine virtues that may be found in the midst of nine corresponding difficulties when the presence of God enters one's soul. These include "silence in tumult, solitude in company, light in darkness, forgetfulness in pressures, vigour in despondency, courage in fear, resistance in temptation, peace in war, and quiet in tribulation."[198] In Wesley's rendition, this list was kept in its entirety except

192. Molinos, *Spiritual Guide*, 158–59; Wesley, *Christian Library* (Molinos), 38:289.

193. Molinos, *Spiritual Guide*, 13.

194. Wesley, *Christian Library* (Molinos), 38:255.

195. Molinos, *Spiritual Guide*, 27.

196. Wesley, *Christian Library* (Molinos), 38:261.

197. Molinos, *Spiritual Guide*, 129; Wesley, *Christian Library* (Molinos), 38:276.

198. Molinos, *Spiritual Guide*, 3.

for "forgetfulness in pressures."[199] Similarly, in the penultimate chapter of the first book, regarding entering a state of recollection, Wesley removed a description that involves remaining at peace when slipping from remembrance into forgetfulness.[200]

Repose and Contentment

John Wesley believed that true repose is not possible in this life. Therefore, we see that he removed or altered Molinos's references to repose, contentment, and peace about nine times, while only keeping the word *repose* in a couple of places or changing the wording to demonstrate a value of contentment over the idea of quiet.

The two places where Wesley preserved the wording of Molinos regarding repose fall within the context of suffering or trials as the outcome produced in the soul as one progresses through such difficulties.[201] In the first, Molinos spoke of "great repose" while in the second he referred to "complete repose." The first referenced more of the contrast between trials and the peace that comes after such trials are endured. This was not as surprising that Wesley left this description in, as opposed to the latter example that speaks of "complete repose." However, in the latter, the description of such peace arrives as a direct outcome of complete mortification of the soul.

Wesley also removed the various mentions of repose as they relate to quietness. This is likely due more to Wesley's issue with Quietism than his issue with repose. Wesley removed an entire paragraph that was in many ways similar to the above where repose is associated with trials. However, a distinct mark of this paragraph as opposed to the above is the statement that Molinos made saying that the "Lord hath his repose no where but in quiet Souls."[202] In the paragraph preceding this, Wesley opted to use the word *content* in place of the words *constant and quiet*. Elsewhere, Wesley interestingly preserved the use of the word *Quietness* as an arrival point, but eliminated the statement immediately following "and supreme internal peace" as an arrival point.[203]

Four times, Wesley completely removed the words *content, peace internal, and repose*.[204] For the first, *content*, Molinos assigned the term to God

199. Wesley, *Christian Library* (Molinos), 38:251.

200. Molinos, *Spiritual Guide*, 57; Wesley, *Christian Library* (Molinos), 38:268.

201. Wesley, *Christian Library* (Molinos), 38:270, 278.

202. Molinos, *Spiritual Guide*, 127.

203. Wesley, *Christian Library* (Molinos), 38:281.

204. Wesley, *Christian Library* (Molinos), 38:264, 274–75, 282.

in his reaction to the soul that is "desirous, humble, quiet and resigned," stating that this is God's "greatest content and glory."[205] It is unclear and merely speculative to guess whether Wesley removed the term because he was uncomfortable using it in reference to God, because of differing views of contentment from those of Molinos, or because he imagined even greater sources of contentment for the Divine. In the two occurrences where Wesley removed *peace internal*, they were for Molinos in direct relationship to the *telos* of the Christian life. In the first, Molinos connected *peace internal* with the "height of perfect Contemplation, to the highest, happiest of the loving Union, and the lofty Throne of Peace Internal."[206] The latter occurrence is connected to an arrival at "perfect Quietness."[207] The separation of "peace internal" from a *telos* point is very much in keeping with the aforementioned statement from Wesley claiming that repose is not possible in this life.

The fourth removal just mentioned, that of *repose*, was found in Wesley's elimination of a complete paragraph on repose. In this paragraph, Molinos described how some people seek after repose and some experience it without looking for it; he then said the same for "pleasure in pain."[208] Perhaps this removal was due to Wesley's perspective leading to the conclusion that seeking after something that is impossible in this life may be an act of futility. Or perhaps the removal of this paragraph was due to Wesley's perspectives on pain and suffering, which will be discussed later. Elsewhere, Wesley also excluded a statement that linked peace in the soul with one's humbling of oneself.[209]

Delight, Pleasure, and Happiness

Upon close inspection of the editorial changes which Wesley made to the writings of Molinos, it becomes clear that the two had very different perspectives on happiness, delight, and pleasure. At times, Wesley removed Molinos's descriptions where happiness was upheld as a virtue; however, he also altered and eliminated references to happiness where it was portrayed more as a vice. Only occasionally did he affirm Molinos's message by preserving the text included. In other words, where Molinos saw happiness as an asset, Wesley saw it as a hindrance and vice versa.

205. Molinos, *Spiritual Guide*, 35–36.

206. Molinos, *Spiritual Guide*, 125.

207. Molinos, *Spiritual Guide*, 142.

208. Molinos, *Spiritual Guide*, 143–44.

209. Wesley, *Christian Library* (Molinos), 38:284.

Two examples of this may be found rather closely together at the end of Molinos's third chapter and just a few chapters later in the beginning pages of his fourth chapter. In the former, as Molinos discussed the spiritual martyrdom, he expressed that the soul in such a state is "it self deprived of the sensible Pleasures" in order to live by faith.[210] In this case, the *sensible pleasures* likely refer to the tangible encounters with the working of God based on sensory reception. Wesley preserved this reference.

However, in that same paragraph, as Molinos urged his readers to quietly persevere in order to attain to happiness, union, rest, and internal peace, the outcomes of which Wesley removed.[211] Early in the next chapter, Molinos went on to portray satisfaction as a vice that may creep in along with presumption if it were not for God hiding the work being done in the soul. Wesley did not alter the description of presumption as such a vice but did eliminate satisfaction from among the lists of vices.[212]

Another phrase pertaining to pleasure which Molinos used on occasion includes "sensible pleasures" or "sensible delight." On a few occasions, Wesley removed these words, even though they were used to reference two very different states of being. The first was used in reference to the Spirit depriving nature of sensible pleasures. This use described nature as an enemy to the Spirit.[213] Therefore, to deprive nature of sensible pleasure would be a positive thing. Similarly, Molinos described the "hunt after sensible pleasures" as a state of being associated with one who gradually falls away from progressing on the spiritual path.[214] Thus, again, sensible pleasures are viewed as a negative and their removal would be an asset. However, in his third book, Molinos spoke of sensible delight as a positive aspect of spiritual fervor.[215] In all of these cases, whether a positive portrayal or a negative, Wesley removed the phrase from the pages of his edition.

Around the previously mentioned paragraph, Molinos also spoke of *despising* "spiritual pleasures" as a virtuous means of ascent toward perfection.[216] Wesley removed this phrasing as well.[217] In places even delights in the broad sense were villainized by Molinos. For example, in a chapter on inward mortification and repose, Molinos stated that a mark of true

210. Molinos, *Spiritual Guide*, 11

211. Molinos, *Spiritual Guide*, 11–12; Wesley, *Christian Library* (Molinos), 38:254.

212. Molinos, *Spiritual Guide*, 13; Wesley, *Christian Library* (Molinos), 38:255.

213. Molinos, *Spiritual Guide*, 32–33.

214. Molinos, *Spiritual Guide*, 36.

215. Molinos, *Spiritual Guide*, 124.

216. Molinos, *Spiritual Guide*, 123.

217. Wesley, *Christian Library* (Molinos), 38:273.

mortification includes "the disesteem of delights, and the counting of 'em torment."[218] Wesley included the link between "the disesteem of delights" with mortification but eliminated the latter phrase of "counting of 'em torment."[219] Thus, Wesley toned down the negativism expressed toward general delights.

Probably one of the most notable editorial adjustments which Wesley made concerning pleasure may be found in his complete removal of the fifteenth chapter in the third book. The chapter examines two means toward contemplation and their accompanying steps toward ascension. These two means include "the Pleasure, and the Desires of" contemplation.[220] This serves as another example of Molinos's positive and negative uses of pleasure and desire, here expressing a positive perspective, while Wesley seems more apt to avoid their uses altogether—either positively or negatively.

JOHN WESLEY ON SPIRITUAL GROWTH[221]

The Stages Summarized

As discussed in the previous chapter, John Wesley had a relatively well developed and quite thorough understanding of the *ordo salutis*, or order of salvation. In Wesley's writings, this order may be categorized into four main themes or stages: (1) The original human state and the working of God available to all people. (2) The process of justification and initial change experienced by all who respond positively to the working and grace of God. (3) The process of spiritual growth. (4) The realization of the climactic state experienced by few, but available to all. Albert Outler offered this summary: "the recovery of the defaced image of God is the axial theme of Wesley's soteriology."[222]

The first stage includes the natural depraved state of every person, though not understood as the total depravity explained by Calvinism. At this stage, God extends prevenient grace to everyone then at some point touches the heart of each person through conviction. When this happens, every person will come to various degrees of an awareness of God and an

218. Molinos, *Spiritual Guide*, 144.

219. Wesley, *Christian Library* (Molinos), 38:282.

220. Molinos, *Spiritual Guide*, 163.

221. Portions of this section were taken from and significantly expanded upon a section from this author's DMin dissertation, "Stages of Spiritual Growth: A Comparative Study of Pseudo-Dionysius, John of the Cross, Teresa of Avila, and John Wesley" (2009, Fuller Theological Seminary).

222. Wesley, *Works* (Outler), 2:185n70.

awareness of one's own fallen state. Again, in Wesley's economy of salvation, these are extended to and experienced by the entirety of humankind. The difference remains in the various responses which people make to this awareness and extension of grace.

At this point, some will reject the grace of God and continue in their own fallen state. However, some will accept God's grace and respond favorably through an act of faith and initial repentance at which point they are justified and made right with God. Upon justification, as initial repentance continues, one begins to experience the initial working of the new birth, a degree of assurance, and an initial sanctification. As these were discussed in the previous chapter, here space is reserved to look primarily at the third phase of this process, and to touch on the fourth phase, which will be addressed more thoroughly in a later chapter.

In the third phase, for those who will continue on the path of spiritual growth and progress, they will begin to deny themselves, live in an ongoing repentance, and grow in faith, hope, and love, along with a further development of peace and joy in the Holy Spirit. Within this process, many will experience what Wesley referred to as the "Wilderness State" and "Heaviness through Manifold Temptations." These are stages marked by suffering and pain yet containing the potential to aid in the process of spiritual growth.

In the fourth and climactic stage, one will be fully born again, receive full assurance, be entirely sanctified, and arrive at a degree of Christian Perfection. Wesley saw this state as a level of completion while allowing room for further growth and development. Again, this will be covered more thoroughly in a later chapter.

Spiritual Growth beyond Justification

Self-Denial

Wesley believed that in order for one to make spiritual progress, one must implement a high degree of self-denial. In his own words, "the 'denying' ourselves and 'taking up our cross,' in the full extent of the expression . . . is absolutely, indispensably necessary, either to our becoming or continuing his disciples."[223] Wesley even drew a direct correlation between the level of self-denial and one's degree to which she or he will follow Jesus. He went on to state that of all the hindrances to growth that occur "in every stage of the

---

223. Wesley, *Works* (Outler), 2:238.

spiritual life," they may be reduced down to the issue that "we do not deny ourselves, or we do not take up our cross."[224]

To Wesley, a significant aspect of the climactic spiritual state includes full and complete submission to the will of God. For this to happen, one must relinquish one's own will. This takes place through self-denial. Wesley saw God's will as "a path leading straight to God" and the human will as a path leading away from God. Therefore, one must choose which to follow and consequently, which to deny.[225]

Wesley went so far as to say that failure to grow in God's grace "is *always* the want of denying ourselves or taking up our cross"; thus, spiritual growth is dependent upon self-denial in Wesley's understanding.[226] Wesley held that lack of forward movement as well as backsliding may result from the degree to which one fails to deny oneself. Such growth, or lack of growth, is also held in close proximity to the works and good deeds one performs in faith, according to Wesley.[227] This combination of self-denial combined with good deeds allows for movement toward the greater spiritual end.

The Wilderness State and Heaviness

On March 28, 1740, in his journal, Wesley referenced a wilderness state which included a "state of doubts, and fears, and strong temptations" after the initial salvation.[228] This was later developed into a sermon preached throughout 1751–52 and published in 1760.[229] Wesley's sermon sought to directly address the common mystical belief of suffering as a God-given means toward maturity, much like that laid out by John of the Cross. To help clarify and supplement his point of view, Wesley developed a follow-up sermon in 1755 titled "Heaviness through Manifold Temptations."[230]

The wilderness state, Wesley argued, is not caused by God's will. He very pointedly asserted that God "never *deserts* us, as some speak: it is we only that *desert* him."[231] Rather, the wilderness state remains the consequence of sin, including sins of commission and omission, inward sin,

224. Wesley, *Works* (Outler), 2:240.
225. Wesley, *Works* (Outler), 2:241–42.
226. Wesley, *Works* (Outler), 2:246 (emphasis mine).
227. Wesley, *Works* (Outler), 2:247–48.
228. Wesley and Sugden, *Works* (*Standard Sermons*), 2:244.
229. Wesley, *Works* (Outler), 2:202–21.
230. Wesley, *Works* (Outler), 2:222–35.
231. Wesley, *Works* (Outler), 2:208.

ignorance of Scripture, ignorance of God's working, and temptation.[232] The result of this state includes a loss of faith, love, desire, joy, hope, peace, and power over sin.[233] Wesley placed the source of this state completely upon the individual as the consequence of his or her own wrongdoing. Although this state is fundamentally a period of backsliding, Wesley held that many people experience it after justification—Edward Sugden noted that Wesley also included himself in this.[234] Therefore, as a result of the frequency of such an experience, the wilderness state serves as a distinctive stage of spiritual progression.

In his follow up sermon "Heaviness through Manifold Temptations," Wesley proposed a stage of spirituality distinct from the wilderness state, yet similarly full of difficulty and various degrees of suffering. As many people experience the wilderness state, Wesley held that even more, in fact, "almost all the children of God experience this," referring to Heaviness.[235] This stage may occur at any point in one's spiritual journey, likely even later in one's growth after one is an "altogether Christian"; however, it is addressed here for the sake of comparison and contrast to the Wilderness state.

In contrast to the wilderness state, heaviness results from temptations, illness, grief, sorrow for lost souls, not from the sovereign will of God, nor from sin. Also, unlike the wilderness state, heaviness does not destroy faith, hope, love, and power over sin, rather this state serves to increase faith, hope, love, and holiness through purification.[236] With these beneficial results, Wesley concluded that there often, but not always, may be a need for people to experience heaviness.[237] These stages will be investigated in greater detail in the next chapter in the context of suffering but are worth noting here as they serve as stages or seasons of spiritual growth.

Ongoing Repentance and Growth in Sanctification

As mentioned earlier, sanctification begins with the new birth, yet in Wesley's perspective, remains gradual and ongoing as a process toward spiritual maturity.[238] During this phase, entire sanctification has not yet occurred. Therefore, Wesley stressed that sin remains in the believer, yet without

232. Wesley, *Works* (Outler), 2:209–12.

233. Wesley, *Works* (Outler), 2:206–8.

234. Wesley and Sugden, *Works* (*Standard Sermons*), 2:244.

235. Wesley, *Works* (Outler), 2:222.

236. Wesley, *Works* (Outler), 2:223, 226–29, 231–33.

237. Wesley, *Works* (Outler), 2:234.

238. See sermon "Scripture Way of Salvation," Wesley, *Works* (Outler), 2:160.

condemnation.[239] Consequently, there also remains the necessity for on-going repentance from both outward and inward sin as a process toward spiritual maturity. In his sermon "The Repentance of Believers," Wesley spelled out this process of repentance as involving conviction of guiltiness, conviction of utter helplessness, followed by repentance.[240]

As one progresses through the state of heaviness, and grows in sanc-tification through ongoing repentance, he or she may grow toward what Wesley viewed as the climax, or *telos*, of the Christian life, entire sanctifica-tion and Christian perfection. To Wesley, the marks of this spiritual growth may be observed through expressions of faith, hope, love, peace, and joy. He summarized well the first three as he reflected on 1 Cor 13 in an open letter to William Warburton, then bishop of Gloucester, in 1763 when he stated, "faith, hope, love, are the sum of perfection on earth; love alone is the sum of perfection in heaven."[241]

The Climactic Stages of Spiritual Growth

Wesley used a few different terms to describe a certain level of arrival to-ward a climactic spiritual state. Although they may point to an overall goal or *telos*, the terms are not fully interchangeable as he sought to communi-cate various aspects of the intended end of the Christian existence. In many cases, he described a more complete realization of that which is experienced in a lesser degree at an earlier stage. For example, as mentioned before, one is born again when one is initially justified. However, Wesley also described a state at which one is *fully* born again. Likewise, coinciding with justifica-tion one becomes a Christian, or follower of Christ. However, through a deeper work of God in the life of the believer closely connected with the level of self-denial, one becomes an *altogether* Christian. Similarly, early on in one's spiritual development, one may experience an assurance that their sins are forgiven and that they may have the hope of eternal life. Yet, as one grows, a *full* assurance may be realized as an outcome of the aforementioned states.

In an earlier chapter, the new birth was addressed as it pertains to jus-tification and the early stages of spiritual growth. Here, it is worth noting a few key aspects of the new birth found in Wesley's theology as it per-tains to the process of spiritual growth and especially to the two levels at which it may be experienced. As mentioned in that chapter, Wesley made

239. See sermon "On Sin in Believers," Wesley, *Works* (Outler), 1:317–18.
240. Wesley, *Works* (Outler), 1:344–45.
241. Wesley, *Works* (Cragg), 11:508.

the distinction between justification and the new birth as the difference between that which God does *for us* and that which God does *in us*, respectively.[242] As a work of God *in us*, the new birth has a certain unpredictability to it. Wesley stated that "the precise manner how it is done, how the Holy Spirit works this in the soul, neither thou nor the wisest of the children of men is able to explain."[243] However, he went on to explain that the outcomes may be explained. Not least of these outcomes is the return to the image of God, which he explained as the moral image, including righteousness, true holiness, love, justice, mercy, truth, and spotless purity.[244]

Wesley also made significant connections between the new birth and religious epistemology. In his article "The New Birth and the Knowledge of God," Douglas Koskela pointed out that "Wesley repeatedly connected the opening of the spiritual senses to the new birth."[245] In other words, the new birth results in a moral change and a deeper spiritual understanding. Larry Wood highlighted how, from 1738 on, Wesley understood this transformation in two different levels, distinguishing "between born 'in the lowest sense' from being 'born in the perfect sense.'"[246] This latter birth then leads toward one living as an *altogether* Christian.

Wesley presented a view of Christianity that included a Christian who is justified and entered into the faith as distinct from an *altogether* Christian who lives out the faith more fully. Some may argue that Wesley lessened the distinction between an *almost* Christian and an *altogether* or *real* Christian over time. However, in his article "Real Christianity as Integrating Theme in Wesley's Soteriology: The Critique of a Modern Myth," Kenneth J. Collins argued that Wesley preserved this distinction and that it remained an important theme in his soteriology. Collins asserted that, early on, Wesley took the definition of a Christian too far by exceeding the essentials of justification and the new birth to also include the language of entire sanctification.[247] This may account for the perceived softening of distinction argued by others. However, in time, his theological development allowed for a distinction between the Christian and the *true* Christian as described as the those who possess the "faith of a servant" and those with the "faith of a

242. Wesley, *Works* (Outler), 2:187.

243. Wesley, *Works* (Outler), 2:191.

244. Wesley, *Works* (Outler), 2:188.

245. Koskela, "New Birth and Knowledge," 13.

246. Wood, "Conflicting Views," 64.

247. Collins, "Real Christianity," 17.

child," respectively. This distinction began to take shape in 1754 according to Collins.[248]

Collins pointed out that by 1740 at the latest, Wesley "began to realize that there are both degrees of faith *and* degrees of assurance."[249] Collins asserted that Wesley held assurance as "a vital ingredient of the true Christian faith."[250] This link remains so crucial that, according to Collins, a mark of real Christianity in Wesleyan soteriology includes "fearlessness in the face of death."[251]

In other words, one becomes a Christian in association with justification. One may be justified without having assurance, yet assurance should follow. As one grows spiritually, there is a point at which one may become a *true* Christian in which state they arrive at a full assurance that their sins are forgiven and of the hope of eternity in heaven. At this stage, one lives in the faith of a child with movement toward the *telos*.

Entire Sanctification and Christian Perfection

John Wesley summarized the goal of the religious life as renewing "our hearts in the image of God, to repair that total loss of righteousness and true holiness which we sustained by the sin of our first parent."[252] To Wesley this end remains obtainable to a very high degree in this life. As sanctification for Wesley remained an ongoing process, he also believed that one could reach this end at a point which he referred to as entire sanctification. Although this theme will be covered more thoroughly in a later chapter, it is worth some attention here as it pertains to the fulfillment of Wesley's soteriological development.

Arrival at such a high climax involves first of all a desire for it, then through self-knowledge and repentance, coming to the awareness for deliverance.[253] Although Wesley gave these prerequisites as the human role toward entire sanctification, he instructed his listeners to "wait in peace for that hour, when 'the God of peace shall sanctify thee wholly,'" stressing that entire sanctification ultimately remains the work of God.[254]

248. Collins, "Real Christianity," 23.
249. Collins, "Real Christianity," 19.
250. Collins, "Real Christianity," 20.
251. Collins, "Real Christianity," 28.
252. Wesley, *Works* (Outler), 2:185.
253. Wesley, *Works* (Outler), 1:351.
254. Wesley, *Works* (Outler), 1:247.

For Wesley, entire sanctification results in perfect love for God and for others a love that expels sin from the soul including pride, self-will, anger, and unbelief.[255] Wesley called the results of entire sanctification *Christian Perfection*. In his sermon by that title, he reserved a portion of the message for a mildly apophatic approach to arrive at what Christian perfection *is* by means of describing what it *is not*. This perfection does not mean one is perfected in knowledge or free from ignorance, nor is one free from mistake, nor infirmities, nor temptation.[256] What Christian perfection *does* involve, according to Wesley, is a freedom from sin—in his words, "a Christian is so far perfect, as not to commit sin."[257] One is also free from evil thoughts and tempers, and free from both outward sin and inward sin.[258]

Although much of Wesley's language seems to allude to *entire sanctification* and *Christian perfection* as arrival points, he acknowledged that there is no such "perfection of degrees."[259] Rather, no matter where one may be in the spiritual journey, there remains a need to "grow in grace," advancing in love for and knowledge of God.[260] Therefore, he concluded that, on earth, there remains no absolute perfection.[261] As mentioned earlier, this idea will be expanded upon later, including some of the more nuanced aspects of Wesley's perspective, but is included here as it pertains to the overall process of spiritual progression.

Heaven

To Wesley, in the stage of entire sanctification ignorance and imperfect knowledge remain, whereas heaven is the place where even understanding becomes perfected and ignorance laid aside.[262] As mentioned earlier, he was reticent to use the word *happiness* in relation to a state of being in this life, yet he had no reservation in using the concept pertaining to heaven. He believed that the "most perfect happiness" rests in the eternal reward of heaven. Using the wording of Revelation, Wesley described the place of true and complete perfection as found only in heaven.[263]

255. Wesley, *Works* (Outler), 2:160.
256. Wesley, *Works* (Outler), 2:100–104.
257. Wesley, *Works* (Outler), 2:116.
258. Wesley, *Works* (Outler), 2:118–19.
259. Wesley, *Works* (Outler), 2:104.
260. Wesley, *Works* (Outler), 2:105.
261. Wesley, *Works* (Outler), 2:104.
262. See sermon "Good Steward," Wesley, *Works* (Outler), 2:290.
263. See sermon "Great Assize," Wesley, *Works* (Outler), 1:370–71.

COMPARISON AND CONTRAST

Ávila, Molinos, and Wesley all viewed the spiritual life as that which ought to include a process of growth toward a specific end or *telos*. Ávila saw learning, the reading of Scripture and historical theological texts, set times of prayer and reflection, and the sacraments as means to growth toward this end. Molinos, on the other hand, emphasized the significant role of the various aspects of prayer as the critical means to spiritual advancement. Wesley tended to align with Ávila in applying multiple disciplines and practices to that which will enable one to develop toward spiritual maturity. All three also strongly emphasized the role and initiation of God in this process.

Although Ávila held to a traditional Roman Catholic soteriology, Molinos a Catholic mystical soteriology, and Wesley a Protestant understanding of salvation, the three maintained a synergistic approach to justification and the spiritual life. Ávila and Wesley placed their emphasis on the role of a free-will response to divine action and saw the exterior and interior, or the senses and the affect, as working together, while Molinos viewed spirituality as a move from exterior to interior, or from the senses to the affect, and from active to passive.

Ávila wrote of a connection with God which develops over time, Molinos stressed the arrival at specific stages, while Wesley proclaimed a Christianity that includes process, progress, and distinct arrival points along the way. All three asserted that self-denial in its various forms is critical for development along these paths. Ávila and Wesley held to the necessity of ongoing self-denial, while Molinos saw purgation, annihilation, and mortification as part of the stages in his economy of salvation and growth which include the two martyrdoms.

Desire serves as an important means toward the end according to Ávila. Wesley, on the other hand, observed the negative outcomes of misguided desire. Both the negative and the positive dynamics of desire worked their way into the writings of Molinos. The three agreed that self-knowledge and awareness empower people to advance spiritually.

These three authors all assigned a great significance to the problem of sin, the fallen nature of humankind, and the ability of God to set people free from sin. Ávila and Molinos wrote on the need for purgation, with the latter carrying the idea of this inner work to the point of annihilation. Wesley proclaimed that one could be free from sin in this life. However, each one also realized that temptation can occur at any time—as a distraction to progress, according to Ávila; sourced in the devil, the world, or the flesh, according to Wesley; and from the devil and the hand of God simultaneously according to Molinos.

All three also addressed the human experience of suffering. Ávila viewed it as a part of the process of spiritual advancement, Molinos as a necessary ingredient to growth, and Wesley as coming from outside forces and a common experience which God may use—yet not absolutely necessary. Each of the above may be used by God to bring about transformation toward a high and lofty goal that is accessible to all, but few attain. Ávila called this *union* with God which leads to active ministry. Molinos opted to describe it as an ultimate level of contemplation (in addition to the arrival at union) which leads to a passive quietude. Wesley applied the terms *Christian Perfection* and *Entire Sanctification* as well as a point of full assurance and becoming an *altogether* Christian which results in perfect love. Although each theological writer maintained his own unique emphasis, terminology, and descriptions based on religious tradition, interpretation, and their own experience, they all expressed an intense commitment to the possibility of a personal experience with God that grows and develops toward a high and lofty end that is available to all and realized by some, with suffering serving (at least in part) as a portion of the means toward that end.

5

Suffering and Divine Withdrawal

SUFFERING IS PART OF the human experience. The theological questions that emerge around pain and suffering do not need to address the matter of *if* people will suffer. Suffering is a given. However, tragedy and hurt force questions about the sources of suffering and whether they may serve a higher purpose. Wesley, Molinos, and Ávila each described a redemptive quality in suffering. They all believed that a higher purpose may be realized through earthly challenges. However, they disagreed in varying degrees on the source of anguish and the extent to which divine involvement plays in causing suffering.

JUAN DE ÁVILA ON SUFFERING

For Juan de Ávila, suffering serves as a means to the end as well as a distinct stage of spiritual progression. He believed that in life, suffering is inevitable, stating that "you will have to suffer trials, sorrows, temptations, and the cross." Though these sufferings may be harsh, he also believed that they were not as severe as they could be, observing that due to the many sins, people "deserve far greater punishments."[1] The intensity of the afflictions faced by people in this life may be very strong according to Juan. He described such a season in a letter to a young woman; though lengthy, it is worth noting here:

> You will be brought to such a pass that you will seem to taste the anguish of death, although death itself would appear less horrible, for you will be terrified by a secret dread that God has abandoned you. These trials will make your soul so dry and hard

1. Ávila, *Confidence* (Benedictines), 14.

that it will seem as dead and as perverse as that of the wicked in hell. You will cry and not be heard, that in which you sought and hoped to find relief will only make you more disconsolate. God will show you no sign of love, but will seem to turn from you in disdain. These and other trials, which are usually suffered in this affliction, will make you so disgusted with yourself, that you would welcome death as gain.[2]

Juan believed that though the suffering can be intense, God also gives consolation, often as a precursor to the trials so that there will be strength to endure.[3]

To Juan, the sources of sufferings may vary. At times, he emphatically declared God to be the source of suffering. He urged his readers not to be discouraged by anything sent by God, but to endure it "because he gives it."[4] He quoted from St. Augustine saying, "blessed is the injury of which God is the cause."[5] As these sufferings come *from* God, Juan even encouraged others to desire such suffering *for* God.[6]

Elsewhere, however, Juan wrote as though such sufferings are not given by God per se, but *allowed* by God for some greater good. For example, in his *Audi, Filia*, he stated, "God permits desolation, darkness of mind, and even sins, so that those so afflicted may humble themselves and be free of the miseries."[7] A bit later he described how God *leaves* people in situations where *the enemies* are the source of tribulation, not God.[8]

Juan also acknowledged that these difficulties may at times be delivered through the actions of others. However, even when the suffering comes from the hand of another, he urged his readers to receive it as from God.[9] He even called for an approach to humility that encourages an allowance of others to be harsh in their treatment of oneself in order to abandon one's opinion and will.[10]

Juan remained clear in acknowledging the pain and intensity of such a season of struggle. However, whereas his contemporary John of the Cross saw the dark night experiences as the soul feeling abandon by God, Juan de

2. Ávila, *Confidence* (Benedictines), 92.
3. Ávila, *Audi, Filia* (Gormley), 98.
4. Ávila, *Audi, Filia* (Gormley), 98.
5. Ávila, *Audi, Filia* (Gormley), 100.
6. Ávila, *Audi, Filia* (Gormley), 211.
7. Ávila, *Audi, Filia* (Gormley), 94.
8. Ávila, *Audi, Filia* (Gormley), 106–7.
9. Ávila, *Confidence* (Benedictines), 13.
10. Ávila, *Audi, Filia* (Gormley), 287.

Ávila often stressed the ongoing presence of God in the midst of the pain. He reminded his readers in the *Audi, Filia* to trust that God will protect people in the trials, even when it feels like the suffering lasts longer than it ought.[11] Juan spoke of God as a friend to those suffering trials, stating that God "dwells with them and provides for them."[12] Even when someone feels abandoned by God, Juan reminded his readers that God "keeps His holy watch over us, and never so faithfully as when we think He has abandoned us."[13] In his sermon on a "Sunday within the Octave of the Ascension," Juan declared that "there is no anguish no matter how great which the Holy Spirit cannot relieve."[14]

In addition to the reminders of God's presence and working within and through suffering, Juan laid out action steps for people who found themselves enduring such trials. In the *Audi, Filia*, he wrote about people enjoying great comfort through what some would refer to as the means of grace, i.e., prayer, the sacraments, God's words, "or by other means that are in the church."[15] He also described the importance of actively aligning one's will to that of God when difficulties come.[16] Juan's counsel included both the affirmation of participation in the means of grace along with the avoidance of that which harms. In a letter to a widow, he directed her during her time of grief to "restrain [the] feelings and make them subservient to reason and to His will."[17] In another letter to a young woman, he advised her to avoid worrying and fretting over the trials, which he saw as a path toward hopelessness. Though he wrote about the human effort during times of struggle, he reminded her that "the remedy comes not from our own power, but from the loving and gracious will of God."[18]

The practice of enduring tribulations to Juan ultimately came down to an expression of love *for* God.[19] He also perceived life's misfortunes as expressions of love *from* God, as discipline from a loving father—referencing

11. Ávila, *Audi, Filia* (Gormley), 108.

12. Ávila, *Confidence* (Benedictines), 36.

13. Ávila, *Confidence* (Benedictines), 94.

14. Ávila, *Holy Spirit* (Dargan), 41.

15. Ávila, *Audi, Filia* (Gormley), 122.

16. Ávila, *Audi, Filia* (Gormley), 98.

17. Ávila, *Confidence* (Benedictines), 34.

18. Ávila, *Confidence* (Benedictines), 95.

19. Ávila, *Confidence* (Benedictines), 71.

Heb 12:6.[20] He often counseled his hearers in their pain to identify with the suffering of Christ since that too was an expression of love.[21]

Juan did not leave his readers without hope in advising them to lovingly endure pain for God's sake. He also pronounced that great afflictions usually "come on the eve of the remedy."[22] For Ávila, the remedy was not just an end to the long, dark season, but a positive outcome of life change. So great is the outcome to Juan, that he stated that trials are the means through which the kingdom of God is entered.[23] However, it is not just for the sake of the afterlife that such sorrows should be endured, but he believed that they "bring great riches to soul," one set of riches being the cleansing from sins of the past.[24] In the *Audi, Filia*, he described the way in which penitents growing in endurance begin to produce "the fruit of the perfect," a greater level of health, and "millions of other blessings," as well as a greater strength over the spiritual enemies.[25] Likewise, in a letter to a young woman, Juan showed how the results of affliction include an utter abandonment of the self to the care of God.[26]

JOHN WESLEY'S EDITING OF JUAN DE ÁVILA ON SUFFERING

As mentioned earlier, Juan de Ávila was a contemporary of John of the Cross. The latter is, perhaps, best known for his work *Dark Night of the Soul*, a commentary on his poem with the same title, in which he described the process through which God works in souls using pain, suffering, withdrawal, and other "dark night" experiences. Juan de Ávila did not place nearly the emphasis that John of the Cross did upon such experiences. However, there were a few occasions when he did use the language of divine withdrawal and divinely initiated punishment, which Wesley carefully removed.

One such occasion appears in the letters that Wesley preserved in his *Christian Library*. It can be found in Ávila's sixteenth epistle, appearing in a section where for two full pages Wesley left the writings mostly intact and unaltered. In one sentence, however, he removed a short phrase of four words. The original from which Wesley drew read, "O that the memory of

20. Ávila, *Love of God, Priesthood* (Fernández-Fígares), 17.
21. Ávila, *Audi, Filia* (Gormley), 234.
22. Ávila, *Audi, Filia* (Gormley), 93.
23. Ávila, *Confidence* (Benedictines), 34.
24. Ávila, *Confidence* (Benedictines), 100.
25. Ávila, *Audi, Filia* (Gormley), 101–2, 107.
26. Ávila, *Confidence* (Benedictines), 91.

that tyme, wherein wee know not God, might serve us now for sharp spurrs, to make us runne greedily after him."[27] Wesley eliminated the phrase "now for sharp spurrs." Although seemingly minor, Wesley was sensitive to wording that would describe God as a causer of suffering or pain. He addressed this in his sermons "The Wilderness State" and "Heaviness through Manifold Temptations," to be explored later.

Other places where Wesley interacted with the issue of divine withdrawal and punishment can be found in his omission of complete letters where Ávila addressed such matters. For example, the second, thirtieth, portions of the thirty-first, the thirty-second, thirty-fourth, forty-first, forty-second, forty-third, forty-fourth, forty-sixth, forty-seventh, forty-eighth, forty-ninth, fiftieth, fifty-first, fifty-second, fifty-third, and fifty-seventh letters all deal with God's temporary departure from people, suffering as given from God for one's growth or endurance through trials, and/or physical illness as a bearing of one's cross. All of these were completely omitted from Wesley's abridgement.

There are a few other places where Wesley eliminated wording concerning the dark night experience from Ávila's letters. Wesley removed wording about divine withdrawal, as seen in Ávila's forty-fifth epistle where Wesley removed the phrase "he estraunged himselfe from you and forgott you."[28] He also cut statements about the obliteration of senses as found in the first letter where he left out the statement "deprived of all sense" and from the fifteenth epistle, "having forgotten themselves."[29]

Wesley also removed a lengthy paragraph describing the "prison of his love" where Ávila compared the restraints of the cross to the bonds of love that tie humans to Jesus.[30] Ávila described this *prison* in very abstract terms without clear definition. It could be that Wesley removed this portion based solely on the abstract nature of it, or perhaps because of Ávila's call to a love separate from liberty, where he stated, "lett our harts be tyed by his love . . . and lett us not desire such liberty, as may carry us out of his prison."[31]

MIGUEL DE MOLINOS ON SUFFERING

Miguel de Molinos placed a much higher emphasis on the role of suffering in one's spiritual progress than did Juan de Ávila. Molinos saw such darkness

27. Ávila, *Selected Epistles*, 137.

28. Ávila, *Selected Epistles*, 343.

29. Ávila, *Selected Epistles*, 5, 109.

30. Ávila, *Selected Epistles*, 20.

31. Ávila, *Selected Epistles*, 20.

as significant means to growth. In fact, he saw it as a necessity to reaching the spiritual *telos*, stating, "In order for the terrestrial soul to be made celestial and to reach the good summit of union with God, it must be purified in the fire of tribulation and temptation."[32] In keeping with the tradition of John of the Cross, Molinos described two distinct stages of darkness, which he referred to as the first and second spiritual martyrdoms. However, he also allowed room for a precursor to these stages of suffering which he referred to as *dryness*.

Molinos understood dryness less as a distinct season, like the two spiritual martyrdoms, and more as momentary experiences. Dryness occurs as a distraction causing difficulty in prayer; it is a time in which the feelings wane and one no longer experiences the same level of affect in prayer. Yet, it is a time in which God is still at work.[33] In the fourth chapter of the first book of his *Spiritual Guide*, Molinos laid out a lengthy list of the fruits of dryness. They include perseverance in prayer, boredom with worldly things, resolve of some flaws, an inner awareness which prevents one from following through on a temptation, grief following sins committed, a desire for suffering and doing God's will, a movement toward virtue, self-knowledge and placement of God as the highest priority, and "a great peace in your soul, a love for humility and mortification, confidence in God, submission and detachment from all creatures, and, finally, the absence of all the sins that you stopped committing when you entered into prayer."[34]

To Molinos, God is the great provider of spiritual consolation; however, either paradoxically or contradictorily, in the first spiritual martyrdom, Molinos attributed the source of anguish as coming from God as he removes all consolation. As God removes consolation, that which carried the soul no longer will; the examples he gave include the reading of books, consideration, and discursive prayer.[35] Without these divine comforts, there exist external demonic torments and internal turmoil. This leads toward another bit of paradox in Molinos's thinking where he declared that God is the source of anguish, yet he also emphasized the place of the devil or demons as the source of pain.[36] An example of this paradox may be found in his assessment on temptations where he stated clearly that the enemy causes them, but they are "at the same time prescribed by the divine hand

---

32. Molinos, *Spiritual Guide* (Baird and McGinn), 147.

33. Molinos, *Spiritual Guide* (Baird and McGinn), 71, 93.

34. Molinos, *Spiritual Guide* (Baird and McGinn), 72.

35. Molinos, *Spiritual Guide* (Baird and McGinn), 65, 67, 147.

36. Molinos, *Spiritual Guide* (Baird and McGinn), 147.

for their gain and spiritual profit!"[37] Molinos saw God's part as a withdrawal more than an active causer of the suffering; the latter he proclaimed to be the role of "the envious enemy" and/or other people who enact persecutions and troubles.[38] These depths of these torments may be realized through the accompaniment of "vehement temptations, painful suspicions, and scrupulous worries."[39] Molinos believed that this first spiritual martyrdom was necessary for the purging of the soul. Such darkness, he stated, will purify both "the senses and sensibilities."[40]

Molinos gave what was probably the most poignant description of this first martyrdom in the eighth chapter of the first book in his *Spiritual Guide*:

> Invisible enemies will persecute you with scruples, with libidinous suggestions and impure thoughts, and with incentives to impatience, pride, rage malediction, and blasphemy of the name of God, his sacraments, and his holy mysteries. You will feel a great tepidity, tedium, and annoyance toward the things of God; an obscurity and darkness in the understanding; a pusillanimity, confusion, and a crush of the heart; and such a coldness and weakness for resistance in the will that a piece of straw will seem to you a beam. The desertion will be so complete that it will seem impossible to have a good desire, and it will seem that for you there is no longer a God. In this desertion you will remain as between two encroaching walls, crushed without any hope of escaping such tremendous oppression.[41]

Although the level of anguish described here is immense, Molinos did not leave his readers in permanent despair. He concluded this chapter with an offer of hope explaining the necessity of such a darkness for the sake of purgation and a deeper revelation of God's mercy. To Molinos, the results of the first season of darkness include a two-fold benefit of the removal of that which is negative to the soul's advancement and the movement toward the positive. For example, he continued the above description explaining the results as an annihilation of desires and passions that do not lead the soul toward God, and a further movement toward perfection, quietude, and inner peace.[42] He saw that the soul that experiences darkness learns to walk in pure faith, it finds itself purged, engaged in deeper prayer, patient,

---

37. Molinos, *Spiritual Guide* (Baird and McGinn), 79.

38. Molinos, *Spiritual Guide* (Baird and McGinn), 64.

39. Molinos, *Spiritual Guide* (Baird and McGinn), 147–48.

40. Molinos, *Spiritual Guide* (Baird and McGinn), 75.

41. Molinos, *Spiritual Guide* (Baird and McGinn), 78.

42. Molinos, *Spiritual Guide* (Baird and McGinn), 78.

happy, intimate with God, effective in good works, interior peace, growing in humility, and ultimately arriving at perfection.[43] Given such outcomes, Molinos described such tribulations as "a great treasure with which God honors his own in this life."[44]

The second spiritual martyrdom, according to Molinos, is for those who have already advanced to a level of "perfection and high contemplation."[45] Molinos's description of this stage was rather brief and abstract; however, he placed a strong emphasis on the existence and driving force of love through this season. He described this state as a time when the soul experiences a level of love which exceeds its own capacity to love, or a deep longing for God's presence when it is not immediately experienced. When this happens, the source of pain in this second state of suffering comes from the depth of an internal longing unfilled, as opposed to external torments from the devil.[46]

JOHN WESLEY'S EDITING OF MIGUEL DE MOLINOS ON SUFFERING

Perhaps the most significant of Wesley's editorial work on the *Spiritual Guide* of Molinos included the topic of suffering. There were over sixty deletions and/or alterations that Wesley made to the original text in his published version concerning the theme of trials, tribulation, torments, temptation, and suffering. This demonstrates a rather strong divergence of thought relating to the role and nature of such difficulties.

Temptation

Whereas Molinos linked temptations and trials closely together in their role in seasons of darkness, Wesley removed a lot of the language regarding the former pertaining to its place in spiritual development. For example, Wesley eliminated a portion of text that linked passing through temptation as a means to arriving at internal peace. Interestingly, however, he kept the paragraph and a half preceding this statement which indicated that the saints passed through intense temptation along their path to holiness, going so far as to claim a direct correlation between the level of holiness and

43. Molinos, *Spiritual Guide* (Baird and McGinn), 56, 139, 144–45, 154, 160.
44. Molinos, *Spiritual Guide* (Baird and McGinn), 153.
45. Molinos, *Spiritual Guide* (Baird and McGinn), 150.
46. Molinos, *Spiritual Guide* (Baird and McGinn), 150–51.

the severity of the temptations. The distinction may be that in the portion removed, the language clearly attributed temptations as necessary means to the *telos*, whereas the section preserved inverted the cause and effect. The difference is that, in the one, temptations cause or result in inner peace; in the other, living in a state of holiness results in great temptations.[47] In the paragraph preceding the two aforementioned, Molinos equated temptation to happiness.[48] This too was excluded from Wesley's version.

A major area of departure for these two spiritual writers included the source of temptation. To Molinos, these seasons are initiated by God even though the temptations themselves come from the devil or one's own drives; Wesley, however, rather consistently removed the language attributing God as the source for trials and temptation. For example, in the fourth chapter of the third book, Molinos described God's two-fold process of cleansing souls and uniting them to himself as occurring through affliction and "the burning fire of inflamed love."[49] Wesley preserved the initial claim but edited out their descriptions. For both stages, Molinos attributed them to God placing people in such states. Molinos did, however, state that these temptations are "caused by the Devil, and received from the hand of God, for their gain and spiritual profit."[50] Wesley removed most of this clause, but kept the words *for, their, spiritual*, and *profit* so that his version read "these temptations are for their spiritual profit," while leaving out the cause.[51]

Another point of difference based on Wesley's editing of Molinos resides in the degree to which God's presence is or is not with someone during periods of temptation. For example, Molinos described those in temptation as having "no light, comfort, nor spiritual sentiment"; later he described seasons of temptation as seasons of "desertion and desolation."[52] Wesley removed both phrases. To Molinos, the level of temptations faced by someone in such a season of darkness were no less than "horrible."[53] However, Molinos believed that these horrendous temptations and "thoughts against the faith" could play a significant role in bringing about self-knowledge and humility.[54] Wesley preserved the place of these temptations in bringing

47. Molinos, *Spiritual Guide*, 29; Wesley, *Christian Library* (Molinos), 38:262.

48. Molinos, *Spiritual Guide*, 28; Wesley, *Christian Library* (Molinos), 38:261.

49. Molinos, *Spiritual Guide*, 125; Wesley, *Christian Library* (Molinos), 38:274.

50. Molinos, *Spiritual Guide*, 26.

51. Wesley, *Christian Library* (Molinos), 38:260.

52. Molinos, *Spiritual Guide*, 32, 138; Wesley, *Christian Library* (Molinos), 38:263, 279.

53. Molinos, *Spiritual Guide*, 25; Wesley, *Christian Library* (Molinos), 38:259.

54. Molinos, *Spiritual Guide*, 25.

about these virtuous results; however, he eliminated the "thoughts against the faith" as something resulting in virtue.[55] As will be discussed later, abandonment of faith is not beneficial, according to Wesley. Molinos saw these temptations as coming from the "quaintness of love" due to the way in which God used them.[56] Wesley, however, affirmed the potential benefit of seasons of temptation, but removed their connection to love, because to him, God is not the source of temptation.[57]

Dryness

As mentioned earlier, Molinos saw dryness as an occasional experience, as opposed to a lengthier season like the two martyrdoms. Wesley also wrote of such dryness in prayer, as will be looked at later. However, Wesley differed from Molinos on the purpose of such moments. This can be seen in his removal of a paragraph in Molinos's fourth chapter of the first book. In it, Molinos described how dryness positively contributes to the removal of all sensibilities and reflection.[58] Right after this paragraph, Molinos continued to describe seven results or "fruits" to dryness. Wesley, however, did some serious editing of these fruits.[59] In some cases, the descriptions were kept, but the terminology eliminated. In three cases, the points were completely removed. The first fruit listed by Molinos was perseverance in prayer, which Wesley excluded from his version. It was not likely that Wesley removed this statement because he was somehow opposed to perseverance in prayer, but because he saw other means to this end than just that of dryness. The second fruit is described as the loathing of worldly things. Wesley did not alter this too much, but only trimmed up the language for brevity. He did the same with the third, which explained the reflection upon one's failings, and the sixth, pertaining to a desire for suffering and doing God's will. Wesley, however, completely removed the fourth and fifth fruits, which respectively dealt with an internal restraint on committing certain sins which previously were committed "without the least Check or Remorse of Conscience" and an internal reproof for the times one falls into "some light fault."[60] In the seventh fruit, Wesley preserved the emphasis on overcoming oneself and

55. Wesley, *Christian Library* (Molinos), 38:259.

56. Molinos, *Spiritual Guide*, 28.

57. Wesley, *Christian Library* (Molinos), 38:261.

58. Molinos, *Spiritual Guide*, 13; Wesley, *Christian Library* (Molinos), 38:255.

59. Molinos, *Spiritual Guide*, 14–15; Wesley, *Christian Library* (Molinos), 38:38, 255–56.

60. Molinos, *Spiritual Guide*, 14–15.

one's passions yet eliminated a statement on the "inclination to Virtue." Similarly, in the eighth, he preserved the portion about holding God in a higher place and creatures in a lesser place but removed a statement about growing in self-knowledge. In the ninth, Wesley preserved the overall focus on humility and trust in God as a fruit of dryness but excluded the summary of these things as being signs of God's working through dryness, even if it isn't felt or realized.[61]

In the seventh chapter of the first book, Molinos described advancement toward union with God through purgation. This, according to Molinos, happens through consent to God's working "by means of the cross, and dryness"; Wesley, however, removed "and dryness" and a connection to consent with "walking through those darksome and desart ways."[62]

Two Types of Darkness

As mentioned earlier, the idea of two types of darkness was a major focus in the writings of Molinos on suffering. In chapter 6 of the first book, Molinos identified the first as coming from sin, which one brings upon oneself, the second being a darkness given by God for one's spiritual progress.[63] However, in chapter 4 of book 3, Molinos described the first spiritual martyrdom more in terms of temptation and external torments, than the committing of sin.[64] Wesley also took a two-type approach to looking at suffering in his sermons "The Wilderness State" and "Heaviness through Manifold Temptations," which will be examined more closely later. Wesley viewed the *wilderness state* as a post-conversion committing of sins which grieves the Holy Spirit and the *heaviness state* as external torments that come through temptation, grief, or some sort of difficulty. Interestingly, however, Wesley did more extensive editing of Molinos's descriptions pertaining to the first martyrdom than his explanation of the second of this two-fold approach to suffering.

Pertaining to the first, Wesley removed much of the language regarding the place of sin, while preserving only a brief description of how to navigate through such difficulties.[65] In the second major description found in book 3, Wesley preserved more of the description of these two forms of dryness. However, he did eliminate a paragraph pertaining to the causes or

61. Molinos, *Spiritual Guide*, 14–15; Wesley, *Christian Library* (Molinos), 38:255–56.

62. Molinos, *Spiritual Guide*, 22; Wesley, *Christian Library* (Molinos), 38:257.

63. Molinos, *Spiritual Guide*, 19.

64. Molinos, *Spiritual Guide*, 125–30.

65. Molinos, *Spiritual Guide*, 13–15; Wesley, *Christian Library* (Molinos), 38:254–56.

sources of darkness.[66] One portion of the description which Wesley kept includes Molinos's use of the word *heaviness*.[67] This likely may be where Wesley obtained the word for his own sermon.

In this latter section, Wesley toned down the language pertaining to the extent of the suffering. For example, he removed the wording of "fire of tribulation and inward torment."[68] In the paragraph following, he preserved the wording of dryness and darkness, while eliminating "anguish, contradictions, continual resistance, inward desertions, horrible desolations."[69] Wesley also removed the wording of desertion, as will be examined later, and that of suffering as punishment.[70]

Extent of the Suffering

Molinos's descriptions of suffering come across as much bleaker than those of Wesley. This is also demonstrated through Wesley's regular elimination of the strongest wording pertaining to the extent of suffering endured in such stages of darkness. For example, in reference to these stages, Wesley left out Molinos's words "bitter sea of sorrows" and "torment," "anguish," "oppression," being "without hope," and the "painful state of fearful desolation."[71] However, the word *melancholy* was an acceptable description for Wesley to keep in his edition.[72]

Desertion

Molinos often described these states of suffering as a perceived, if not actual, near, if not full, desertion of God from the human. Wesley, however, was more apt to remove an over-use of the language of desertion, although he did not completely remove the concept. One example of these includes an altering of Molinos's description of desertion in his fourth chapter of the third book. Wesley preserved the statement that one is not "at any time

---

66. Molinos, *Spiritual Guide*, 12–15, 19–20; Wesley, *Christian Library* (Molinos), 38:107, 78.

67. Molinos, *Spiritual Guide*, 129; Wesley, *Christian Library* (Molinos), 38:276.

68. Molinos, *Spiritual Guide*, 128–29; Wesley, *Christian Library* (Molinos), 38:275.

69. Molinos, *Spiritual Guide*, 129; Wesley, *Christian Library* (Molinos), 38:276.

70. Molinos, *Spiritual Guide*, 129; Wesley, *Christian Library* (Molinos), 38:276.

71. Molinos, *Spiritual Guide*, 23, 24, 134; Wesley, *Christian Library* (Molinos), 38:258, 278.

72. Molinos, *Spiritual Guide*, 33; Wesley, *Christian Library* (Molinos), 38:264.

nearer to God, than in such cases of desertion," while in the next sentence he eliminated "painful desertion in thy Soul," which are permitted by God.[73]

In the next chapter, which through editing Wesley included as the same stream of thought, Molinos stated that the suffering would *seem* to be beyond consoling. Wesley kept this statement, but removed the rest of the clause, stating "and that Heaven rains no more upon thee."[74] Similarly, Wesley later removed an entire paragraph in which Molinos described a desire for suffering devoid of comfort from God as being too far advanced and risking unjust attacks from others.[75]

Elsewhere, Molinos described the need to draw close and to look at God "in the time of strong temptation, desertion and desolation."[76] Here Wesley maintained the description as a time of strong temptation but eliminated the latter two words.[77] To Molinos, following "Christ crucified" is done "with simpleness and bareness of Spirit." Wesley, however, eliminated bareness as a mode for following Christ.[78]

Results of Darkness

Molinos saw these tribulations as "profitable and meritorious," the second one being more so than the first; Wesley, however excluded this contrast of measures between the two martyrdoms.[79] The profits, according to Molinos, were no less than perfection and union with God.[80] An understanding of the benefits of difficulties and a doctrine of perfection were certainly not foreign to Wesley. However, Wesley frequently seemed to remove such a direct correlation between darkness and the *telos* that Molinos seemed so quick to connect. For example, Wesley removed a strong statement and the ensuing paragraphs written by Molinos, stating that "to the end that the Soul of Earthly may become Heavenly, and may come to that greatest good of Union with God, it is necessary for it to be purified in the Fire of

73. Molinos, *Spiritual Guide*, 130; Wesley, *Christian Library* (Molinos), 38:276.

74. Molinos, *Spiritual Guide*, 131; Wesley, *Christian Library* (Molinos), 38:276.

75. Molinos, *Spiritual Guide*, 140; Wesley, *Christian Library* (Molinos), 38:280.

76. Molinos, *Spiritual Guide*, 138.

77. Wesley, *Christian Library* (Molinos), 38:279.

78. Molinos, *Spiritual Guide*, 139; Wesley, *Christian Library* (Molinos), 38:280.

79. Molinos, *Spiritual Guide*, 278; Wesley, *Christian Library* (Molinos), 38:278.

80. Molinos, *Spiritual Guide*, 11, 130–31.

Tribulation and Temptation."[81] He also removed connections of darkness with those described as spiritually proficient.[82]

Elsewhere, Wesley also eliminated the link between suffering and souls becoming "heavenly," the connection of pain with "glory," and the pairing of the necessity of tribulation with being made acceptable to God.[83] In addition, Molinos saw darkness as the means to blotting out sin, which Wesley excluded, and the primary mode of bringing about purgation, which Wesley also altered.[84]

Cause

The source of suffering is probably one of, if not *the* main point of contention that Wesley had with the mystical perspective on this topic; this will be further developed in the next section. In short, to Wesley, trials, pain, and temptations come from evil sources like the devil and demons, worldly sources like griefs and influences from the fallen world around, and one's own sinful actions. To many of the mystics, however, experiences of dark times are given from the hand of God. This difference in understanding is reflected in Wesley's editorial work.

For example, in the third book, Molinos attributed "horrible torments" to being "ordained by his hand."[85] Wesley maintained the description of the transforming power of the "fire of tribulation."[86] However, he removed the aforementioned attribution to the hand of God.

A similar statement was removed in a chapter on persevering through temptations in the first book. Molinos described the benefit all would have if they believed that "all these temptations are caused by the Devil, and received from the hand of God, for their gain and spiritual profit."[87] Wesley reduced this sentence to explain the benefit all would have if they believed that "all these temptations are for their spiritual profit."[88] Thus, Wesley shared a positive outlook on the results of temptation, but saw a broader number of sources, while rejecting one of the sources being God's hand. In

81. Molinos, *Spiritual Guide*, 130–31; Wesley, *Christian Library* (Molinos), 38:276.

82. Molinos, *Spiritual Guide*, 15 20; Wesley, *Christian Library* (Molinos), 38:256.

83. Molinos, *Spiritual Guide*, 126, 134, 140; Wesley, *Christian Library* (Molinos), 38:275, 278, 281.

84. Molinos, *Spiritual Guide*, 126; Wesley, *Christian Library* (Molinos), 38:274.

85. Molinos, *Spiritual Guide*, 117.

86. Molinos, *Spiritual Guide*, 117; Wesley, *Christian Library* (Molinos), 38:270.

87. Molinos, *Spiritual Guide*, 26.

88. Wesley, *Christian Library* (Molinos), 38:260.

the paragraph following, Wesley also edited out a description of how the sins of others may serve as a spiritual benefit. Although Molinos was careful to state that God doesn't will another's sinful behavior, he did declare the resulting impact on one's soul as part of God's will.

JOHN WESLEY ON SUFFERING

John Wesley's most direct and thorough publication addressing the concept of mystical darkness and suffering may be found in his two sermons "The Wilderness State" and "Heaviness through Manifold Temptations." Wesley did not take issue with the idea that Christians suffer, nor did he disagree with the thought that God may use such difficulties to produce greater growth in the life of the believer. Wesley's main point of tension with the mystical writers was the concept that God is the source of such pain. In brief, the *Wilderness State* placed the responsibility of the cause of darkness on the individual as an issue of sin which grieves the Holy Spirit. In his sermon on *Heaviness*, Wesley perceived the cause as worldly or demonic pressures endured by the individual. These themes were touched upon in the previous chapter as they pertain to the stages of spiritual progression; here, they are expanded upon as they relate to suffering.

Wilderness State

In his "Wilderness State" sermon, Wesley began with a brief summary of the issue. He stated that such a state occurs after justification and happens to the "greater part" of Christians, though it is often greatly misunderstood.[89] He then went on to describe the nature, the causes, and the cure of this state. To this experience, Wesley applied the mystical term *darkness*.

The nature of this state, Wesley saw as a loss of faith, love, joy, peace, and power. The loss of faith he described as a lack of experiential evidence and the witness of the Spirit, with an ensuing weakness. Due to the inseparable connection of faith and love, according to Wesley, along with the loss of faith comes a loss of love for God. Accompanying this lack of love comes a diminishing of happiness and the death of desire for the Divine. Evangelical zeal and compassion also fade away as anger increases.[90]

To Wesley, joy is the expected outcome of the love of God. Therefore, the loss of love consequently will result in the loss of joy. In his words, "for

89. Wesley, *Works* (Outler), 2:205.
90. Wesley, *Works* (Outler), 2:206–7.

the cause being removed, so is the effect."[91] Similarly, with the loss of the above, so comes the loss of peace, according to Wesley. In its stead enter doubt and fear. Accompanying all these is the elimination of power over sin, resulting in a returned struggle with sin.[92]

Wesley believed that the primary causes of this wilderness included sin, ignorance, and temptation. To the result of these means, Wesley had no problem attaching the mystical term *darkness*. The causes associated with sin encompass sins of commission, sins of omission, and inward sin. Sins of commission he defined as those that are known, willful, or presumptuous.[93] Sins of omission, he attributed to a willful "train of omissions" including a "neglect of private prayer" and a failing to rebuke others.[94] To inward sin, Wesley linked the entertaining of pride, anger, desiring things other than the Divine, and spiritual sloth. In such cases, God gradually withdraws his light and darkness increases.[95]

To the cause of ignorance in bringing about this dark wilderness, Wesley included the ignorance of Scripture and the ignorance of God's work within one's soul. In this section, he went on to defend against some of the mystical teachings. Regarding the former, he stated that those who remain ignorant of Scripture accept a form of the mystical teaching on darkness, concluding that darkness is a necessary and unavoidable state for every believer to endure. In the latter, Wesley refuted the assertion that darkness is a higher state than walking in the light, arguing that darkness is a loss of the light of God and is therefore detrimental. He also denied the role of darkness in the purging of the soul.[96]

The third cause of darkness according to Wesley includes temptation. Wesley observed that early in one's relationship with God, temptations quickly fade away when resisted. However, there often arrives a time when peace flees and temptations intensify and persist. This, he stated, comes from demonic hands.[97]

When looking at the cure to darkness, Wesley was careful to indicate that one size does not fit all. He noted that just as cures to bodily diseases are numerous, so too are cures to darkness. He did provide a list of such cures, asserting them within provisional statements as reactions to the various

91. Wesley, *Works* (Outler), 2:207.

92. Wesley, *Works* (Outler), 2:207–8.

93. Wesley, *Works* (Outler), 2:208.

94. Wesley, *Works* (Outler), 2:209.

95. Wesley, *Works* (Outler), 2:210–11.

96. Wesley, *Works* (Outler), 2:212.

97. Wesley, *Works* (Outler), 2:213.

causes. For example, if the cause of darkness included sin or sins of com-mission, then the cure would include repentance; on the other hand, if the cause is a sin of omission, then the remedy would include diligently walking in the light. If the cause is pride, then the medicine is humility; if anger, then forgiveness; if sloth, then active prayer; if ignorance, then learning; if temptation, then teaching to expect it.[98]

In explaining the various cures to the wilderness state, Wesley took opportunity to reiterate his primary objections to the mystical teachings on darkness. His most passionate oppositions included the teaching that every believer must endure such a season and, secondly, that God's withdrawal is more effective than "joy in the Holy Ghost" in producing internal purity.[99]

Heaviness through Manifold Temptations

Wesley began his sermon on *Heaviness* by explaining the existence of simi-larities and differences between heaviness and darkness, or the *wilderness state*. He stated that for believers, heaviness is more common than darkness and that "almost all the children of God experience this in an higher or lower degree."[100] He explained how the two states often get confused for the other due to their similarities, yet, to Wesley the differences far outnumber the similarities.

Quoting 1 Pet 1:6, which says, "now for a season, if need be, ye are in heaviness through manifold temptations," Wesley continued the sermon by explaining to whom this referenced, a further description of heaviness, the causes, and the outcomes of this state. Drawing upon other statements in 1 Peter, Wesley asserted that the audience to whom Peter wrote were people of faith, already believers in Jesus, and filled with the Holy Spirit.[101]

He went on to show a significant difference between darkness and heaviness by stating that in heaviness one does not lose faith, hope, joy, love, power over sin, or holiness.[102] The reason for this, according to Wesley, comes from the respective sources of the two states. To him, wilderness or darkness are a direct result of one's own sin. Heaviness, however, comes from sources outside of oneself or outside of one's control. Wesley referred to the Greek word λυπηθεντες, used by Peter and translated as *heaviness*.

98. Wesley, *Works* (Outler), 2:214–20.
99. Wesley, *Works* (Outler), 2:218–19.
100. Wesley, *Works* (Outler), 2:222.
101. Wesley, *Works* (Outler), 2:223.
102. Wesley, *Works* (Outler), 2:223–24.

He defined this as "made sorry" or "grieved."[103] Thus, Wesley deduced that heaviness is a state of sorrow or grief, including a deep and prolonged grief that may even impact one's physical health, yet remaining not devoid of joy.[104]

Wesley believed that this state may be caused by a wide variety of temptations which come through physical ailments, pain, and "nervous disorders," poverty and its ensuing troubles, the death of a loved one, and the grief over the poor spiritual condition of another, spiritual battles, and the awareness of one's own depravity.[105] Throughout this description of the causes of heaviness, he made poignant distinctions between this and the former states. One such distinction includes the assertion that "there may be sorrow without sin."[106] Likewise, he clarified the peculiarities of his view from the mystics, proclaiming "that [God] ever withdraws himself because he *will*, merely because it is his good pleasure, I absolutely deny"; he then followed it up with an appeal to the Bible.[107] However, Wesley did not shy away from the terminology of permission, stating that there are great results through "God's permitting the temptations which bring heaviness on his children."[108]

Wesley concluded his sermon on *Heaviness* by reiterating the differences between the two states, concluding that heaviness may, but not necessarily, be needed, while there is never a need for darkness. Although Wesley may have differed with the mystics as to the source and causes of the various sorts of suffering, he would agree that great benefits may be realized through the challenges of life, so much so that they are "unspeakable gain." To him, this "trial of their faith" may serve to increase faith, hope, joy, love, and holiness, while also serving to benefit others who may observe one's reaction to this grief.[109]

COMPARISON AND CONTRAST

From the writings of Ávila, Molinos, and Wesley, five main sources of suffering emerge—God, demons and devils, other people, one's own sin, and life's broader challenges. Although there exists relative agreement regarding

103. Wesley, *Works* (Outler), 2:224.
104. Wesley, *Works* (Outler), 2:225.
105. Wesley, *Works* (Outler), 2:226–30.
106. Wesley, *Works* (Outler), 2:228.
107. Wesley, *Works* (Outler), 2:229.
108. Wesley, *Works* (Outler), 2:231.
109. Wesley, *Works* (Outler), 2:232–33.

most of the sources as given by these three authors, the main point of contention remains in their perspective of the role of the Divine in bringing about such trials. Ávila believed that God both gives and allows such suffering, Molinos mostly wrote about God as the giver of such suffering while preserving some room for allowance, while Wesley only relegated such painful situations to all the other sources except God.

All three saw some forms of suffering as distinct stages or states along the path of spiritual growth, though they differed in their definitions. Both Molinos and Wesley divided the experiences of suffering into two different categories. Molinos taught that there are two martyrdoms or *darkness* toward which *dryness* serves as a precursor. One form of darkness is the result of sin while the other is a result of God-given distress. Similarly, Wesley categorized suffering into *heaviness* and the *wilderness state*. The former is a result of one's sin and grieving the Holy Spirit, which in turn results in darkness, divine withdrawal, and a loss of faith, love, joy, peace, and power. The latter is a season of temptation, grief, and/or stress which results in greater closeness to God and spiritual growth as one continues to walk in the light, not darkness.

In such states of trials, Molinos believed that God may still console while remaining withdrawn; Ávila held that God consoles while remaining present, though seeming distant; Wesley taught that God consoles and remains present through sufferings that come from the outside and not as a result of one's own sin. Ávila saw such trials and temptation as a loving discipline from God, Molinos viewed them as means toward growth in virtue, while Wesley deemed temptations as a response from the outside toward one's holiness, not the producer of holiness. Even given such varied perspectives, all agreed and provided the often-needed reminder that God may redeem and create beauty out of the pains of life in mysterious ways.

6

Prayer, Meditation, Contemplation, and Mystical Language

LIKE OTHER PHILOSOPHICAL AND theological traditions, mysticism has its share of variety, nuance, plurality, and micro-traditions within the meta-tradition. Consequently, forming a conclusive definition of mysticism poses a challenge. Add to this the essence of the tradition's namesake—*mystery*—and the difficulty is compounded. The following examines the theological themes that generally fall into the category of mysticism, as addressed by the three authors at hand. Here, we see the nuance and breadth of perspective from three theologians who, arguably, may each don the label of Christian mystic.

JUAN DE ÁVILA ON PRAYER AND MYSTICISM

Prayer

Juan de Ávila often stressed the high importance of prayer in the spiritual life with great passion. He urged his readers to pray with care and frequency because through prayer many have "been enriched and helped in their poverty."[1] He saw prayer as a crucial weapon against impurity.[2] He also went so far as to quote Origen in saying that prayer is *necesaria*, even necessary in bringing about that which had been previously prophesied.[3] He

---

1. Ávila, *Audi, Filia* (Gormley), 207.

2. Ávila, *Audi, Filia* (Gormley), 58.

3. Ávila, *Audi Filia*—Spanish, capítulo 70; Ávila, *Audi, Filia* (Gormley), 209.

saw prayer as means for seeing Jesus accurately and for understanding and doing the will of God.[4]

He often encouraged his readers to set aside specific times and specific places for the sake of prayer, while also acknowledging the apostle Paul's call to "pray in every place."[5] In his *Audi Filia*, he laid out a pattern for daily prayer that begins with penance, moves to thanksgiving, then shifts to reflection upon the crucifixion of Jesus while designating a different aspect to each specific day of the week.[6] In the chapter that followed, he proposed a slightly altered structure progressing through recollection, confession, prayers pertaining to self-knowledge, reading, then reflection upon Jesus' love and compassion expressed through the cross.[7]

Ávila saw prayer as a mutual communication between a person and God. He urged others to assume a posture of listening in prayer. Examples of this may be found in his *Audi Filia* and in a letter to a friend.[8] In addition to listening prayer, he also valued intercession, especially among the priests. He exhorted priests to intercede for cities, the unconverted, and for their parishioners, to the point of even *pestering* God.[9] However, he also believed that there are many times when God initiates such intercession by placing certain people or circumstances on one's mind.[10] Thus, prayer, to Ávila, is a reciprocated divine and human interaction.

Meditation, Contemplation, and Mysticism

Although Juan did not travel theologically as far down the trail of mysticism as his contemporaries John of the Cross or Teresa de Ávila, et al., he did remain quite comfortable with the language of mysticism. For example, in a chapter on hearing God's voice through faith in his *Audi Filia*, Juan described the mystery of seeing God in darkness and understanding God beyond the use of reason. He stated that God "is said to dwell in darkness because he is Light, so bright and so excellent that, as Saint Paul says, he dwells in a light that no one can reach." He then continued, "It is not that the light is dark, but that it is a light that in every way exceeds all understanding."[11]

4. Ávila, *Audi, Filia* (Gormley), 205, 219.

5. Ávila, *Audi, Filia* (Gormley), 210.

6. Ávila, *Audi, Filia* (Gormley), 210–13.

7. Ávila, *Audi, Filia* (Gormley), 214–15.

8. Ávila, *Audi, Filia* (Gormley), 246; Ávila, *Confidence* (Benedictines), 90.

9. Ávila, *Love of God, Priesthood* (Fernández-Fígares), 46, 50–51.

10. Ávila, *Love of God, Priesthood* (Fernández-Fígares), 48.

11. Ávila, *Audi, Filia* (Gormley), 113.

As described earlier, this then became the platform for some of his concepts on the role of suffering much like the *dark night* experiences explained by John of the Cross.

Juan also frequented the use of the words *meditation* and *contemplation*. Juan, however, focused more on the practice of meditation and contemplation rather than the two as stages in the journey as found in the writings of John of the Cross. For example, in his section on self-knowledge, he urged his readers to "cease from praying vocally. Place yourself in the very depth of your heart, realizing that you are alone in the presence of God."[12] Later, he encouraged the practice of meditation as a break from busyness, describing it as one of a diverse group of exercises.[13]

JOHN WESLEY'S EDITING OF ÁVILA ON PRAYER AND MYSTICISM

Mystical Language

John Wesley was strongly influenced by Catholic mystical theology; however, on November 23, 1736, in a letter to his brother Samuel, he stated that in his early years of ministry, "I think the rock on which I had the nearest made shipwreck of the faith was in the writings of the mystics."[14] As Wesley edited the words of Ávila, he displayed this ongoing struggle with the language of mystical theology. Like the mystics that preceded him, Wesley's view of the climactic *telos* of the Christian life was quite lofty. However, where the mystics used words like *union, divination,* and *enlightenment,* Wesley preferred the terms *Christian perfection, entire sanctification,* and being *perfected in love.* To Wesley, the former placed humans too much on the same level with God, whereas the latter spoke of a high level of attainment that remained within the realm of human potential.

One place that demonstrates this struggle may be found in Wesley's editing of Ávila's words found in his thirty-ninth epistle. In this letter, Ávila yearned for all to be transformed and for all to "growe, to be one and the self-same Spirit with God."[15] Wesley certainly shared the yearning for transformation, and he also preserved the idea of being one spirit with God;

---

12. Ávila, *Audi, Filia* (Gormley), 182.

13. Ávila, *Audi, Filia* (Gormley), 234–35.

14. Wesley, *Works* (Baker), 25:487.

15. Ávila, *Selected Epistles,* 306.

however, by removing the words "and the self-same," Wesley shifted the emphasis away from mystical union, or God-oneness, and placed it more on God-likeness. Interestingly, however, Wesley did preserve Ávila's quote of the famous saying "He makes himselfe man, that hee may make us Gods."[16]

Part of the broader mystical experience includes genuine encounters with the presence of God. Wesley would not disagree with this possibility. However, Wesley did alter the language of ecstatic experience by changing the wording from "raptures" to "ecstasies."[17]

Another theme with which Wesley took issue was the idea of a mystical dark night experience as popularized by Ávila's contemporary John of the Cross. Wesley was comfortable with the concept of God using difficult situations for the individual's growth, yet he did not like the idea that God caused these things to happen. In direct response to the teachings circulating about this darkness, Wesley preached his sermons "Heaviness through Manifold Temptations" and "The Wilderness State." These were evaluated earlier but are briefly summarized here for the sake of context; in the former, Wesley spoke about the difficulties people face from external temptations, grief, etc. In the latter, he talked about the times when people grieve the Holy Spirit through committing sin post salvation.

There are a few places where Wesley eliminated wording concerning the dark-night type of experience from Ávila's letters. Wesley removed wording about divine withdrawal as seen in Ávila's forty-fifth epistle where Wesley removed the phrase "he estraunged himselfe from you and forgott you."[18] He also cut statements about the obliteration of senses as found in the first letter where he left out the statement "deprived of all sense" and from the fifteenth epistle, "having forgotten themselves."[19]

Wesley also removed a lengthy paragraph describing the "prison of his love" where Ávila compared the restraints of the cross to the bonds of love that tie humans to Jesus.[20] Ávila described this *prison* in very abstract terms without clear and definitive definition. It could be that Wesley removed this portion based solely on the abstract nature of it, or perhaps because of Ávila's call to a love separate from liberty, where he stated, "lett our harts be tyed by his love . . . and lett us not desire such liberty, as may carry us out of his prison."[21]

16. Ávila, *Selected Epistles*, 137; Wesley, *Christian Library* (Ávila), 46:299, 320.

17. Ávila, *Selected Epistles*, 262.

18. Ávila, *Selected Epistles*, 343.

19. Ávila, *Selected Epistles*, 5, 109.

20. Ávila, *Selected Epistles*, 20.

21. Ávila, *Selected Epistles*, 20.

Many of the mystics often wrote of the removal of affection as a stage of one's spiritual growth. The goal is so that one may love God more interiorly, beyond feeling and affect, thus loving God more deeply and intimately. The affect was seen, by many, as helpful in the early stages of spirituality, but limited in their ability to draw the soul toward a greater union with God. In Ávila's fifteenth epistle, he described why Jesus told John "behold your mother" and why Jesus spoke "with lesse tendernes" to his mother as a limiting of attachment in order to model for others how "to keepe our selves cleere from particular affection."[22] Wesley eliminated this paragraph.

Eros Language

In the mystical tradition, it is quite common for descriptions regarding the relationship between God and his people to use the language of lover and beloved—common also for many of the contemporaries of Ávila. For example, the poetry of John of the Cross portrays lover and beloved meeting on a park bench where the lover gently strokes the hair of the beloved before breaking her neck, suspending all feeling as a description of the dark night experience. In Teresa de Ávila's *Interior Castle*, she described the most interior room as the place where lover and beloved meet.

In the letters of Juan de Ávila which Wesley included, the language of eros is not very strong. However, there were four times in which Wesley saw fit to alter Ávila's wording concerning the love relationship between God and his people. As Ávila described how the love of Christ made some people "to endure prisons, torments, dishoners," he stated how "the great worth of the beloved has been placed before the eyes of the lover."[23] Wesley, however, removed "the eyes of the lover" and replaced it with "their eyes"—thus changing the audience from God to other people.[24]

In the Christian mystical and affective traditions, it was common to interpret the Song of Solomon as an allegorical description of God's love for his people or Christ's love for the church. Ávila used such an allegorical approach to the Song of Solomon in his sixteenth letter. Here, Wesley removed a very large section of text in his publication of Ávila's letters. Four main themes emerge here with which Wesley may have taken issue. First is the allegorical approach to interpreting the biblical text, second is the idea that God wounds the heart which Wesley addressed in his sermon "The Wilderness State," third is the idea that God must be hunted which Wesley

---

22. Ávila, *Selected Epistles*, 129.

23. Ávila, *Selected Epistles*, 70.

24. Wesley, *Christian Library* (Ávila), 46:276.

often refuted by placing the emphasis on God's pursuit of people, and fourth is the idea that God cannot leave people once he is found.

In Ávila's forty-fifth letter, to a "lady who was religious woman and in great affliction," he likened the relationship with God to that of spouse. Two paragraphs use such language. In both places, one near the beginning of the letter and the other toward the end, Wesley removed these lengthy sections altogether.[25]

MIGUEL DE MOLINOS ON PRAYER AND MYSTICISM

Prayer and Quietism

As mentioned, Molinos divided prayer into two stages including the *animal life* for beginners and the *human life* for those more advanced.[26] The latter, he linked to quietude. When entering the higher level, he believed that one should resist the urge toward vocal prayer and remain quiet in order to hear from God.[27] He went on to support this position by referencing three insights from Francisca López. The first of her instructions he described, saying:

> Fifteen minutes of prayer that included the recollection of the senses and powers, resignation, and humility benefited the soul more than five days of penitential exercise, hair shirts, disciplines, fasts, and sleeping on planks. This is because the latter afflict the body, while recollection purifies the soul.[28]

This description places López and Molinos (through his affirmation) distinctly separate from the ascetic movement, aligning more closely to the affective tradition. Similarly, the next two points of instruction continue to reiterate this affective expression over and above ascetical spirituality. He continued, "The second was that his Majesty is more gladdened when the soul gives itself in quiet and devout prayer for one hour than when it partakes of great journeys and pilgrimages." The third affirmed "affect of the will" over "an effort of understanding."[29]

Although Molinos tended to focus on the theoretical and the broadsweeping generalities of spirituality, he also made sure to address the

25. Ávila, *Selected Epistles*, 343, 352.

26. Molinos, *Spiritual Guide* (Baird and McGinn), 70.

27. Molinos, *Spiritual Guide* (Baird and McGinn), 85.

28. Molinos, *Spiritual Guide* (Baird and McGinn), 85.

29. Molinos, *Spiritual Guide* (Baird and McGinn), 85, 86.

everyday struggles commonly endured. Regarding prayer, his first book addressed the challenge of the wandering mind and how to live in a perpetual
state of prayer while still tending to the common everyday tasks, among
others.[30] Yet ultimately, his thrust was to move his reader toward the climactic state of prayer, which to him was closely linked to quietude and solitude.

An apophatic summary, which also alludes to the process, of interior
solitude may be found in the twelfth chapter of the third book, where he
described it as consisting "in the forgetting of all created things, in detachment, and in the perfect shedding of all affects, desires, thoughts, and will."[31]
In this *via negativa* path, one arrives at what Molinos saw as a destination
point of quietude, or "mountain of tranquility." Here, he believed that the
experience of God is so intense that it *overflows* from the interior to the
exterior. In a more affirmative way, he described this state as a phase when

> the soul, which has already entered the heaven of peace, recog-
> nizes itself to be full of God and his supernatural gifts because
> it lives founded in a pure love. To it, light is as agreeable as
> darkness, night as day, affliction as consolation. In this holy and
> celestial indifference it loses no peace in adversity or tranquility
> in tribulation. Indeed, it appears full of ineffable joys.[32]

This, is a description of the highest of what he described as the three types
of silence—silence of words, desires, and thoughts.[33]

Meditation and Contemplation

Molinos adhered closely to the Christian mystical tradition in relation to
the respective places of meditation and contemplation. To many of the
mystics, spiritual progression consists of a movement through stages,
where each stage moves a soul closer to the Divine while offering a season
of preparation for the next level. Many drew from the three-fold-way of
Pseudo-Dionysius, who viewed this ascent as a journey through *purgation*,
then *illumination*, and climaxing with *enlightenment*. Later authors would
develop the themes of meditation and contemplation as they relate to this
triad of spiritual growth. The mystics believed that the early purgation both
leads one into and is facilitated by a state of meditation. As the work of
purgation has acted sufficiently, then one is illumined and begins to make

---

30. Molinos, *Spiritual Guide* (Baird and McGinn), 91, 93.
31. Molinos, *Spiritual Guide* (Baird and McGinn), 162.
32. Molinos, *Spiritual Guide* (Baird and McGinn), 181.
33. Molinos, *Spiritual Guide* (Baird and McGinn), 98.

progress in contemplation. To many of the mystical writers, contemplation is both a process toward union with God, or enlightenment, as well as an arrival point closely connected with divine union. This movement through meditation and contemplation is also a progression from active to passive and from exterior to interior spiritual expression and experience. Molinos held closely to this mystical tradition.

Meditation

In his *Proem*, Molinos began his treatise with a summary of some terms and themes found throughout his book, especially offering clarity to his perspective on meditation and contemplation. In the opening paragraph he identified these as the two means of approaching God. Meditation, he described, as belonging to beginners, to the senses, and consisting of "*consideracion y discurso.*"[34] Robert Baird translated *discurso* into English as "discursive prayer." He described the use of this word as including, but "not limited to, the scope of our 'discourse,' which generally refers to speech." He went on to state that "to Molinos, *discurso* refers to a general category of prayer that involves leading the mind from one mental object to another."[35]

As Molinos developed the treatise itself, he continued the concept of meditation being reserved for the beginner. In fact, he asserted that "the soul cannot arrive at perfection and union with God by means of meditation and discursive prayer. These are only useful in beginning the spiritual path."[36]

Molinos continued in his *Proem* to associate four actions with the practice of meditation—*considerar*, to give *atención*, *discurrir*, and *ponderar*.[37] These three verbs and one noun all allude to cognitive actions involving an active reflection upon something. The objects of these ponderings include "the mysteries of our holy faith," "the knowledge of its truths" and "particularities," and "the circumstances for moving the affects of the will."[38]

He believed that these cognitive acts were important for beginning the spiritual life but will only carry someone so far down the path. As one transitions to the next stage—contemplation—Molinos observed a shedding of the previous as the means toward the next state. He described this process as something which God does in a person "when he deprives it of

---

34. Molinos, *Guia Espiritual*, 5.

35. Molinos, *Spiritual Guide* (Baird and McGinn), 207.

36. Molinos, *Spiritual Guide* (Baird and McGinn), 68.

37. Molinos, *Guia Espiritual*, 6.

38. Molinos, *Spiritual Guide* (Baird and McGinn), 57.

consideration and discursive prayer. Thinking that it cannot do anything and that it is lost, the soul finds itself detached and perfect in a time of growth without having ever hoped for such a thing."[39] Upon coming to such an experience, he believed that through perseverance, one may soon enter into contemplation.

Contemplation

In the opening statements of his *Proem*, Molinos connected contemplation with "purity of faith, a general, indistinct, and confusing knowledge" and with "interior recollection." He believed that contemplation was not for the beginners, but for the *aprovechados*, or the hard-working and diligent. Where meditation is experienced in the senses, he viewed contemplation as being "more naked, pure, and interior."[40] He continued to associate three interchangeable terms with that of contemplation, these include *oración de fe, oración de quietud*, and *recogimiento interior* or *prayer of faith, prayer of quietude*, and *interior recollection* respectively.[41]

Although it was quite common among the Spanish mystics to use the word *oración* for meditative and contemplative prayer, it is still interesting that Molinos chose to use this term as opposed to the other Spanish words for prayer like the verbs *rezar, rogar*, or the nouns *ruego* or *súplica*. This may be due to the nature of these other forms all indicating an asking, begging, or plea for something, whereas *oración* refers more to a generalized interaction.

Molinos also included in his *Proem* a connection of three verbal actions to contemplation and the way one relates to the truth discovered through meditation. These include *amando, admirándose*, and *gozándose*, or to love, admire, and enjoy the truth.[42] Where the acts of meditation are more cognitive in nature, to Molinos, the acts of contemplation are more affective in nature. In the fifteenth chapter of the third book, he maintained this position by stating that there are two means toward this contemplation—"*el gusto y los deseos*."[43] To Molinos, this *pleasure* and *desire* are the affective means through which one encounters the depths of divine love.

As Molinos divided prayer into two categories, meditation and contemplation, he then subdivided contemplation into two categories—active

39. Molinos, *Spiritual Guide* (Baird and McGinn), 67.
40. Molinos, *Guia Espiritual*, 5; Molinos, *Spiritual Guide* (Baird and McGinn), 55.
41. Molinos, *Guia Espiritual*, 6.
42. Molinos, *Guia Espiritual*, 6.
43. Molinos, *Guia Espiritual*, 53.

and passive.[44] Though he believed that the overall movement from meditation to contemplation is a movement from active to passive, with contemplation being more passive in nature, he also believed that contemplation
may have an active form to it. This dynamic will be explored more later, but
it is worth noting here.

Molinos stated that the more active form of contemplation may be
reached by *diligencia*.[45] He then went on to support his case by quoting from
a sermon by Bernard of Clairvaux on Mary and Martha. It is interesting that
he referenced Bernard to support active contemplation in connection with
diligencia. In his treatise *De Diligendo Deo*, Bernard laid out four stages of
loving God—loving self for the sake of self, loving God for the sake of self,
loving God for God's sake, and loving self for the sake of God. In the original
Latin, Bernard used forms of the word *amor* to refer to the first two levels
of love and reserved the word *diligendo* for the higher two states.[46] Thus, to
Bernard *diligence* is a part of the highest spiritual state; to Molinos, however,
diligence is relegated merely to the penultimate stage.

In describing the second type of contemplation, Molinos described it
as "perfect and infused," then referenced Teresa of Ávila for authoritative
support. His quote from Teresa included a relatively lengthy description of
how God suspends cognitive understanding and removes words from the
means of communication, thus bringing a person to a passive enjoyment of
God's presence.[47]

As mentioned earlier, Molinos equated contemplation with interior
recollection. As he entered into the first book of his treatise, he laid out
one of the purposes of this interior recollection as pacifying "that throne of
your heart so that the sovereign king may rest upon it."[48] It is also a state
in which God's wisdom is immeasurably poured into one's soul and one
remains resigned to the will of God.[49]

As mentioned above, Molinos made the distinction between meditation and contemplation, then divided contemplation into two forms (the
active and passive); he then divided the second form—infused contemplation—into three grades: *la hartura*, *la embriaguez*, and *la seguridad*, or satiety, intoxication, and security. The first is when the person hates worldly

44. Molinos, *Spiritual Guide* (Baird and McGinn), 59.

45. Molinos, *Guia Espiritual*, 7.

46. Clairvaux, *Diligendo*.

47. Molinos, *Spiritual Guide* (Baird and McGinn), 61.

48. Molinos, *Spiritual Guide* (Baird and McGinn), 64.

49. Molinos, *Spiritual Guide* (Baird and McGinn), 94–95, 97.

things and is filled with the Divine, the second is when the mind is full of love, and the third is when all fear is expelled.[50]

Molinos held that the means of entry into this infused contemplation were strictly by the action of God. In his first book, he stated that "God alone, and not the guide, causes the soul to pass from meditation to contemplation."[51] He maintained this position in the third book stating that this contemplation "is an experiential and intimate manifestation that God gives of himself" with God being the sole object and actor.[52]

JOHN WESLEY'S EDITING OF MOLINOS ON PRAYER AND MYSTICISM

Prayer

In general, there exist many aspects to prayer—especially to Molinos and the writings of Christian mysticism. In keeping with the mystical tradition, Molinos conveyed a progressive layering in prayer beginning with mental prayer, progressing through meditation to contemplation, and climaxing in silence and quietude. Wesley demonstrated his divergence from Molinos in the frequency of alterations he made to the original text, especially regarding silence. As some of the specific aspects to prayer are evaluated elsewhere, this section looks at the changes made by Wesley as they pertain to prayer in a more general sense.

Quite a few editorial removals were made to Molinos's second chapter, which deals with perseverance in prayer. More notably is Wesley's elimination of the word *discourse*. In the chapter's opening paragraph, Molinos alerted his readers that they would be "full of confusion and doubts, because in Prayer thou hast failed in Discourse."[53] Wesley removed the latter clause while keeping the ensuing description of this state.[54] Likewise, Wesley excluded the paragraph that followed which described the process of "enlarging thy self in mental Discourse."[55]

Midway through the chapter, Wesley preserved a paragraph instructing the readers to persevere in prayer, yet he removed a statement regarding

---

50. Molinos, *Guia Espiritual*, 53; Molinos, *Spiritual Guide* (Baird and McGinn), 167–68.

51. Molinos, *Spiritual Guide* (Baird and McGinn), 96.

52. Molinos, *Spiritual Guide* (Baird and McGinn), 165.

53. Molinos, *Spiritual Guide*, 4.

54. Wesley, *Christian Library* (Molinos), 38:251.

55. Molinos, *Spiritual Guide*, 4–5; Wesley, *Christian Library* (Molinos), 38:251.

an inability to "enlarge in Discourse."[56] Again, he eliminated a similar statement in the chapter's closing paragraph.[57] It is a bit perplexing as to why
Wesley removed the word *discourse* so frequently from the *Spiritual Guide*
as he himself was not averse to using the word in his own writings. In fact,
the word *discourse* appears in his published works more than a couple
hundred times. Mostly, he used the term in reference to person-to-person
conversation; however, he also used it in reference to person-to-God conversations found in the Bible.

In addition to the varied perspectives on discourse and the divergent
points of view explored elsewhere regarding meditation, contemplation,
and silence, a couple other differences pertaining to prayer are revealed between the Methodist and the Quietist through Wesley's editorial alterations.
One very notable difference may be found in the expression of the climactic
state of prayer. To Molinos, the "perfect and spiritual way of Praying" is "Internal recollection."[58] This thesis examines internal recollection elsewhere,
but here it is worth noting in its role pertaining to the *telos* of prayer. In his
thirteenth chapter of the first book, Molinos provided a lengthy defense of
his case. Although Wesley included the opening paragraph of this chapter in
his version and spliced in half of a later paragraph, he excluded the remainder of this chapter.[59]

In Molinos's third book, Wesley removed a paragraph of interest in a
chapter on mortification and resignation.[60] The paragraph describes people
who do not reach mortification, purity, peace, or resignation. Wesley was
not averse to any of these ends in and of themselves as he preserved many
of Molinos's uses of them. Wesley also would not have been opposed to
the idea that not everyone reaches such an end. Therefore, it was likely not
Wesley's issue with these ends that led him to remove this paragraph, but
perhaps it was an issue with the opening prerequisite. Here, Molinos stated
that people fail to reach these ends no matter how dedicated they are to
prayer. Perhaps it is because to Wesley, dedication to prayer will lead a person toward the goal.

56. Molinos, *Spiritual Guide*, 6.

57. Molinos, *Spiritual Guide*, 8.

58. Molinos, *Spiritual Guide*, 39–41.

59. Wesley, *Christian Library* (Molinos), 38:266.

60. Molinos, *Spiritual Guide*, 138; Wesley, *Christian Library* (Molinos), 38:280.

Meditation and Contemplation

Passive Nature

Within mystical theology, the language of meditation and contemplation has remained a common, if not ubiquitous, theme. The concept of spiritual progression into meditation as an earlier stage followed by contemplation as a climactic, or at the very least the penultimate, state of being was shared by many authors within the tradition. However, there was a point of variance that developed into a debate in Christian Mysticism—that is, the active and passive natures of contemplation. For example, two predecessors of Molinos and contemporaries of Juan de Ávila, John of the Cross and Teresa de Ávila, varied on this point. To John of the Cross, contemplation is a passive state of being to which there was no greater goal. To Teresa, however, contemplation compels the person toward active service toward God and one's fellow human beings. This was also a point of variance for John Wesley and Miguel de Molinos.

This deviation from one another was expressed in Molinos's frequent use of the language of passivity found in book 3, especially as it relates to contemplation, and Wesley's correspondingly frequent removal of such language from his published version of the *Spiritual Guide*. One example may be found where Molinos described the beginnings of the state by means of tribulation. Molinos described the way in which one's only active participation is consent and from there, God will "dispose thee and prepare thee passively."[61] Wesley excluded the idea of passive preparation in his edition, however.[62] Likewise, in the paragraph that follows, Wesley preserved the statement "thou wilt find within thy self a passive dryness, darkness," while leaving out the word *passive*.[63]

In the thirteenth chapter of the same book, Molinos linked passive contemplation directly with union with God, in the mystical sense of union. Wesley preserved much of this description, though removing the word *union*. What was quite notably left out of this description was the opening sentence to the paragraph that likened this experience to a stage of God-induced sleep and the words *passive state* in the sentence that follows.

Molinos continued this theme into the fourteenth chapter. In this chapter, Wesley only kept two of the seven paragraphs. The first of these two paragraphs describes the light and love which God gives to a soul who makes spiritual progress and the willingness of the soul to receive whatever

---

61. Molinos, *Spiritual Guide*, 128–29.

62. Wesley, *Christian Library* (Molinos), 38:275.

63. Molinos, *Spiritual Guide*, 129; Wesley, *Christian Library* (Molinos), 38:276.

God gives, even if it includes trials. The second paragraph which Wesley kept describes a state of *perfect prayer* which includes "a total and absolute consignment of thy self into the hands of God."[64] This sort of complete abandon to God was a strong part of Wesley's teachings. In fact, later adherents to Wesleyan theology would emphasize surrender as a primary means toward the climactic spiritual state as expressed through the Holiness Movement. However, Wesley did remove two adjectives which preceded and qualified this state of perfect prayer—*pure* and *passive*.[65]

Meditation and Recollection

As mentioned above, the two-fold process of spiritual maturation through meditation and contemplation was a common theme in the Christian mystical tradition. Interestingly, however, Molinos rarely used the word *meditation* and opted for an alternative—*recollection*. In fact, the word meditation doesn't occur in Wesley's rendition and may only be found a couple of times in the earliest English translation of Molinos's original. In these occurrences, meditation is closely linked to contemplation and recollection.

Molinos often linked the *interior way* with the practice of recollection. Wesley had a tendency of removing many references to recollection, though not all. He removed some references to recollection where it was closely linked to things internal, yet he also eliminated references to recollection where it was linked directly to the senses and faculties.

Wesley's editorial treatment of *internal recollection* may be found in the opening chapter. Molinos urged his readers "to pacifie that Throne of thy Heart" by means of *internal recollection*.[66] In the Methodist's edition, the strong urging toward heart pacification was perpetuated; however, this portion of the means was expelled. It is likely that Wesley removed these means not due to the concept of recollection itself, but the emphasis on the internal aspect of it. This may be seen in the way that Wesley maintained the next clause stating that "thy protection is to be Prayer and a loving recollection in the Divine Presence."[67] In the next paragraph, Wesley then proceeded once again to remove a statement about *internal recollection* being the means toward a soul's experience of divine peace.

In removing two nearly consecutive statements about this internal recollection serving as a means to an end but preserving a statement about

64. Molinos, *Spiritual Guide*, 161.

65. Wesley, *Christian Library* (Molinos), 38:289.

66. Molinos, *Spiritual Guide*, 3.

67. Wesley, *Christian Library* (Molinos), 38:250.

recollection as a way of existence in between, demonstrates that there was a certain aspect of recollection which Wesley was editing out of the text. If not the internal nature, then perhaps it was the idea of recollection serving as a means to something else, instead of an end to itself. In the unaltered wording, "Prayer and a loving recollection in the Divine Presence" are themselves one's protection, not the means to one's protection.

As alluded to earlier, Wesley also eliminated some reference to recollection as it pertains to the external. In the twelfth chapter of the first book, Molinos included a relatively lengthy description of prayer according to Francesca Lopez of Valenza. In the opening instructions, Francesca affirmed the practice of beginning prayer with fifteen minutes of "recollection of the senses and faculties, and with resignation and humility."[68] Wesley excluded the former clause while including the latter.[69] Thus, it was not merely the internal nature of recollection with which Wesley took issue. This may also be found in his removal of the closing paragraph of this chapter which states that in internal recollection, "the faculties operate not, and that the Soul is idle and wholly unactive." Yet, Molinos continued to express that which is active and that which is inactive pertaining to the faculties both external and internal.[70] Wesley's removal may have been due to his opposition to the idea of such a strong bifurcation between the soul and body, even though Wesley was a dualist in this sense.

Contemplation

Wesley's theological parting from Molinos may be observed rather strongly in looking at their respective treatments of contemplation. To Molinos, contemplation is closely associated with, if not actually is *the* ultimate of spiritual development. Wesley, on the other hand, removed most of the references to contemplation, with only a couple exceptions. Wesley's first removal of the word *contemplation* may be found in the thirteenth chapter of the first book. There, Molinos urged his readers to pray for their experiences of *divine presence, repose, quietness,* and *tranquility* to endeavor "for a whole day, a whole year, and thy whole life," which he regarded as "that first act of Contemplation, by faith and love."[71] Wesley preserved this call to perpetual communion but edited it to be "that first act of faith."[72]

68. Molinos, *Spiritual Guide*, 36.

69. Wesley, *Christian Library* (Molinos), 38:265.

70. Molinos, *Spiritual Guide*, 37–38.

71. Molinos, *Spiritual Guide*, 38.

72. Wesley, *Christian Library* (Molinos), 38:266.

Similarly, in the third book, Wesley reworked Molinos's writings to alter the goal. In the conclusion of chapter 3, Molinos described the hindrance that self-love may play on reaching one's end. To Molinos, that end includes *perfect contemplation, loving union,* and *peace internal.*[73] From this trio, Wesley only allowed for *loving union* to enter his edition.[74] A couple chapters later, Molinos again correlated perfection with contemplation in "souls already advanced" by means of *martyrdoms.*[75] Wesley continued the concept of martyrdom, advancement, and the "fire of divine love" while divorcing these from perfection and contemplation.[76] His removal of contemplation was in keeping with his practice elsewhere, but it is interesting that he also chose to remove the word *perfection* here, as *Christian perfection* was a resounding theme in much of his theology and writings.

As the third book unfolded, Molinos encouraged his readers who found themselves in a season of temptation to "get close into thy center, that thou may'st only look at and contemplate God, who keeps his throne and his abode in the bottom of thy Soul."[77] Wesley tweaked this statement to read ". . . look at God, who keeps his throne in the bottom of thy soul," thus eliminating contemplation as a part of this process.[78] Likewise, Wesley also excluded contemplation, along with habitual recollection, from the process of mortification, whereas Molinos saw these as all part of the means toward a certain point of arrival.[79]

To Molinos, speculation and contemplation are means to knowing God. In the eighteenth chapter of his third book, Molinos addressed such knowledge of the Divine. Wesley preserved a large portion of this chapter, keeping the notion that such knowledge does not come through one's own learnedness or mere curiosity, but by denying oneself and through the revelation given from the Holy Spirit. However, Wesley edited out the first four paragraphs of the chapter which addressed contemplation as the primary means toward this knowledge of God. Here, Wesley did not completely eliminate the word or idea of contemplation. In one paragraph which Wesley kept in his edition, Molinos addressed those of learning to use their understanding where appropriate, but always to return "their minds to the simple and naked Contemplation of God, without form, figure or consideration."

---

73. Molinos, *Spiritual Guide,* 125.

74. Wesley, *Christian Library* (Molinos), 38:274.

75. Molinos, *Spiritual Guide,* 135.

76. Wesley, *Christian Library* (Molinos), 38:278.

77. Molinos, *Spiritual Guide,* 138.

78. Wesley, *Christian Library* (Molinos), 38:279.

79. Molinos, *Spiritual Guide,* 158; Wesley, *Christian Library* (Molinos), 38:128.

These instructions Wesley preserved, save the final phrase "without form, figure or consideration."[80]

Mystical Theology

Although influenced by many aspects of mystical theology, Wesley also demonstrated through his editing his disdain for certain extremes. Notably, he removed the word *mysticism* and its various forms from the writings of Molinos many times. For example, in the second chapter of the first book, Molinos included a quote by the fourteenth- to fifteenth-century French theologian Jean Charlier de Gerson which recounted his experiences in reading and prayer. Gerson stated that the most effective way "for attaining to Mystical Theology" includes becoming "like a young Child and Beggar in the presence of God."[81] Wesley preserved Gerson's counsel for prayer yet removed its end as the attainment of *mystical theology*.[82] Likewise, Wesley spared a quote by St. Augustine regarding seeking God, while removing Molinos's preliminary commentary concerning God leading Augustine "to the Mystical Way."[83] Although preserving these quotes, with alterations, later in the same book Wesley removed two paragraphs which included the entirety of a quote attributed to "the mystical Falcon" which likened spiritual attainment to a gift of a jewel.[84]

In the third book, Wesley removed a paragraph in which Molinos instructed his readers to "die in himself by the total denying of sense, and the reasonable appetite" as means to thinking and living mystically.[85] The concept of dying to oneself and self-denial were not out of Wesley's vocabulary. Therefore, it is likely that his removal of this paragraph was due to the corresponding goal as being the mystical life and the elimination of sense.

Three times, Wesley also altered the use of the term *mystical science*. Once he changed it to read "Divine wisdom" as something which belongs "to the humble and simple."[86] In the same chapter, Wesley eliminated the second half of a paragraph which spoke of moving toward *mystical science*; however, unlike the paragraph mentioned above, he preserved the stated

---

80. Molinos, *Spiritual Guide*, 173–77; Wesley, *Christian Library* (Molinos), 38:290–91.

81. Molinos, *Spiritual Guide*, 5.

82. Wesley, *Christian Library* (Molinos), 38:252.

83. Molinos, *Spiritual Guide*, 9; Wesley, *Christian Library* (Molinos), 38:253.

84. Molinos, *Spiritual Guide*, 39; Wesley, *Christian Library* (Molinos), 38:266.

85. Molinos, *Spiritual Guide*, 143; Wesley, *Christian Library* (Molinos), 38:281.

86. Molinos, *Spiritual Guide*, 174; Wesley, *Christian Library* (Molinos), 38:290.

importance of total self-denial.[87] Likewise, he removed another paragraph toward the end of the same chapter that stated five things which need to be removed from someone seeking to "attain to the Mystical Science."[88]

In addition to the word *mysticism* and its various forms, Wesley also eliminated some of the concepts of mysticism from his rendition of the *Spiritual Guide*. The wording of *union* with God was an idea with which Wesley was quite selective. At times he maintained the wording, while at other times he removed it. However, with great consistency Wesley always excluded the word *deified* and its forms from his publication of the various mystical theologians. For example, in the *Spiritual Guide*, Wesley altered the word *deified* to "into his likeness" concerning a soul who has been purged and transformed.[89] Interestingly, Wesley's tendency was to keep Molinos's use of the word union. In four cases where Wesley kept the word *union*, two of them deal with mortification and the denial of self-love, which Wesley preserved. These two also linked union with perfection, the latter of which Wesley eliminated.[90] Similarly, the third occurrence pertains to continual perseverance through these difficulties.[91] The fourth, on the other hand, is a description of arrival at the state of union where God possesses mastery over the soul.[92] The place where Wesley eliminated the word *union* occurs in the same paragraph as the fourth occurrence; therefore, it may have been merely an editorial move to eliminate repetition.

Silence and Quiet

If one were to summarize Wesley's main point of contention with Molinos, it would be on the issue of silence and quiet. Though Wesley saw enough value in the *Spiritual Guide* to include it in his *Christian Library*, he also spent a lot of time writing against the extremes of the Quietist Movement of his time—the movement that was birthed out of Molinos's *Guide*. These writings will be explored in further detail later, but here it is worth noting the numerous changes which Wesley made in his edition of the original English translation of Molinos's treatise regarding this theme—mostly, the removal of the word *silence*.

87. Molinos, *Spiritual Guide*, 175; Wesley, *Christian Library* (Molinos), 38:290.

88. Molinos, *Spiritual Guide*, 176; Wesley, *Christian Library* (Molinos), 38:291.

89. Molinos, *Spiritual Guide*, 27; Wesley, *Christian Library* (Molinos), 38:261.

90. Molinos, *Spiritual Guide*, 21, 125; Wesley, *Christian Library* (Molinos), 38:257, 274.

91. Molinos, *Spiritual Guide*, 133; Wesley, *Christian Library* (Molinos), 38:277.

92. Molinos, *Spiritual Guide*, 158–59; Wesley, *Christian Library* (Molinos), 38:289.

The first occurrence of these editorial alterations pertaining to quietude may be found in Molinos's second chapter of the first book, where he urged his readers who desire to grow in prayer with God to "walk by Faith and Silence in His Divine Presence."[93] Wesley removed the words "and silence" from this clause.[94] A few paragraphs later, Molinos elevated silence, along with *humble resignation*, to the means through which one draws close to God. Wesley removed the word *silent* as one of the defining adjectives for the state of resignation, yet he kept the word *humble*.[95] The intentionality of Wesley's editing may be seen here through his consistency as he removed *silence* and kept *faith* as a means to growing in prayer one more time in this chapter and later in the eleventh chapter.[96]

In the chapter following the above mentioned, Molinos continued the same theme, describing how one ought to continue in prayer, especially in the dry seasons. In closing out the chapter, he encouraged his audience in such times to "be quietly silent, and patiently persevere" while moving toward divine union. Wesley preserved the terminology of union and perseverance yet eliminated the instruction to be *quietly silent*.[97] In this same sentence, Wesley also excluded the equating of divine union with *eminent rest*.

In the twelfth chapter of the first book, Wesley removed relatively large portions, if not the whole, of every chapter except one. In the one exception, he removed only two nouns and their respective accompanying conjunction or preposition and changed the wording of one other noun. The latter word change was relatively inconsequential as he altered the word *sentiment* to *joy*. The words removed include a reference to God's *contentment* in seeing a "Soul in silence, desirous, humble, quiet, and resigned."[98] Wesley, however, removed the word *content* and the word *silence*. Interestingly, he kept the word *quiet* here.[99]

Likewise, in the chapter which followed, Wesley again edited out the majority of the text, keeping only one and a half paragraphs. The paragraph which he mostly preserved in its entirety spoke of offering oneself fully to God and coming to the point of resting in "holy repose, with quietness,

93. Molinos, *Spiritual Guide*, 5

94. Wesley, *Christian Library* (Molinos), 38:251.

95. Molinos, *Spiritual Guide*, 6; Wesley, *Christian Library* (Molinos), 38:252.

96. Molinos, *Spiritual Guide*, 6, 32; Wesley, *Christian Library* (Molinos), 38:252, 263.

97. Molinos, *Spiritual Guide*, 11–12; Wesley, *Christian Library* (Molinos), 38:254.

98. Molinos, *Spiritual Guide*, 35–36.

99. Wesley, *Christian Library* (Molinos), 38:264.

silence, and tranquility" and living every day of one's life in "that first act of Contemplation, by faith and love."[100] In this paragraph, Wesley again made three alterations, removing the nouns *silence, contemplation*, and *love*. Yet again here, Wesley kept the word *quietness*.[101]

A similar pattern may be found in Molinos's seventeenth chapter of the first book where Wesley again removed most of the text and kept only a portion of three out of the eight paragraphs. Again, the words pertaining to silence were removed from the *Christian Library* edition. In this chapter, however, it is noteworthy that the opening two paragraphs were completely removed, especially when looking at their content. Molinos opened the chapter with a description of three types of silence including that of the words, desires, and thoughts. Wesley, however, eliminated all of these.[102]

As the third book unfolded, Molinos stressed the withdrawal into the interior and the accompanying silence as people progress in their spiritual journey. In the two opening chapters, Wesley edited out both the call to enter the interior and the accompanying aspect of silence and quiet.[103] This is likely due to Wesley's stress on the place of external works as will be explored later.

In addition to linking silence with interior spirituality, Molinos also necessitated a connection between silence and spiritual progression through trials and suffering. Though Wesley saw the potential for divine involvement during times of struggle, he eliminated the connection with silence and quiet in his edition of Molinos's work. For example, in the fourth chapter, Molinos encouraged people who knew "how to be constant and quiet in the Fire of Tribulation," whereas Wesley changed "constant and quiet" to the word *content*. In that same chapter, Wesley removed the next paragraph in its entirety which places God's repose in the souls that are quiet and whose passions have been burnt up by "the Fire of Tribulation and Temptation."[104]

In the fifth chapter, Molinos addressed what he considered to be the first martyrdom—a stage of spiritual growth which necessarily involved suffering. Again, Wesley preserved some of the original descriptions about the divine working in the midst of struggle but eliminated the word quiet in connection. He also removed Molinos's instructions to "afflict not thy self

100. Molinos, *Spiritual Guide*, 38.

101. Wesley, *Christian Library* (Molinos), 38:266.

102. Molinos, *Spiritual Guide*, 56–59; Wesley, *Christian Library* (Molinos), 38:268.

103. Molinos, *Spiritual Guide*, 117–20; Wesley, *Christian Library* (Molinos), 38:270–71.

104. Molinos, *Spiritual Guide*, 127; Wesley, *Christian Library* (Molinos), 38:275.

too much, with inquietude" and his description of all good consisting "in being silent."[105]

Wesley was not completely opposed to the idea of silence, quiet, and solitude. There were places where he opted to keep the word *quiet* and others where he removed it. He did the same with the word *solitude*. For example, he kept the explanation that through dying to self, one may reach "perfect quietness"; however, shortly thereafter he removed the word *quietness* from Molinos's description of one who stands in "Peace and Quietness" in the midst of trials.[106] The distinction here may be that to Wesley, quietness is a peaceful outflow of the Christian life, not a state to be sought out. This will be explored later. The other example, that of *solitude*, may be found where Wesley removed Molinos's description of solitude as the "giver of eternal Blessings" and the "Mirrour, in which the eternal Father is always beheld," and the assessment that "there is not a more blessed Life than a solitary one"; however, in the same chapter he kept the connection between solitude and union, along with the acknowledgment that few arrive at it.[107]

Elsewhere, Wesley preserved Molinos's instructions to "look not upon other mens faults, but thine own" while removing connection to do this by keeping "silence with a continued internal conversation."[108] However, once again Wesley kept the concept of quiet where Molinos listed the virtues that may be found in "the throne of quiet" where "magnificent [*are*] the perfections of spiritual beauty," yet removed "silence and internal solitude" from among the list of virtues.[109]

JOHN WESLEY ON PRAYER AND MYSTICISM

In his book *Mysticism in the Wesleyan Tradition*, Robert G. Tuttle Jr. tracked the theological development of Wesley in relation to mysticism as he described the ways in which Wesley separated the *gold* from the *dross* of mysticism—picking up on the language Wesley used in the preface to his abridgment of Madame Guyon and a letter written on September 8, 1773.[110] Tuttle described two main branches of mysticism which influ-

---

105. Molinos, *Spiritual Guide*, 133; Wesley, *Christian Library* (Molinos), 38:277.

106. Molinos, *Spiritual Guide*, 142, 150; Wesley, *Christian Library* (Molinos), 38:281, 284.

107. Molinos, *Spiritual Guide*, 156, 157; Wesley, *Christian Library* (Molinos), 38:287–88.

108. Molinos, *Spiritual Guide*, 144; Wesley, *Christian Library* (Molinos), 38:282.

109. Molinos, *Spiritual Guide*, 187; Wesley, *Christian Library* (Molinos), 38:292.

110. Tuttle, *Mysticism*, 126.

enced eighteenth-century England. One aligned with an attempt toward syncretism with Neoplatonism and the other emerged out of the Counter-Reformation within Roman Catholicism. Tuttle placed Wesley in closer alignment to the latter as reflected in the works of those whom he abridged, including Ávila and Molinos.[111]

Tuttle's hypothesis is worth noting in its entirety as it is solidly supported throughout his work and captures well Wesley's relationship to mysticism. Tuttle postulated:

> Of the five mystical stages (1. awakening, 2. purgation, 3. illumination, 4. the dark night of the soul, and 5. union with God), Wesley continued to practice and encourage the "tools" known to the first three stages. He also admired and commended the many other practical outworkings of these stages manifested in the lives of the mystics whose utter devotion to God was a continual inspiration to him. Similarly he continued to uphold the mystical concept of perfection (mystical fifth stage) as the end of religion. Yet Wesley detested the vain irrational philosophy that sought to link the noble beginnings of religion (stages one to three) to the ultimate end of religion (stage five) by the dark night of the soul (the mystical fourth stage involving a lifeless theory of "in orco"), and it was precisely at this point that he substituted the Aldersgate experience of justification by faith in Christ.[112]

As Tuttle theorized, it was precisely at Wesley's soteriology in the early stages of spiritual growth in which he adopted a more Lutheran understanding while holding to the mystical views of the latter stages of spirituality (with some alterations as discussed elsewhere).

Tuttle went on to chart Wesley's relationship with mysticism, approaching it at face value, then applying his hypothesis above. At the surface, Tuttle showed how Wesley displayed a strong and growing affinity to mysticism from his studies at Oxford through his time spent in Georgia from 1720 through 1736. After this time, he began to react against the extremes of mysticism as demonstrated in a letter to Samuel in 1736, followed by a growing distancing from mysticism following his Aldersgate experience in 1738 and climaxing with the Moravian "stillness controversy" of 1740. However, Wesley returned to the mystics in his publishing of an abridgement of de Rentry in 1741 and his *Christian Library* from 1749 through 1755. He then rejected some of the teachings of William Law's mysticism in an open

---

111. Tuttle, *Mysticism*, 26.

112. Tuttle, *Mysticism*, 127.

letter written in 1756, yet published an abridgement of Madame Guyon in 1776, followed by some strong thoughts of opposition to the writings of Behmen in 1780.[113] As Tuttle applied his theory to Wesley's seemingly back-and-forth relationship with mysticism, he demonstrated how John really had an increasing rejection of the "dross" of mysticism while simultaneously embracing a rising affinity for the "gold" of mysticism.[114]

Prayer

John Wesley placed a high value upon the place of prayer as means of grace, essential for the establishment and continuation of a relationship with God, and a vehicle for transformation and ministry impact. In fact, the word *pray* and its forms appears in Wesley's works well over three thousand times, not including his *Christian Library*. This alone highlights the centrality at which Wesley placed prayer in living out the faith. It is also noteworthy that Wesley frequently linked prayer with fasting and study, emphasizing a broader approach to spiritual disciplines beyond prayer alone.

In brief summary of Wesley's approach to prayer and its evolution over time, he began his ministry as a high-churchman in the Church of England. Thus, his practice was to pray the prescribed prayers in the *Book of Common Prayer* for public worship and private devotion. In time, Wesley shifted, opting for the practice of extemporaneous prayers both publicly and privately.

Wesley's use of extemporary prayer was not without its critics. In his journal entry dated November 28, 1740, he recounted a conversation with a gentleman who felt that Wesley was leaving the church because he prayed extemporaneously. His argument was that one "cannot do two things at once," which he identified as thinking and praying. Wesley defended extemporary prayer by making the argument that "reading and praying are two things."[115] Wesley also spent a fair amount of space in his writings defending extemporary prayer against the naysayers. This may be found in his *Farther Appeal to Men of Reason and Religion*, his *Minutes of Several Conversations between the Rev. Mr. Wesley and Others: From the Year 1744, to the Year 1789*, and *Principles of a Methodist Farther Explained*.[116]

In 1750, Wesley left off public extemporary prayer for a brief time. Yet even in the midst of this phase, recollecting a communion service with

113. Tuttle, *Mysticism*, 184.

114. Tuttle, *Mysticism*, 185.

115. Wesley, *Journal* (Curnock), 404.

116. Wesley, *Works* (Cragg), 11:185–86; Wesley, *Works* (Davies), 9:187, 195; Wesley, *Works* (Jackson), 8:321.

a person who had fallen ill recorded in his journal dated April 30, he marveled at the work of God in spite of the lack of a more spontaneous form of prayer.[117] In his later years, Wesley defended the Methodists as adhering to the Church of England on the major points and only veering slightly on a few matters of pragmatism. One of these latter items includes employing extemporaneous prayers, as seen in his journal entry for August 4, 1788, which he deemed a shift made "out of necessity, not choice."[118]

Although Wesley opted toward an extemporaneous form of prayer as time passed, he also called for and practiced a methodical approach to scheduling prayer. For example, later in life in a letter to Zechariah Yewdall dated October 9, 1779, Wesley urged his reader, "you would do well to read every morning a chapter in the New Testament with the *Notes*, and to spend the greatest part of the morning in reading, meditation, and prayer."[119]

The Senses and the Interior

Many among the mystics, like Molinos, saw the spiritual life as a progression from the exterior to the interior, from the outward senses to the interior, and from cognition to affect. Wesley also had his own version of this. He articulated his understanding of this shift most clearly in a sermon published late in his life in 1788, later titled by Joseph Benson as "On Discoveries of Faith."[120]

Wesley began this sermon by quoting a Latin saying "*Nihil est in intellectu quod non fuit prius in sensu*," which he proceeded to translate, "There is nothing in the understanding which was not first perceived by some of the senses."[121] He believed that knowledge and the senses are directly related. He even ranked the senses in a hierarchy of ability to produce knowledge from sight at the top, to hearing, then taste and smell, followed by feeling.[122]

However, like many mystics who preceded him, Wesley saw limits to the senses. He connected the senses to the way in which one understands the physical world, while understanding of the spiritual realm requires a different vehicle. This is where faith enters. Wesley continued to explain how faith serves as the means to belief in and understanding of angels, God, the

---

117. Wesley, *Works* (Ward and Heitzenrater), 20:334.
118. Wesley, *Journal* (Curnock), 422.
119. Wesley, *Letters* (Telford), 6:357.
120. Wesley, *Works* (Outler), 4:28.
121. Wesley, *Works* (Outler), 4:29.
122. Wesley, *Works* (Outler), 4:29–30.

Triune nature of God, the eternal world including heaven and hell, Christ's return, final judgment, and spiritual world.[123]

Like the mystics, Wesley saw spiritual progression as a move from the senses to "this interior kingdom."[124] Robert G. Tuttle Jr. defined mysticism as "anything that gets one in touch with reality beyond the physical senses."[125] Using this as a definition, it may be concluded that Wesley was—at least to some degree—a mystic. Unlike many mystics, however, Wesley emphasized faith as the means to arriving at such an end, not contemplation or darkness. However, faith is not the sole means, as this is brought about only by the work of the Holy Spirit in connection to this faith.[126]

Meditation and Contemplation

Wesley viewed meditation as one of the means of grace and a vehicle through which one may advance spiritually. This view remained consistent throughout his life. In an early sermon titled "Self-Denial"—which had its beginnings while he was in Savannah and was preached multiple times later—Wesley described someone who was "not 'going on to perfection.'" Among the primary reasons which he attributed to this lack of growth was the failure to participate in meditation.[127] In his treatise published in 1757, *The Doctrine of Original Sin: According to Scripture, Reason, and Experience*, Wesley expressed that the cure for "detain[ing] the carnal mind 'before the Lord'" is through "fix[ing] it in the meditation of spiritual things."[128] Similarly, in a later sermon titled "On Family Religion," which he preached in 1783, Wesley encouraged people to instruct the respective members of their households to commit to daily "reading, meditation, and prayer."[129] Likewise, an even later sermon that first appeared in the *Arminian Magazine* in 1787, titled "The More Excellent Way," counseled readers and hearers who were accustomed to reciting pre-written and memorized prayers to "add to your other devotions a little reading and meditation," thus again affirming meditation as an important spiritual exercise.[130]

123. Wesley, *Works* (Outler), 4:30–34.
124. Wesley, *Works* (Outler), 4:34.
125. Tuttle, *Mysticism*, 22.
126. Wesley, *Works* (Outler), 4:34.
127. Wesley, *Works* (Outler), 2:247.
128. Wesley, *Works* (Maddox), 12:461.
129. Wesley, *Works* (Outler), 3:340.
130. Wesley, *Works* (Outler), 3:268.

In addition to these examples, throughout many of his letters, Wesley continued to encourage his readers to engage in meditation, often linking it to prayer, reading, and/or study. The difference, however, between Wesley and other mystics was his working definition of *meditation*. Whereas the mystics generally viewed meditation as a distinct stage in spiritual development leading toward contemplation and ultimately union with God, Wesley considered meditation as an exercise of the intellect, or an action of reflection and consideration upon a particular text, attribute, or directly upon God.

Regarding contemplation, Wesley often addressed it with the mystical understanding as a distinct state of being which moved people closer to the climactic stage of spirituality. However, his handling of the term often coincided with a critical analysis of the mystical use. An example of this may be found in a sermon titled "Upon our Lord's Sermon on the Mount, Discourse the Fourth." Here, Wesley picked up on the theme of outward verses inward religion. He acknowledged that "the root of religion lies in the heart, in the inmost soul; that this is the union of the soul with God, the life of God in the soul of man."[131] However, he went on to defend the place of outward works, stating that "contemplation is only one way of worshipping God in spirit and in truth."[132]

This displays that Wesley was not completely opposed to contemplation. This may also be observed in his sermon on "Wandering Thoughts" developed in the late 1750s and early 1760s; in it, he addressed the way in which wandering of thoughts may interrupt prayer and even "the steadiest of contemplation."[133] He worded this in such a way as to affirm contemplation as an expression of prayer.

Likewise, in his treatise on *Original Sin*, written in 1757, Wesley described the process and effects of turning away from God after having an established relationship. In this treatise, he quoted from Howe's *Living Temple* where he described part of this falling away, stating, "The noble powers which were designed and dedicated to *divine contemplation* and *delight* in God, are alienated to the service of the most despicable idols, and employed in the vilest embraces." Wesley described this as a "beautiful description," thus giving an endorsement to Howe's description of the place of contemplation and the lament of that which diverts from such a state or practice.[134]

131. Wesley, *Works* (Outler), 1:541.

132. Wesley, *Works* (Outler), 1:541.

133. Wesley, *Works* (Outler), 2:131.

134. Wesley, *Works* (Maddox), 12: 271–72.

Eros Language

For the most part, Wesley did not follow his mystical predecessors in employing the use of erotic language when speaking of the relationship between
God and people. In fact, one would be somewhat hard-pressed to find such
language in the writings of Wesley. However, Wesley was not completely
averse to the use of marital language for describing the divine to human
relationship. This may be observed in a few places, most notably in his *Notes
on the Song of Solomon* and his sermon "On the Wedding Garment."

In Wesley's *Notes on the Old Testament*, he introduced the Song of
Solomon with these words:

> The design of the book in general is to describe the love and
> happy marriage of two persons, but it is not to be understood
> concerning Solomon and Pharaoh's daughter, (although the oc-
> casion may be taken from that, or rather he makes an allusion to
> that) but concerning God, or Christ, and his church and people
> . . . . Hence it follows, that this book is to be understood al-
> legorically concerning that spiritual love and marriage which is
> between Christ, and his church.[135]

This allegorical interpretation of the Song of Solomon was quite prevalent throughout the history of the Christian church, which Wesley also
perpetuated.

In his sermon "On the Wedding Garment," Wesley examines some of
the Scripture passages that call upon marriage imagery in describing the
relationship between God and humankind or individual people. When
comparing and contrasting the wording in Jesus' parable on the wedding
garments found in Matt 22 with the wedding supper described in Rev 19,
he noted that "the supper mentioned in the parable belongs to the Church
Militant; that mentioned in the Revelation, to the Church Triumphant: The
one, to the kingdom of God on earth; the other, to the kingdom of God
in heaven."[136] He continued to describe the garments as representing the
righteousness which is given by Jesus.

Thus, we see that Wesley was comfortable with the language of marriage as allegorical for God's relationship with people. However, Wesley
seemed to keep to the specifics of the symbolism represented while often
avoiding the use of marriage as a description of the love relationship between the Divine and human. In particular, he strictly evaded the use of

---

135. Wesley, "Notes on the Song of Solomon."

136. Wesley, *Works* (Outler), 4:143.

erotic language in describing this spiritual connection, with the perceived allegory found in the Song of Solomon being the exception.

The *Telos* or Goal and Quietism

The theme of *union with God* may be understood as a key tenet of mysticism. In fact, it is often preceded with the adjective *mystical* union. This is a doctrine with which Wesley held great affinity as well as great contention. Since this is critical in understanding Wesley's relationship to mysticism and mystical language, it will be handled in the next chapter to give it the attention it deserves. However, here, it is worth examining the tension brought about by the writings of Molinos, the ensuing development of Quietism in Great Britain, and Wesley's opposition to the extremes that emerged over time.

Quietism was not exclusive to Molinos nor his Spanish contemporaries, nor was it new to the seventeenth century in which he lived. To this point, Robert Tuttle stated that the term, and perhaps the founding, may be traced back to the Hesychastai of the fourteenth century.[137] Quietism found its way into France and the broader continent in the sixteenth and seventeenth centuries, but with precursors perhaps measurable in centuries. However, it was the seventeenth century that saw a certain form of Quietism arise in Great Britain, arguably climaxing in the mid-eighteenth century (although precursors may also be found back to the fourteenth century, for example, in the writings of Walter Hilton). Much of this form of Quietism and its influence in Great Britain may be connected to the events in 1685 when King James II ascended to the throne of England, Scotland, and Ireland as the last Roman Catholic monarch. With him came a relative religious tolerance (emphasis on *relative*). This opened the door for a greater breadth of religious publications in the English language. Not least of these was the translation of Miguel de Molinos's *Spiritual Guide* in 1688. Consequently, Roman Catholic mystical theology found its way even further into British Protestantism, especially Molinos's ideas of stillness and quietude.

Although Wesley was heavily influenced by mysticism in general, it was particularly the Quietism brand of mysticism upon which Wesley felt that he almost made shipwreck his faith. It is interesting that Wesley traversed down the Quietist path so far during his years in Oxford and Savannah when his father warned and cautioned against such extremism. Samuel Wesley's understanding of the issues in Molinos's form of Quietism may be

137. Tuttle, *Mysticism*, 37.

found in a poem which he wrote upon the death of Mr. Morgan of Christ Church. Reflecting on Mr. Morgan's piety, Samuel wrote:

> To means of grace the last respect he show'd,
> Nor sought new paths, as wiser than his God:
> Their sacred strength preserved him from extremes
> Of empty outside or enthusiast dreams;
> Whims of Molinos, lost in rapture's mist,
> Or Quaker, late-reforming quietist.[138]

Although John Wesley did not start out his ministry at the same place as his father on this matter, in time he came to embrace a similar caution on Molinos, the Quakers, and the Quietists in his midst.

Wesley's disdain for Quietism developed after his return to England from Georgia. In an article titled "The Stillness Controversy of 1740: Tradition Shaping Scripture Reading," Mark K. Olson recounted the start of the stillness controversy within Methodism as beginning in the Fetter Lane Society in November of 1739 when Philipp Molther accused some of the members of practicing a works-righteousness by their engagement in the means of grace. Molther then blamed the brothers Wesley for their emphasis on the sacraments and certain spiritual practices.[139] Philipp Molther was the key influencer in leading the Methodists of Yorkshire to the Moravians. Wesley identified the Moravians' version of Quietism as a "new-reformed" variety. Although the conflict reached a sort of climax within the Fetter Lane Society near the end of 1739, Wesley expressed his contentions with the Moravians in a letter which he began in September 1738 and brought to completion on June 24, 1744. In that letter, he asserted that the books which they were publishing in England nearly all contained the three errors of "*Universal Salvation, Antinomianism*, and a kind of new-reformed *Quietism*."[140]

Wesley recounted what he heard from Mr. Molther on December 31, 1739, in a letter written to Benjamin Ingham dated September 8, 1746. His recollection identifies his primary points of contention with the Moravian form of Quietism. There, he recalled Molther as saying that:

> To attain faith is "to be still," that is,
> Not to use (what we term) the means of grace;
> Not to go to church;
> Not to communicate;

138. Wesley, *Works* (Ward and Heitzenrater), 18:135.

139. Olson, "Stillness Controversy," 120–21.

140. Wesley, *Journal* (Curnock), 2:498.

Not to fast;
Not to use *so much* private prayer;
Not to read the Scriptures;
Not to do temporal good; and
Not to attempt to do spiritual good.[141]

As described earlier, Wesley viewed such spiritual practices as *means of grace*. To Wesley, these very exercises may serve as vehicles through which people may encounter the grace of God. To throw off such practices, to Wesley, is to miss out on significant aspects of the transformational working of God. Olson identified the primary issue leading to this conflict as being a matter of hermeneutics informed by tradition—the Moravians shaped by the pietistic Lutheran view of spontaneous regeneration and Wesley by his Church of England view of degrees of faith.[142] However, it may not be quite as simple as merely the pietistic influence upon the Moravians—rather, the strong Quietist influence may have served as an even greater influence at these points. Tuttle noted that the Moravians combined the Lutheran soteriology of salvation by faith with the Quietism of the mystics, particularly the variety found in Molinos.[143]

By June 5, 1742, Wesley's caution against the mystics grew strong and harsh. After reading a couple of works by Jean Guyon, he pondered:

> The very words I have so often heard some of you use, are not your own, no more than they are God's. They are only retailed from this poor Quietist; and that with the utmost faithfulness. O that ye knew how much God is wiser than man! Then would you drop Quietists and Mystics together, and at all hazards keep to the plain, practical, written word of God.[144]

Even given this harsh assessment, Wesley would go on to publish abridgments to Guyon's works. Yet, he maintained his strong criticism of her and the accompanying Quietism which she promoted. As late as September 9, 1773, Wesley offered the following critique in a letter to Mary Bishop:

> Madam Guyon was a good woman, and is a fine writer, but very far from judicious. Her writings will lead anyone who is fond of them, into unscriptural Quietism. They strike at the root, and tend to make us rest contented without either faith or works.[145]

141. Wesley, *Works* (Ward and Heitzenrater), 20:136–37.
142. Olson, "Stillness Controversy," 126–27.
143. Tuttle, *Mysticism*, 102–3.
144. Wesley, *Journal* (Curnock), 3:18.
145. Wesley, *Letters* (Telford), 6:44.

It is important to note, however, that Wesley was not completely opposed to stillness in all its forms. On September 8, 1746, he wrote a letter asserting:

> First, as to "stillness": The thing meant hereby is, that man cannot attain to salvation by his own wisdom, strength, righteousness, goodness, merits, or works; that therefore, when he applies to God for it, he is to cast away all dependence upon everything of his own, and trusting only to the mercy of God, through the merits of Christ, in true poverty of spirit, to resign himself up to the will of God, and thus quietly wait for his salvation. I conceive this to be the first mistake. I have nothing to object to this "stillness." I never did oppose *this* in word or deed. But this is not "the thing meant thereby," either by Molther, or the Moravians, or the English Brethren, at the time that *I* (and *you* at Mr. Bowers's) opposed them.[146]

Examining Wesley's oppositions mentioned above, his particular issues with Quietism may be categorized at the levels of soteriology, ecclesiology, sacramental theology and the means of grace. At the level of soteriology, Wesley was concerned that Quietism set stillness as a goal that undermined the place of salvation by faith expressed through works. He was concerned that stillness would lead to apathy and sloth as it came to performing good deeds. Regarding his ecclesiology, Wesley was distraught by those who stopped attending church and meeting together under the guise of being still before God. Wesley held a high view of the sacraments of baptism and the Lord's Supper. His sacramental theology viewed these acts as strong means of grace through which one encounters God. However, beyond the sacraments, Wesley also saw spiritual disciplines like the reading of Scripture, prayer, fasting, etc. as means of grace, but on a different plane. The "newly reformed" Quietists of his time abandoned such practices, also in the name of stillness. To Wesley, such neglect was minimizing one's ability and opportunity to encounter the grace of God more fully, thus hindering spiritual growth.

COMPARISON AND CONTRAST

Regarding the topic of mysticism, Ávila, Molinos, and Wesley may be arranged in a scale of progression. Molinos would certainly be further toward the Mysticism end of the scale than the other two. Ávila and Wesley would remain relatively close to one another on a more centrist position with

---

146. Wesley, *Works* (Ward and Heitzenrater), 20:136.

mystical leanings, with the former leaning slightly more toward the mystical end of the scale than the latter.

Molinos adhered quite closely to the Pseudo-Dionysian three-fold way of purgation, illumination, and enlightenment while assigning meditation to the state of illumination and contemplation to the climactic level of enlightenment. Ávila and Wesley were both less likely to view meditation and contemplation as distinct stages and more apt to assign them to actions taken at any stage. Wesley in particular used the words to describe acts of intellectual reflection.

Molinos held to the mystical tradition of seeing spiritual progress as a movement from active to passive existence, while Ávila and Wesley maintained an interplay of the active and passive throughout one's spiritual journey. This is much of the reason for Wesley's distaste for Quietism. However, Wesley did write of the movement from the senses to a life of faith, as mentioned earlier. This was different than Molinos's perspective which understood spiritual progress as a move from the senses to the interior life. For Wesley, this move was more about epistemology than a form of devotion. For Wesley, the senses serve as the vehicle through which knowledge is obtained, while faith is the means through which knowledge of the Divine is realized.

Another notable distinction among these three authors may be found in their handling of the theme of suffering. Molinos described suffering and darkness as necessary means to growth closely linked to the progression from meditation to contemplation. Similarly, Ávila also wrote of darkness as a means to seeing God beyond reason. Wesley, on the other hand, wrote against using the wording of darkness in describing the work of God because God is light. He was not, however, averse to acknowledging that God can and does redeem suffering as a tool for spiritual growth as seen in his sermons on *heaviness* and *wilderness*.

Differences may also be found in their treatment of asceticism. Ávila believed that some asceticism can be helpful yet cautioned against extremes. Molinos found greater value in recollection over ascetic practices. Wesley encouraged certain spiritual practices yet denounced taking it to the point of asceticism.

Regarding the climactic stage, their written expressions differed. Molinos was quite comfortable with the figurative use of erotic language, Ávila utilized some romantic language allegorically, while Wesley seemed to avoid it nearly altogether (with the exception of some marriage allegories). Beyond their tools of description, the three veered from each other in the substance of the spiritual *telos*, or goal. Molinos held to the traditional view of mystical union with God, perhaps just shy of divination. Ávila was quite comfortable with the terminology of *union* while describing it as a connection of the "self-same spirit." Wesley, however, opted to speak of *God-likeness* over *God-oneness*. Interestingly, all three viewed the climactic spiritual stage as an arrival at a state of perfect love (as will be further examined in the next chapter).

7

The *Telos*

ANECDOTALLY, THE ULTIMATE PHILOSOPHICAL question is often quoted as "what is the meaning of life?" It follows that if life has an ultimate meaning, then life has an end goal or what the Greeks called a τελος (*telos*). Though an overwhelmingly strong consensus exists among various Christian traditions, with few exceptions, that the ultimate human *telos* is realized after death in heaven, the extent to which one may experience a *telos* in this life remains debatable. It is this latter point at which Ávila, Molinos, and Wesley maintained differences of opinion. However, they all remained in agreement that the level to which one may attain a spiritual climactic state is significantly high.

JUAN DE ÁVILA ON THE *TELOS*

The *Telos*

In a sermon preached on Pentecost Sunday, Juan de Ávila presented his understanding of the whole purpose of humankind. He explained how purpose may be found as one "might love God, and loving Him possess Him, and possessing Him, enjoy Him, and enjoying Him, become blessed."[1] In his *Audi Filia*, he laid out for his readers a description of the outcomes of spiritual growth. He described the ultimate goal, or *telos*, as a state in which one enters into a "union with the divine will," "*unión con la divina voluntad*" such that there is no interior tribulation.[2]

---

1. Ávila, *Holy Spirit* (Dargan), 51.
2. Ávila, *Audi Filia*—Spanish, capítulo 26; Ávila, *Audi, Filia* (Gormley), 99.

According to Gormley's translation, this is also a state in which one's thinking moves toward conformity with that of God;[3] however, Ávila's original wording went deeper than merely thinking. Rather, it is a state in which one's sensory experiences, perceptions, and feelings align with the Divine, "*pues de Dios debemos sentir conforme a Dios*" (note his use of *sentir*, not *pensar*; feeling, not thinking), and one's abilities are moved to a higher plane, "*que es cuanto más alto pudiéremos*."[4] He described this transformation as a "*perfecta liberación*," or "perfect liberation," and possession of "*perfecta virtud*," or "perfect virtue," both of which come from the hand of God.[5] This state, according to Ávila is so lofty that when one arrives, one reflects the very beauty of Jesus.[6]

The levels at which one may progress spiritually, according to Ávila, are quite lofty and therefore require great courage. In his *Audi Filia*, he described the goal as one's arrival at the fulfillment of the desires "to possess incorruption in corruptible flesh . . . to have as your way of virtue what the angels have by nature . . . [and] to aspire to a special crown in heaven."[7] The word which Ávila used, *queréis*, translated by Gormley as *desire*, may mean a *wanting*, but may also be used as a term of affection, fondness, or love.[8] The latter definitions seem consistent with Ávila's overall perspectives on spiritual progression, where spiritual growth is mostly about developing a loving relationship with God. In other words, although he wrote of self-abandonment and suffering as means to progress, he aligned more with the affective tradition than the *via negativa* or the ascetic traditions.

Though virtue has its prominent place in the spiritual *telos*, Ávila saw this climactic spiritual state as more than merely an exhibition of goodness; he saw it as a perfecting of friendship with God, out of which develops the outcome of perfect virtue.[9] This perfection of virtue to Ávila is not a mere imputation of righteousness, but an actual impartation of holiness (if the terminology of later Protestant debates may be used). In referencing the apostle Paul's words to the Colossians to "live worthily of God," Ávila responded that Paul would not have expected such a thing if it were not possible for one to fulfill it, yet Ávila saw it as a "work of God not [the people]."[10]

---

3. Ávila, *Audi, Filia* (Gormley), 127.

4. Ávila, *Audi Filia*—Spanish, capítulo 39.

5. Ávila, *Audi Filia*—Spanish, capítulo 36–37; Ávila (Gormley), *Audi, Filia*, 122–24.

6. Ávila, *Audi, Filia* (Gormley), 311, 316.

7. Ávila, *Audi, Filia* (Gormley), 65.

8. Ávila, *Audi Filia*—Spanish, capítulo 11.

9. Ávila, *Audi, Filia* (Gormley), 90–91.

10. Ávila, *Audi, Filia* (Gormley), 257.

Whereas some within the mystical tradition emphasized the immediate entry into the highest spiritual phase of union with God, Ávila was more apt to stress the lengthy process through which one treks toward such an end. In his *Audi Filia*, he cautioned his readers not to despair "if integrity of life and the remedy you desire do not come as soon as you would like."[11] In fact, in reference to the apostle Paul's statement concerning the crucifying of one's flesh "with its vices and desires" found in Gal 5, Ávila asserted that "what is said in only one word is accomplished in many years."[12]

Another area in which Ávila stands out from some of the other mystical writers may be found in his perspective on one's movement toward an *active* spirituality at the higher levels. In the section meditating on and imitation of Christ's Passion, he insistently asserted that "they think wrongly that one who experiences greater sweetness and spends more hours in prayer is the greater saint. But, in reality, the greatest is the one who, with profound contempt for himself, has the greatest charity."[13] Thus, to Ávila, *caridad*, or charity, took precedence over spiritual consolations.

Ávila's alignment with the affective and active traditions may also be seen throughout many of his personal letters. Both of these affinities are expressed in one of his letters to Teresa de Ávila, where he stated succinctly, "even though it be certain that the favors come from God, do not let your mind dwell on them with complacency, for holiness does not consist in such things, but in a humble love of God and our neighbor. Fear all ways other than this, and practice humility, the virtues, and the love of our Lord."[14] Teresa, in turn, also took this position of an active and affective spirituality, especially expressed in her *Interior Castle*.

Another expression of Ávila's affective emphasis may be found in a letter to one of his friends where he described how perfection and holiness emerge out of love. This is an interesting assertion, though not completely unique as will be shown later; often spiritual writers may view love as the outcome of holiness and perfection, whereas here Ávila places love as a means toward those ends. He concluded this same letter declaring that love is also the means to producing the outcome of "perfect charity toward our neighbor."[15]

He understood love to be the driving force in the alignment of one's will with the will of God. He proclaimed that "the love that the saints bear

11. Ávila, *Audi, Filia* (Gormley), 93.

12. Ávila, *Audi, Filia* (Gormley), 224.

13. Ávila, *Audi, Filia* (Gormley), 219.

14. Ávila, *Confidence* (Benedictines), 7.

15. Ávila, *Confidence* (Benedictines), 79–80.

toward God transforms their will, so that it becomes one with His: that is, they can wish, or not wish, only what He does." He went on to reference Pseudo-Dionysius as stating that an effect of love is the uniting of the wills of the two who love.[16] This, however, does not happen completely passively. One must also renounce one's own will in order for the alignment to happen.[17]

Although love moves one toward perfection, charity, the alignment of one's will, and holiness—the latter of which he claimed is "a higher gift than mere existence"—these are not ends in themselves according to Ávila, but penultimate to the climax. This love for God and others ultimately results in God being *praised and worshiped*.[18]

In addition to those just mentioned, the outcomes of arriving at union with God are plentiful according to Ávila. Referencing Bernard of Clairvaux, he described this state as one in which "God and the soul speak in accord."[19] It is a level at which one participates in the divine nature, one's understanding is enlightened, one will burn with love for Jesus, and be given grace and glory.[20] In a sermon on Pentecost Tuesday, he described union with God as despising "everything on earth that is not of God, and your one thought will be to love and please Him, as your only good," and continuing to state that one would be "filled with joy and fervor" and know that all is well.[21] In his *Treatise on the Love of God*, Ávila explained the benefits of union by saying that "if you are united to Him in this way, be certain that what belongs to Him will belong to you; what belongs to the Father will belong to the children."[22] In his *Treatise on the Priesthood*, he went so far as to say that there are no longer two, but one.[23] He even likened this union to the incarnation, but given the uniqueness of the incarnation, he instead applied the term "*spiritualization* by the Holy Spirit."[24]

All of this, he attributed to the inner working of the Holy Spirit.[25] Ávila believed a high degree of union with God is possible in this life through

16. Ávila, *Confidence* (Benedictines), 104.

17. Ávila, *Confidence* (Benedictines), 136.

18. Ávila, *Confidence* (Benedictines), 98, 109.

19. Ávila, *Confidence* (Benedictines), 118.

20. Ávila, *Confidence* (Benedictines), 133; Ávila, *Holy Spirit* (Dargan), 98.

21. Ávila, *Holy Spirit* (Dargan), 143.

22. Ávila, *Love of God, Priesthood* (Fernández-Fígares), 35.

23. Ávila, *Love of God, Priesthood* (Fernández-Fígares), 56, 72.

24. Ávila, *Holy Spirit* (Dargan), 83.

25. Ávila, *Confidence* (Benedictines), 133; Ávila, *Holy Spirit* (Dargan), 98, 118, 143.

this working of the Holy Spirit, but only as the beginning of that which will be fulfilled in the life to come.[26]

Death, Purgatory, and Heaven

Juan de Ávila held relatively closely to a traditional Roman Catholic perspective on heaven, purgatory, and hell. In his *Audi Filia*, he recounted the process leading just prior to death. He saw this process as including an awareness of the gravity of one's sins, but one's senses and ability to confess will flee. Then, God will command the soul to leave the body and tell it "'Depart from me into eternal fire,' or 'Remain with me in a state of salvation, in purgatory or in paradise.'"[27] Ávila believed that the fulfillment of union with God is realized in heaven and thus there remains a need for a final purgation in the state of purgatory. However, he also believed that the degree to which one experiences purgatory, or the time spent there, may be reduced through proper endurance through the sufferings faced in this life.[28]

Ávila saw heaven as the place of reward for hard work done on earth and satisfaction for the self-denial endured in life. In a sermon on Pentecost Sunday, he even went so far as to state imperatively that

> the harder you work here below, the more magnificent and the larger will be your chain of gold in heaven. Deprive yourself here on earth, that you may have wealth in there! If you are lonely on earth, you will later be the companion of those who enjoy God; if you close your eyes here, you will see God in the next life; if you work here below, you will rest in glory for ever.[29]

Likewise, in a letter to a friend, he urged his reader not to seek honors in this life, for God will heap them upon the person in Paradise.[30] For Ávila, there was no greater expression of union with God than that which may be experienced in the eternal heavenly dwelling.

26. Ávila, *Confidence* (Benedictines), 139–40.

27. Ávila, *Audi Filia*—Spanish, capítulo 61; Ávila, *Audi, Filia* (Gormley), 183–84.

28. Ávila, *Audi Filia*—Spanish, capítulo 22; Ávila, *Audi, Filia* (Gormley), 89.

29. Ávila, *Holy Spirit* (Dargan), 70.

30. Ávila, *Confidence* (Benedictines), 136.

JOHN WESLEY'S EDITING OF JUAN DE ÁVILA ON THE *TELOS*

As mentioned earlier, Wesley's editing of Juan de Ávila often included the removal of words, phrases, and themes that reflected the theology of mysticism. Wesley often opted for terms like *Christian perfection, entire sanctification*, and *perfected in love* over ideas of *union* and *divination*. He preferred to think of the goal more in terms of God-likeness than God-oneness.

Purgatory

The letters from Ávila which Wesley published only contain two references to purgatory. Both references appear near the end of the same letter—a follow-up letter to a woman who was facing affliction. Wesley altogether eliminated the mention of purgatory. In the first, he omitted a lengthy statement describing that "afflictions of this world prevent Purgatorie, and entitle us to heaven."[31] Here, Ávila pondered how people should logically love such afflictions and even feel sorrow when such afflictions are not present. Based on Wesley's sermon "Heaviness through Manifold Temptations," it is likely that Wesley was not taking issue with the source of affliction (i.e., the world) as he clearly refuted the idea that God is the giver of affliction. It is also unlikely that he rejected the notion of some sort of redeeming value in affliction. Therefore, it is more likely that Wesley was rejecting the idea of affliction preventing purgatory, if not the concept of purgatory altogether. The latter seems most likely given the next elimination of the word *purgatory* a few paragraphs later; Wesley changed "I desire that you would encourage your selfe to suffer the Purgatorie of your sinnes" to "I desire that you would encourage yourself to suffer the Remedy of your sins."[32]

MIGUEL DE MOLINOS ON THE *TELOS*

The *Telos*

In writing about the climactic phase of spiritual growth, Molinos held relatively closely to the broader Christian mystical tradition, especially that of the *via negativa*. He believed that union with God is the ultimate level of Christian spirituality. Like Ávila and Wesley, the word *perfection* and its

---

31. Ávila, *Selected Epistles*, 88.
32. Ávila, *Selected Epistles*, 89; Wesley, *Christian Library* (Ávila), 46:281.

forms also appear with relative frequency in speaking of this state. He believed that this is such a high state that few arrive. He described a lengthy and harsh process of moving toward this end yet held that full arrival may happen in an instant. One area in which Molinos may have been relatively unique within the mystical tradition includes his strong emphasis, or arguably his over-emphasis, on quietude and silence as going hand-in-hand with the spiritual climax.

To Molinos, one cannot arrive at union by means of meditation; rather, perfection is obtained through a four-fold process of *oración*/prayer, *obediencia*/obedience, *frecuente communión*/frequent communion, and *interior mortificación*/interior mortification.[33] That being said, he held that it was really the latter along with other forms of trials and suffering by which one enters the state of mystical union. To Molinos, this involves being deprived of spiritual delights, the painful process of purifying the soul's "disordered passions, its concupiscence, its self-esteem, its desires, its cares (even spiritual ones), and all the other attachments and hidden vices." He relegated the extent of this purgation to the point of annihilation, the martyrdoms, and even losing oneself in God through nothingness.[34] In fact, Molinos stated that "*es necesario*" (it is necessary) to "suffer to arrive at . . . high contemplation and loving union." He continued to emphasize this point by claiming that no one has arrived without passing through "spiritual martyrdom and painful torment."[35]

Given the intense sufferings necessary in order to arrive at perfection and union, along with other factors, Molinos believed that arrival at such a high state is only experienced by a few people. He believed that few arrive because of the unwillingness of many to "strip themselves of imperfect reflection and sensible pleasures," and because they don't "embrace scorn and allow themselves to be wrought and purified" or "embrace the cross."[36] He also saw the unwillingness to deny oneself and one's will as hindrances to progress for many people, thus resulting in a small and limited number of those who arrive to such spiritual heights.[37]

In addition to the two spiritual martyrdoms and detaching oneself from all worldly things Molinos asserted that in order to arrive at the *telos*, one also must attach oneself to contemplation and submit oneself completely

33. Molinos, *Guia Espiritual*, 35; Molinos, *Spiritual Guide* (Baird and McGinn), 68, 125–26.

34. Molinos, *Spiritual Guide* (Baird and McGinn), 70, 145, 177, 179–80.

35. Molinos, *Guia Espiritual*, 45; Molinos, *Spiritual Guide* (Baird and McGinn), 150.

36. Molinos, *Spiritual Guide* (Baird and McGinn), 89, 141, 143.

37. Molinos, *Spiritual Guide* (Baird and McGinn), 153, 183.

to "the divine hands and . . . his most holy Will."[38] When engaging in these active steps, one can then move more passively into the higher states where God takes the soul toward its end. Upon arrival at this mystical union, according to Molinos, one comes to a level at which one has "no support but God alone," and the ability to find God in all things.[39] It is a state in which one finds new depths of love for God and others, they are in a perfect habit of humility, a perfect and peaceful mystical silence, and their will aligns with the will of God.[40] He saw it also as a stage at which one arrives where one's knowledge is enlightened and one's love inflamed; in this, one possesses a "great hunger to suffer for God" along with a certainty of hope that God will always be near. These in turn result in three outcomes, a "fortitude of spirit" to reject sloth and neglect, to repel concupiscence, and to leave behind all negativity toward others.[41]

In his penultimate chapter, Molinos provided additional and lengthy descriptions of the outcomes of such a state. There he described the movement from active to passive as the soul arrives at a holy indifference in difficulties, a resistance to evil attacks, and in these sufferings "the superior part of the soul, the true sun enlightens, inflames, and illuminates it, and so it remains clear, peaceful, resplendent, tranquil, and serene, a sea of happiness."[42] He saw it as a state where one resides in perpetual and perfect quietude, infused and passive contemplation, a purgation of vice and life of virtue.[43]

JOHN WESLEY'S EDITING OF MIGUEL DE MOLINOS ON THE *TELOS*

John Wesley was certainly not opposed to a climactic spiritual state which involves a form of perfection. In fact, one of his most widely circulated works was titled *A Plain Account of Christian Perfection*—which will be explored later. However, there is clear divergence of thought between the eighteenth-century Anglican and the seventeenth-century Spanish Catholic. This may be seen through the more than twenty alterations pertaining to the word *perfection* which Wesley made to the works of Molinos in publishing his *Christian Library*.

38. Molinos, *Spiritual Guide* (Baird and McGinn), 166.
39. Molinos, *Spiritual Guide* (Baird and McGinn), 90, 152.
40. Molinos, *Spiritual Guide* (Baird and McGinn), 98, 151, 158.
41. Molinos, *Spiritual Guide* (Baird and McGinn), 170.
42. Molinos, *Spiritual Guide* (Baird and McGinn), 181.
43. Molinos, *Spiritual Guide* (Baird and McGinn), 164, 181–82.

Though Wesley adhered to a spiritual *telos* involving perfection, he parted ways with Molinos regarding certain means and outcomes concerning this lofty end. For example, in his *Spiritual Guide*, Molinos described a stage through which one no longer experiences the enjoyment it once had, he continued by instructing his readers how to navigate through such a season. Wesley preserved much of this text; however, he left out a portion of the description which included the means through which one progresses, "through the dark, and desert Paths of Perfection."[44] A similar example may be found in Molinos's third book where Wesley removed a reference to trouble, temptation, and dryness stating that they are necessary prerequisites to perfection.[45]

In the paragraph that followed, Molinos gave an explanation of two types of prayer. Wesley preserved these distinctions yet left off the statement that "the first is of Beginners, the second of Proficients, who are in the progress to Perfection."[46] This alteration makes sense for Wesley as he would not have designated certain forms of prayer to specific stages of growth (this will be explored later); however, he also made alterations that seem a little more perplexing based on the corpus of his writings. One example of the latter may be found in Molinos's seventh chapter of the first book where he described the outcome of mortifying the "external senses" as making advancement "towards the high mountain of perfection, and union with God."[47] In his own writings, Wesley's preference was to speak of the climactic spiritual state more in terms of perfection than union. However, in his rendition of the *Spiritual Guide*, here, he opted to protect the wording of union while jettisoning the language of perfection.[48]

At first glance, another somewhat perplexing alteration Wesley made may be found a little later where Molinos described the plethora of temptations faced by those who "have attained to holiness and perfection."[49] Though Wesley held the concepts of holiness and perfection as very closely related, here he chose to eliminate the word *perfection* while keeping the word *holiness*.[50] In addition to the link between perfection and holiness, Wesley also linked perfection—and holiness for that matter—to the expression of love. It is especially telling that Wesley kept Molinos's definition of

44. Molinos, *Spiritual Guide*, 11; Wesley, *Christian Library* (Molinos), 38:254.

45. Molinos, *Spiritual Guide*, 124; Wesley, *Christian Library* (Molinos), 38:273.

46. Molinos, *Spiritual Guide*, 12; Wesley, *Christian Library* (Molinos), 38:254.

47. Molinos, *Spiritual Guide*, 21.

48. Wesley, *Christian Library* (Molinos), 38:257.

49. Molinos, *Spiritual Guide*, 29.

50. Wesley, *Christian Library* (Molinos), 38:262.

perfection as consisting "not in speaking not in thinking much on God, but in loving him."[51] Though in this paragraph, Wesley only kept a few altered sentences, it is likewise telling that he also preserved the adverb *perfectly* in connection with the verb *love* which one expresses toward God.[52] In other words, to Wesley *and* Molinos, a major aspect of the climactic stage involves a perfect expression of love for God.

To Molinos and Wesley, love may be both the outcome and a means toward this end. Interestingly, however, Wesley removed one reference where Molinos indicated that love is a means through which God leads the soul toward perfection, while keeping another where Molinos attributed affliction and love as two means through which God leads one toward perfection.[53] To Molinos, an expression of this "humble and perfect love" may be found in one's dying alone, only in the presence of God. Curiously, Wesley kept this statement yet changed the word *perfect* to *contrite*, perhaps because he thought that there are other, more effective ways of demonstrating a *perfect* love, as will be explored later.

There were a few times when Wesley removed the word *perfect* and its forms when it was used as a point of certain arrival for the reader. These may be found in the third book. For example, in the second chapter, which explores the outward and inward distinctions, Molinos referred to people who have entered the inward way as "though thus Perfect." He continued to describe how such people have a deep awareness of their "weakness and imperfections" and what is still needed in order to arrive at perfection. Here, it seems as though Molinos may be explaining a point of arrival at the *telos* within which one still may progress. This idea was not foreign to Wesley, yet he did remove the first statement about being perfect while keeping the second statement regarding walking toward perfection.[54] Likewise, in the chapter following, Wesley removed a clause about coming to perfection in the context of abandoning one's will as a necessary part of following Jesus, and elsewhere, he eliminated the adverb to Molinos's statement "unless thou dost perfectly overcome thy self."[55]

To Molinos, the idea of perfection was also closely linked to humility. This may be seen especially in chapter 10 of his third book. In this chapter, Molinos described the existence of a "true humility." Wesley preserved

---

51. Molinos, *Spiritual Guide*, 57; Wesley, *Christian Library* (Molinos), 38:268.

52. Molinos, *Spiritual Guide*, 58; Wesley, *Christian Library* (Molinos), 38:268.

53. Molinos, *Spiritual Guide*, 125, 133; Wesley, *Christian Library* (Molinos), 38:274, 277.

54. Molinos, *Spiritual Guide*, 119–20; Wesley, *Christian Library* (Molinos), 38:271.

55. Molinos, *Spiritual Guide*, 122, 137; Wesley, *Christian Library* (Molinos), 38:272, 279.

much of the description; however, he excluded an important phrase which followed—"which have gotten a perfect habit of it."[56] Like the above, Wesley was comfortable with a degree of arrival, but to claim a perfect arrival at humility may not have sat well with him. The consistency which Wesley used in removing such statements of a definite arrival at perfection may be found in his treatment of Molinos's climactic chapter. Molinos concluded his treatise with a brief four-paragraph description of the few who arrive at perfection. Wesley opted to exclude this chapter in its entirety from his rendition. As a further example of Wesley's tendency to remove references to perfection as a definitive arrival, he preserved the statement made by Molinos, that "many are they who are call'd to perfection, but few are they that arrive at it."[57] Thus, it is not necessarily the possibility of such an arrival with which Wesley differed, but perhaps more the claim of certain arrival. This will be explored later.

Wesley also removed a couple of references to perfection as they were connected closely to contemplation by the Quietist. Wesley's editing of Molinos regarding meditation, contemplation, and quietude were explored in another chapter, but it is worth noting a few other examples here. The first may be observed where Molinos described the hindrance which self-love serves in preventing one from reaching the ultimate state. Here, he described this highest level in terms of both contemplation and union with God. Wesley preserved the phrasing of union while eliminating the wording of "perfect contemplation."[58] Note the adjectival use of *perfect* linked to contemplation. The second example may be found at the beginning of the sixth chapter of the third book where Molinos discusses the second martyrdom. Here, he explained the benefits to the soul of those "already advanced in perfection and deep contemplation."[59] Wesley, however, ended this clause after the word *advanced*.[60] In this case, Wesley's rendition described the benefits of such a martyrdom to any who had made significant spiritual progress, removing the specifications of perfection and contemplation.

JOHN WESLEY ON THE *TELOS*

Of all the volumes of John Wesley's writings, the most systematic address of his perspective on the spiritual *telos*, or end goal, is his treatise *A Plain*

56. Molinos, *Spiritual Guide*, 148; Wesley, *Christian Library* (Molinos), 38:283.

57. Molinos, *Spiritual Guide*, 123; Wesley, *Christian Library* (Molinos), 38:273.

58. Molinos, *Spiritual Guide*, 125; Wesley, *Christian Library* (Molinos), 38:274.

59. Molinos, *Spiritual Guide*, 135.

60. Wesley, *Christian Library* (Molinos), 38:278.

Account of Christian Perfection. In it, he defended his perspective on Christian perfection, claiming that his doctrine remained consistent from 1725 through the date of his writing of the treatise in 1765, which was then published the year following. However, it may be more accurate to say that the consistency developed in 1738 and following. According to Mark K. Olson, in Wesley's pre-1738 Aldersgate experience, he held more to the Church of England teaching that what begins at baptism reaches its culmination in final justification and the fulfillment of the new birth, though some signs of his consistent doctrines existed early on in his preaching.[61]

Wesley began this treatise by laying out some of the influences upon his theological formation. Included in this list are Jeremy Taylor's *Rule and Exercises of Holy Living and Dying*, which shaped Wesley's emphasis on "purity of intention"; Thomas à Kempis's *Christian Pattern*, which influenced Wesley's ideas of inward religion; William Law's *Christian Perfection* and *Serious Call*, which drove him toward an all-in devotion; and the deeper study of the Bible, from which he observed a call to complete alignment with Christ and his ways.[62] From there, Wesley chronicled his various sermons, notes, and publications offering summaries and direct quotes emphasizing his doctrines.

According to Wesley, the starting point of his teaching on the subject began with his sermonic address to the University Church of St. Mary in Oxford on the first of January, 1733, when he delivered his message "The Circumcision of the Heart." Interestingly, this sermon was given years before his own heart was "strangely warmed" at Aldersgate on May 24, 1738. Yet, throughout his life he praised it as a sermon that captured well his understanding of Christian perfection. In his *Plain Account*, Wesley recorded a few quotes from the sermon that summarize his views. The first not just connected, but equated *circumcision of the heart* with *holiness*. There, he summarized this work as "being cleansed from sin," "being endued with those virtues which were also in Christ Jesus," and "to 'be perfect, as our Father in heaven is perfect.'"[63] In addition to holiness, the other quotes also continue to equate *circumcision of the heart* to *love*. This is a complete and full love for God from which Wesley did not shy away, applying the word *union* with God. The final quote included here reflected upon the full extent of devotion to God that is called for when one's heart is circumcised.[64] Wes-

---

61. Olson, "New Birth," 82, 83, 86.

62. Wesley, *Plain Account* (Maddox and Chilcote), 33–34.

63. Wesley, *Plain Account* (Maddox and Chilcote), 35; Wesley, *Works* (Outler), 1:402–3.

64. Wesley, *Plain Account* (Maddox and Chilcote), 35–37; Wesley, *Works* (Outler), 1:407–8, 413–14.

ley did, however, leave out of his *Plain Account* some of the means toward arrival at this state which are contained in his sermon. To Wesley, humility, faith, the inward working of the Holy Spirit, and purgation of sin are all necessary to bring one to this highest degree of spirituality.[65]

After quoting from a couple of hymns, Wesley then referenced his first interview with someone who attested to an assurance of faith in keeping with that for which Wesley longed up to that year. Shortly after his Aldersgate experience, Wesley visited the Moravians in Germany. In his journal, and later in his *Plain Account*, Wesley recorded the words of Arvid Gradin who described "the full assurance of faith" as "repose in the blood of Christ. A firm confidence in God, and persuasion of his favour; the highest tranquility, serenity, and peace of mind, with a deliverance from *every fleshly desire*, and a *cessation of all, even inward, sins*."[66] In his journal entry regarding May 29, 1738, however, Wesley translated the same Latin as saying "serene peace and steadfast tranquillity of mind," instead of "the highest tranquility, serenity, and peace of mind," and "from every outward and inward sin" instead of "a cessation of all, even inward, sins." Interestingly, though Wesley used this quote in support of his view of Christian perfection, elsewhere, he asserted that he did not believe that full repose is possible in this life. In fact, as late as 1782 in a journal entry for the days following Wednesday, July 17, he wrote of his belief that even just a brief momentary repose was not for him in this world.

In 1741, Wesley began more formally and directly to address the topic of Christian perfection by publishing his sermon by that title in response to the encouragement from Bishop Edmund Gibson. This was then followed by the publication of his tract *The Character of a Methodist* in 1742, though Maddox and Chilcote point out that he mistakenly placed it chronologically before the aforementioned sermon in the respective summaries found in his *Plain Account*.[67]

In Wesley's summary of the sermon on "Christian Perfection" found in his *Plain Account*, he began with an apophatic approach explaining what perfection *is not* and followed it up with a brief description of what perfection *is*. Wesley stressed that perfection is not perfection in knowledge, nor freedom from ignorance, mistake, or infirmities.[68] Although he gave a few illustrations in his summary, the full text of his sermon expanded upon more specific examples. For instance, Wesley expressed the limits of

---

65. Wesley, *Works* (Outler), 1:401–14.

66. Wesley, *Plain Account* (Maddox and Chilcote), 39.

67. See footnote 81 of Wesley, *Plain Account* (Maddox and Chilcote), 41.

68. Wesley, *Plain Account* (Maddox and Chilcote), 48.

knowledge in this life as it pertains to the mysteries of God, *viz.* understanding the full extent of the Trinity, knowing the "times and seasons" of God's working, or even understanding the reasons for God's working, etc. This being said, Wesley affirmed a level of knowledge that is possible, including "the general truths which God hath revealed"; to a great extent, but not perfectly, the love of God; and the working of the Holy Spirit "in their hearts."[69]

Regarding mistakes, Wesley continued his sermon on "Christian Perfection" by noting his observation that these are a frequent occurrence. He believed that even people who have been perfected in Christian love may still be mistaken about certain facts pertaining to the details of things that have occurred, or the reason behind them, and even the interpretation of Scripture. However, he asserted that those who have been thus perfected will not be mistaken on matters necessary for salvation.[70]

Wesley went on to describe that people who have been perfected are not free from infirmities. He unequivocally warned not to apply this to known sins. The infirmities of which he spoke were those of a physical nature pertaining to both bodily and cognitive limitations. He then added *temptation* to this list as something from which perfected persons are not free, but perhaps for a season.[71]

Wesley then shifted from the *via negativa* to a *via positiva* description of Christian perfection. Wesley began with the assertion that Christians may be made perfect so as "not to commit sin," stating that even "babes in Christ" are in such a sense perfect. His sermon ensued with a lengthy apologetic defending this claim.[72] From there, Wesley claimed that Christians who are "strong in the Lord" are also "freed from evil thoughts and evil tempers," followed by a brief description expounding upon some key biblical texts.[73] Intriguingly, he only made brief mention in this sermon about being perfected in love, as he remained committed to staying on task in addressing the concept of perfection as pertaining to freedom from sin.

In Wesley's *Character of a Methodist*, like his sermon on "Christian Perfection," he again began with an apophatic approach to describing what a Methodist *is not*, followed by a discourse on what *is* a Methodist. Unlike the sermon, however, this treatise went beyond merely freedom from sin and focused more on the virtues of perfection. Drawing from the apostle Paul's wording in his Epistle to the Philippians, he subtitled his treatise "not

---

69. Wesley, *Works* (Outler), 2:100–101.
70. Wesley, *Works* (Outler), 2:102–3.
71. Wesley, *Works* (Outler), 2:103–4.
72. Wesley, *Works* (Outler), 2:105–16.
73. Wesley, *Works* (Outler), 2:117–21.

as though I had already attained"; thus, the treatise is not so much about the benchmarks one must reach in order to become a Methodist, but the goal toward which they strive. Therefore, much of his description is about the virtuous aspects of the spiritual *telos*.

Wesley began his affirmative description of a Methodist equating salvation with "holiness of heart and life."[74] Though Wesley wrote of various stages in spiritual progression elsewhere, he also held them all together in one complete package. He then continued to describe the various components of this holiness. To Wesley, the spiritual climactic state results in, is driven by, and hinges upon one having "the love of God shed abroad in [one's] heart," which includes a complete love for God with all one's heart, soul, mind, and strength.[75] Out of this love flows a perpetual happiness in God, continual gratitude, an unceasing state of prayer, love for others, purity of heart, the sole desire to do God's will, obedience to the commandments of God, doing all things for the glory of God, and doing good to all people.[76] Note how his progressions ends in an active spirituality and not a passive contemplation, setting him apart from Molinos. Wesley also took a different approach to the will of God than Molinos, in that Wesley wrote of a desire to do the will of God as well as the ability to do so, but did not go as far as Molinos in merging the divine and human wills together in a union.

As Wesley continued his *Plain Account*, in addition to quoting from a number of hymns written by Charles and him, he referenced the first four conferences beginning with that of 1744, and at length, two seminal publications on the topic—*Thoughts on Christian Perfection* and *Farther Thoughts on Christian Perfection*—all of which took an interrogation or question-and-answer approach to addressing the topics of sanctification and perfection. In the first conference, the *telos* was described as being "renewed in the image of God, 'in righteousness and true holiness,'" in regards to sanctification; "the loving God with all our heart, and mind, and soul," pertaining to perfection; and being "saved from all our uncleanness," in relation to inward sin.[77] As these doctrinal statements were brief, they were expanded upon at the conference the following year to include the beginning point of sanctification as connected with justification, the gradual dying to sin until one is "sanctified throughout," and the possibility of being thus sanctified well before the point of death.[78] The third conference merely affirmed the

---

74. Wesley, *Character of a Methodist*, ¶4.

75. Wesley, *Character of a Methodist*, ¶5.

76. Wesley, *Character of a Methodist*, ¶¶6–16.

77. Wesley, *Plain Account* (Maddox and Chilcote), 70.

78. Wesley, *Plain Account* (Maddox and Chilcote), 71.

doctrinal statements of the previous two, while the fourth conference—that
of 1747—went into greater depth regarding the breadth of what may be allowed for those who disagree. In the latter, there was nothing new added
to the content of the teachings, but Wesley and the conference did stress
the importance of maintaining and protecting the doctrine that one may be
"saved from *all* sin before the article of death."[79]

Wesley's *Thoughts on Christian Perfection* were birthed out of the conference of 1759 and later published. Here, he expanded the definition of
Christian perfection. He included "loving God with all our heart, mind,
soul, and strength," as previously defined, but added, "this implies that no
wrong temper, none contrary to love, remains in the soul; and that all the
thoughts, words, and actions, are governed by pure love."[80] From that point,
Wesley further developed the place of mistakes and ignorance which may
still remain in someone perfected in love—much of which he borrowed,
at least in concept, from his aforementioned sermon on "Christian Perfection." The main reason Wesley could hold these together was due to his definition of sin as being a "voluntary transgression of a known law"; in other
words, involuntary "sins" would be committed out of ignorance or lack of
knowledge, not disobedience.[81]

Wesley later wrote his *Farther Thoughts on Christian Perfection* in response to the growing number of people who were claiming to be freed
from all sin. Here, Wesley didn't introduce any new doctrine as much as
he explained in more detail the previous teachings. Unique to this work, as
distinct from the previous works on the topic, was his thorough explanation
of the relationship between the Mosaic Law and the "Law of Christ," as he
called it. Regarding the *telos*, Wesley again declared love as the fulfillment
of the Law and the highest state of the Christian life. He expounded upon
Paul's writing on love in the thirteenth chapter of his First Epistle to the
Corinthians as the description of the ways in which this love is expressed
through the followers of Jesus who have been thus perfected. He summarized this a few paragraphs later addressing the depths of sincerity as "love
filling the heart, expelling pride, anger, desire, self-will; rejoicing evermore,
praying without ceasing, and in everything giving thanks."[82]

In this treatise, Wesley also laid out the soteriological process of the
saving work of Christ, the sanctifying work of Christ, the sustaining work
of Christ, and the inner witness of the Holy Spirit in leading one to and

---

79. Wesley, *Plain Account* (Maddox and Chilcote), 73.

80. Wesley, *Plain Account* (Maddox and Chilcote), 82.

81. Wesley, *Plain Account* (Maddox and Chilcote), 85.

82. Wesley, *Plain Account* (Maddox and Chilcote), 118.

keeping one in this climactic stage. To Wesley, the inner witness of the Holy Spirit serves in knowing one's salvation and understanding one's spiritual state. However, this inner witness does not merely exist as an epistemological tool, but also confirms these things through external fruit. Drawing from Paul's letter to the Galatians, he described the fruit of this highest level as

> *love*; *joy*; *peace* always abiding; by invariable *longsuffering*, patience, resignation; by *gentleness*, triumphing over all provocation; by *goodness*—mildness, sweetness, tenderness of spirit by *fidelity*, simplicity, Godly sincerity; by *meekness*, calmness, evenness of spirit; by *temperance*, not only in food and sleep, but in all things natural and spiritual.[83]

Wesley believed that one could fall away from this state; therefore, he spent a great deal of space concluding this work with cautionary instruction about the situations, experiences, and attitudes that may potentially lead one astray.

Wesley concluded his *Plain Account* with a summary he wrote in 1764, which he outlined in eleven propositions. Though lengthy, they are worth including in their entirety here:

1. There is such a thing as *perfection*; for it is again and again mentioned in Scripture.

2. It is not so early as justification; for justified persons are to "go on to perfection."

3. It is not so late as death; for St. Paul speaks of living men that were perfect.

4. It is not *absolute*. Absolute perfection belongs not to man—no, nor to angels; but to God alone.

5. It does not make a man *infallible*—none is infallible while he remains in the body.

6. Is it *sinless*? It is not worthwhile to contend for a term. It is *salvation from sin*.

7. It is *perfect love*. This is the essence of it. Its *properties*, or inseparable fruits, are "rejoicing evermore," "praying without ceasing," and "in everything giving thanks."

8. It is *improvable*. It is so far from lying in an indivisible point, from being incapable of increase, that one perfected in love may grow in grace far swifter than he did before.

---

83. Wesley, *Plain Account* (Maddox and Chilcote), 124.

9. It is *amissible*, capable of being lost; of which we have numerous instances. But we were not thoroughly convinced of this till five or six years ago.

10. It is constantly both preceded and followed by a *gradual* work.

11. But is it in itself instantaneous, or not?[84]

From there, Wesley continued to expand upon the potential for an instantaneous change. He attested that this transformation was instantaneous for some, but gradual for others, yet arrives at a particular moment for all who experience it. The marks of arrival at this *telos* of perfect love may be found as people are able to live out the words of the apostle Paul in his Epistle to the Thessalonians as "they rejoice evermore, pray without ceasing, and in everything give thanks."[85]

COMPARISON AND CONTRAST

Juan de Ávila, Miguel de Molinos, and John Wesley all maintained a strong emphasis on the place of love in one's spiritual progress and arrival at the Christian *telos*. All three expressed that the goal of this life and the life eternal is to experience and live in a *perfect* love for God and others. Each one viewed love as one of the primary means toward the spiritual end and also the end itself, though they may have differed on some of the other means (Molinos's emphasis on the two spiritual martyrdoms, for example). Wesley's emphasis on love was so strong that he preferred to identify the climactic state as *Christian perfection*, while at times substituting *entire sanctification*, and holding these synonymous with *holiness*. Ávila and Molinos, on the other hand, opted for the terminology of *union* with God; Molinos especially favored this word.

These authors, in their own unique ways, closely connected movement toward and arrival at this highest stage with one's dealing with sin. Molinos preserved teaching from the Dionysian tradition on purgation, where God obliterates sin within a person through painful sufferings. Ávila drew some from the three-fold way of Dionysius but did not adhere as strictly to this pattern as did Molinos. To Ávila, through confession, repentance, and a bit of ascetic self-dealings, one progresses and eventually may arrive at a *perfect liberation* accompanied by *perfect virtue*. For Wesley, this level is nothing less than a freedom from *all* sin.

---

84. Wesley, *Plain Account* (Maddox and Chilcote), 155–56.

85. Wesley, *Plain Account* (Maddox and Chilcote), 156.

Each also included humility as a necessary ingredient to one's growth. Wesley described humility as a necessary means to advancement, whereas Molinos held humility as both a means to growth and an end result (though Wesley would not disagree), yet Ávila placed the emphasis on humility as the outcome of holiness. Given these unique emphases, each expressed the need for individuals to humbly set aside one's own will in order to seek the will of God. To Molinos, this meant an annihilation of one's will in order to reach an alignment and union with the will of God. Ávila likewise called for a complete alignment and union with God's will. Wesley, however, remained a bit reserved in going so far as the other two in the uniting of one's will with that of the Divine. Instead, Wesley maintained that one's will still existed in a unique and individual state apart from the will of God; rather, he called for one to will to do the will of God.

This willing to *do* the will of God, also serves as one of many demonstrations of Wesley's emphasis on an active spirituality—*doing* over mere *being*. Ávila also held that movement toward union results in an active, lived-out, faith, whereas Molinos believed that the passive state of silence and quietude remain superior to active spiritual expression.

All held to a lofty *telos* for the Christian life. Each of these authors drew from the biblical text to support their perspectives, yet Ávila and Wesley both explicitly asserted that the Scriptures would not command such high expectations if it wasn't possible to attain such heights. Though all agreed to such possibilities, Molinos and Wesley stated that few arrive, while Ávila stressed the lengthy process often necessary if one ever arrives. Like Ávila, Molinos and Wesley also made room for a gradual process toward arrival, yet the latter two were much more apt to support the possibility of an instantaneous arrival; and for Wesley, those who attain through gradual process still arrive at a particular moment. With this being said, each of these authors allowed for room to grow, even after a particular entrance into the *telos*.

The affective Ávila, the mystical Molinos, and the Protestant Wesley each expressed a more synergistic approach to spiritual growth in various ways, although each were also very emphatic about the working of God throughout all stages. To Ávila and Wesley, it is the inner working of the Holy Spirit and to Molinos it is the hand of God causing and working externally and internally which moves people forward. Each had particular ways in which a person allows for the working of God, but ultimately it is the work of the Divine which leads one to the *telos*.

8

Concluding Thoughts

THIS THESIS CLOSELY EXPLORED Wesley's editing of a couple selections out of his voluminous *Christian Library*—particularly, the non-biographical writings of two Spanish mystics. His editorial approach reflected his ability to critically analyze various perspectives. His removal of words, phrases, and paragraphs demonstrated his capacity to lay aside perspectives which, in his mind, did not align with Scripture, tradition, or reason, while remaining open to fresh insights offered by people from varied traditions—or, as Robert Tuttle Jr. stated it, separating the *dross* from the *gold*.

This study highlighted the strong influence of Catholic Mysticism on Wesley's understanding of spiritual growth and Christian perfection while also demonstrating, through his critique of the mystics, his commitment to a solidly Protestant soteriology and bibliology. His editorial interactions on the topic of suffering displayed Wesley's understanding of a purely benevolent and loving God. In addition to these themes, a greater understanding of his overall theological perspectives on many topics were examined based on his thorough work on these two abridgments. However, it is worth spending a bit more time summarizing the theological distinctions that emerged from the study of these three writers pertaining to spiritual progression.

As referenced earlier, Pseudo-Dionysius the Areopagite—often considered the father of the Christian mystical tradition—proposed a three-fold process for spiritual progression that involved *purgation, illumination,* and *enlightenment.* Though respectively unique, each of the three authors in this study also followed a three-fold process of growth including an early stage when a person comes to faith and experiences the beginnings of a transformed life, a middle stage that involves deeper growth and understanding, and a climactic stage that realizes a richly intimate relationship with God through which one arrives, at least in part, at their *telos*.

SOTERIOLOGY AND THE EARLY STAGES

Ávila, Molinos, and Wesley all wrote of the first stage as a season when God deals with the issue of sin in a person. Ávila and Wesley both taught that God initiates this season by revealing one's sinfulness to the person. This divine revelation results in greater self-knowledge, which all three believed to be necessary to lead one toward greater knowledge of God. All three also believed that there remains a need for human response in a synergistic working with the initiation of God; this comes in the form of faith expressed through works. Although, in the case of Ávila, works is linked to faith as requisite to this human response. All three also understood that some form of confession and repentance are necessary for beginning this relationship with the Divine, then the human realizes a God-given forgiveness.

Wesley and Ávila stressed the role of confession, with the latter adding in penance, as means toward or a precursor of repentance. Molinos would agree with these two that repentance is needed for further spiritual growth. Interestingly, Wesley and Ávila both understood assurance and consolation, respectively, to be outcomes of these early soteriological experiences following this initial repentance.

The following chart places the soteriological order according to these authors in a side-by-side comparison. Note that similar stages or events are set in the same row, while those which are unique to the respective authors stand in rows by themselves.

Soteriology and the Early Stages

	John Wesley	Juan de Ávila	Miguel de Molinos
God's Initiation	Prevenient grace	God's reprimand	
	Spirit of God brings self-knowledge and awareness	Self-knowledge and acknowledgment	Self-knowledge connected to awareness of one's sinfulness
	Self-knowledge leads to divine knowledge	Self-knowledge leads to divine knowledge	Self-knowledge leads to divine knowledge

Initial Human Response	Faith of a servant (broad)	Faith and works	Faith with works as expression
	Almost Christian		
	Confession	Confession	
		Penance	
	Initial repentance	Repentance	External repentance
	Faith of a servant (narrow)		Surrender of will
Results and Outcomes		Grace	
	Forgiveness	Forgiveness	
	Justification		
	Saved from sin	Initial cleansing	External purgation
	Faith of a child		
	New birth		
	Initial sanctification		
	Initial assurance	Consolation	

At first glance, it is noticeable that Wesley communicated more stages and events in his *ordo salutis*, while Molinos kept it simple. Wesley also tended to call upon more terminology to describe the multiple and somewhat complex aspects of the process of entering into a relationship with God. There are two main take-aways regarding this matter. The first may be found in the commonalities shared by these three, namely, that sin must be dealt with in the early stages. Whether it is forgiveness, being freed, cleansed, purged, or a combination of these, according to these spiritual writers, one must come to terms with one's own shortcomings, failures, and sins if one desires to progress spiritually. The second take-away pertains to the respective traditions held and maintained by these authors. Wesley was clearly Protestant, if not *nearly* Lutheran and *mostly* Arminian in his soteriology; Ávila was unashamedly Roman Catholic; and Molinos rested in the Christian mystical tradition. Yet, all had a uniqueness about them as discussed throughout this thesis. Wesley's Protestantism set him apart from the mystics regarding his soteriology; his doctrine of prevenient grace and the distinction between the faith of a servant and the faith of a child made him unique among those from his own tradition.

MIDDLE STAGES AND GROWTH

In looking at the middle stages and the long-term growing process, it is interesting that compared to their respective soteriological perspectives, the roles were switched—Wesley took a more minimalist approach and Molinos added further sub-stages and events. Like above, the following chart aligns the stages and events of the middle stages of growth with one another according to the writings of Wesley, Ávila, and Molinos. Interestingly, for each of the categories identified in Wesley's editing and works, Ávila and Molinos held their nearly direct counterpart—albeit a different take on the matter.

For example, Wesley identified the *wilderness state* as a season when one grieves the Holy Spirit through the committing of a known sin after one is justified. This may lead one to a deeper repentance and, thus, further spiritual growth. Similarly, Ávila wrote about a season of serious lament and self-accusation of sins which then leads to an amending of one's deeds and further spiritual growth. Likewise, Molinos referenced an experience of significant temptation which leads toward external repentance and additional growth.

Wesley, Ávila, and Molinos also believed that self-denial and/or the surrender of the will is a critical factor determining the level to which one will experience a more significant inner working of God. They also understood that suffering and either perceived or real divine abandonment may significantly lead one toward their ultimate spiritual *telos* (note that Wesley did not perpetuate the doctrine of divine withdrawal; rather he saw such seasons as only *perceived* withdrawal). Other nuances may be observed below.

Middle Stages and Spiritual Growth

	John Wesley	Juan de Ávila	Miguel de Molinos
Beginning of Deeper Growth		Gratitude	
		Imagination and desire	Active meditation
	Wilderness state (cause: one's sin)	Lament, self-accusation of sins	Temptation
	Ongoing repentance	Amend one's deeds	External repentance
			Purgation
	Self-denial	Self-denial	Surrender of will

	Heaviness (cause: world, demons, infirmities, etc.)	Divine abandonment and suffering	Suffering and divine withdrawal
Outcomes			Annihilation and mortification
	Growth in faith, hope, love, and joy	Growth in outward virtues	
		External to internal	Meditation

Here, we may find three take-aways: (1) suffering often plays some significant part in spiritual growth, (2) one may grow in virtues and good deeds after dealing with the issue of sin, and (3) suffering comes from various sources and determining the cause may be difficult. At this level, that which made Wesley distinct from the mystics and others was his development of the concepts of *wilderness* and *heaviness*. Ultimately, his issue regarded the source(s) of suffering. To the Methodist preacher, God is not the cause of suffering. Rather, committing a known sin(s) results in a wilderness state, while the world, the devil, physical ailments, grief, etc. may lead one into a season of "heaviness through manifold temptations."

FINAL STAGES AND THE *TELOS*

Regarding the final stages of spiritual progression, this may arguably be the phase that finds the most points of *near* convergence, while also carrying the most theological weight in the differences from one writer to the next. The chart below tracks some of these comparisons.

Final Stages and the *Telos*

	John Wesley	Juan de Ávila	Miguel de Molinos
Entry	Self-denial	Self-denial	Self-denial and surrender of will
	Divine action	Divine action	Consent to divine
	Instant and process	Process	Instant and process
	To will God's will	Human will aligns and unites with divine will	Internal surrender of will, divine will takes over

			Active contemplation
Outcomes and Evidence	Free from sin	Perfect liberation and virtue	Annihilation and hatred of worldly things
	Active in nature	Active in nature	Active to passive External to internal Senses to affect
	Born again		
	Altogether Christian		
	Full assurance		Removal of fear
	Perfect love	Perfect love	Perfect love
Telos **Terminology and Arrival**	Christian Perfection	Union	Union
	Entire Sanctification		Passive and infused contemplation
			Quietude
	God-likeness	God-oneness	God-oneness

This chart shows that all three believed that movement toward the *telos* involves a synergistic process of self-denial and divine action leading toward an alignment of one's will with the will of God, freedom from sin, and perfect love. However, Wesley and Molinos held that all this may potentially happen in an instant, not merely through lengthy process, whereas Ávila emphasized the aspect of a lengthy process which moves one toward a religious climax. Another key difference may be found in the way in which Wesley wrote of a human will that does not disappear or become absorbed into the divine will; rather, human will remains individual while willing God's will with increasing regularity. A significant difference setting Molinos apart includes the way he uniquely saw this stage as a movement from active to passive spirituality, whereas the others called people to a relationship with God that results in active expressions through love and good deeds. It is also noteworthy that Wesley avoided terminology that spoke of *God-oneness* and opted to urge his readers toward *God-likeness*.

Many of these nuances may be summarized in one key word—*autonomy*. Wesley believed that humans remain completely autonomous in relation to God, though potentially very close, if not spiritually intimate. Though greatly influenced by Christian Mysticism regarding the *telos*, Wesley stood apart from the mystics in his unwillingness to use the language of *union* and especially *divination*. To Wesley, autonomy of the human soul is a vital Christian doctrine. Although the spiritual goal includes a demonstration of the fruit of the Holy Spirit and a perfection of love, the person maintains differentiation in relation to its creator; the mystics believed that at the *telos*, a person becomes one with their creator. Thus, in many ways Wesley was an *almost mystic*, but not fully.

FINAL THOUGHTS

Wesley's editing of the Spanish mystics in his *Christian Library* highlights the ways in which Wesley was Protestant in his bibliology, mostly Lutheran and Arminian in his soteriology, somewhat Moravian in his spirituality, *almost* Roman Catholic mystic in his teleology, and uniquely Methodist throughout. However, John Wesley's *Christian Library* was vast. The breadth of topics included in it are nearly immeasurable. To fully grasp the multi-layered and nuanced theology of Wesley, further examination of his *Christian Library* remains necessary to appreciate the abundant influences and critical considerations which formed his theology. Whether he was abridging the Spanish mystics, the Cambridge Platonists, the early church fathers, or his contemporaries in the Church of England, one thing remained consistent and clear: to Wesley, the Christian *telos* is high and lofty, yet attainable. He desired all who are willing to reach their God-given end.

Appendix

OTHER EDITING OF ÁVILA

Other Theological Issues with Ávila

A FEW OTHER THEOLOGICAL issues emerge out of Wesley's editing that are not addressed in this thesis. These changes tend to be unique in that they are the only alteration pertaining to that particular theme, or they do not have the same bearing as the others addressed earlier. Some themes may be found with the slight change of a sentence or phrase, maybe even in only one occurrence. However, even the slightest mending may point to a greater theological disagreement between the two authors here observed. The following are some of these examples.

In the seventh letter, Ávila urged his reader to "laugh at the temptation of vainglory."[1] To Wesley, laughter was serious business. In a stoic manner, he often admonished people away from laughter and frivolity in general; temptation for sure would be no laughing manner.

In an epistle to a woman who had become ill, Ávila described certain people who "arrive to know at length, both what God is; and what hee is to them who seeke him."[2] Wesley amended this by eliminating the words "arrive to." The difference between arriving to know at length and knowing at length may seem inconsequential, but Wesley's meticulous scrutiny of the texts led him to make such a change. Perhaps it was the idea of complete attainment of such knowledge that seems to be conveyed in the word *arrive*.

Later in that same letter, Ávila encouraged the woman to adhere to his advice "till you have perfect health." Wesley preserved the encouragement and even the hope of healing which followed; however, he edited out the words pertaining to *perfect health*. Wesley's writings on issues of physical

---

1. Ávila, *Selected Epistles*, 53.
2. Ávila, *Selected Epistles*, 64.

health were numerous. He often counseled people in various remedies through letters, publications, and face-to-face which he later recorded in his journal. However, he remained reticent to perpetuate a concept of perfection as it pertained to health.

In the twelfth letter of Ávila, he described the process of God's refinement of a soul by using the analogy of the polishing of stones. As stones are polished through pounding against other stones, he told how God polishes souls by giving "them new blowes, without compassion."[3] Wesley kept thirty-one lines of this section intact before removing the two words "without compassion." This may be due to the way he took seriously the biblical text which says "God is love" and the compassion that God shows out of such love.

In a letter to a friend regarding growing cold in virtue, Ávila described how God meets those who move toward him and will "cover us close with the mantle of his pitty, & goodness."[4] Wesley removed the word *pity*.

In Ávila's fifteenth letter, he described how Jesus "hath wrought our redemption; and salvation by a way, which put him to soe much cost."[5] Wesley certainly would have agreed that salvation and redemption came through Jesus and that the cost was great through his death on the cross. Interestingly, however, Wesley removed the words "and salvation." This was likely because Wesley saw redemption and salvation as the same work.

Later, in this same letter, Ávila explained what God did for humankind through Jesus's death on the cross. Wesley preserved much of this description but did eliminate the words describing that God "punished with soe great severity his onely begotten sonne."[6]

Toward the end of this same letter, Ávila discussed actions of right verses wrong and the accompanying reward or punishment to ensue. In describing those who do more right, he stated that they will be "more favoured, and beloved."[7] Wesley kept the word *favored* but removed the word *beloved*. This was perhaps because Wesley saw all people as beloved of God, irrespective of works or doing right; however, being favored by God could be earned through right living.

Immediately following the above discourse on doing the right, Ávila encouraged his reader to let others see the good in him so that they too could follow his example. Wesley removed this paragraph. Perhaps this

3. Ávila, *Selected Epistles*, 86.

4. Ávila, *Selected Epistles*, 98.

5. Ávila, *Selected Epistles*, 121.

6. Ávila, *Selected Epistles*, 128.

7. Ávila, *Selected Epistles*, 130.

was due to Wesley's emphasis on Jesus's words in his Sermon on the Mount stressing not to "do one's acts of righteousness before others to be seen by them."

A curious topic removed by Wesley from the letters includes God's omnipotence. One such example appears in Ávila's letter to friends who were being persecuted. Wesley removed a portion of a paragraph that pronounced God's omnipotence, alluded to God's omniscience, and concluded declaring that God has "infinite power, an infinite wisdom, and an infinite love."[8]

In a letter to a recent widow, Ávila offered words of comfort. In describing the pain which she was facing, he explained that she was either a sinner who was being cleansed through affliction or a just person facing a trial. Although Wesley preserved this assessment, he did alter the language a bit. Instead of a sinner being "cleansed by this affliction," Wesley changed the words to read "must be brought to repentance by this affliction."[9] Finally, in a letter to some disciples in Ezija, Ávila described God as "the pardoner of them who are converted towards thee"; Wesley altered this to read "the Pardoner of them who believe in Thee."[10] Again, some of these editorial alterations show that Wesley's changes did not just pertain to the topics addressed in the chapters of this thesis but covered a wide breadth, not to mention the adjustments to bring the translations in line with the standardization of spelling that emerged at the turn from the seventeenth to the eighteenth centuries.

8. Ávila, *Selected Epistles*, 178.

9. Ávila, *Selected Epistles*, 188; Wesley, *Christian Library* (Ávila), 46:310.

10. Ávila, *Selected Epistles*, 307; Wesley, *Christian Library* (Ávila), 46:321.

Bibliography

Abelove, Henry. *The Evangelist of Desire: John Wesley and the Methodists*. Stanford, CA: Stanford University Press, 1990.

Abraham, William J. *Aldersgate and Athens: John Wesley and the Foundations of Christian Belief*. Waco, TX: Baylor University Press, 2009.

Ávila, Juan de. *Audi, Filia, et Vide*. Ivory Falls, 2017.

———. *Certain Selected Spirituall Epistles*. Rouën: by the widdow of N. Courant, 1631.

———. *Finding Confidence in Times of Trial*. Edited by Benedictines of Stanbrook Abbey. Manchester, NH: Sophia Institute, 2012.

———. *The Holy Spirit Within: Homilies at Ascension and Pentecost*. Edited by Ena Dargan. New Rochelle, NY: Scepter, 2012.

———. *John of Ávila: Audi, Filia—Listen, O Daughter*. Edited by J. F. Gormley. New York: Paulist, 2006.

———. *Obras Completas del Santo Maestro*. Edited by F. Martin Hernandez and L. Sala Ballust. Madrid: Biblioteca de Autores Cristianos, 1970.

———. *On the Love of God, On the Priesthood*. Edited by I. Fernández-Fígares. New York: IVE, 2012.

Baker, Frank. *John Wesley and the Church of England*. London: Epworth, 1970.

Baker, Frank, and John Stacey, eds. *John Wesley: Contemporary Perspectives*. London: Epworth, 1988.

Barambio Descalzo, Francisco. *Discursos, Philosophicos, Theologicos, Morales, y Misticos, Contra los Proposiciones del Doctor Miguel de Molinos*. Madrid: for Ivan Garcia Infanzon, 1691.

Bigelow, John. *Molinos the Quietist*. New York: Scribner's, 1882.

Bond, B. W. *Life of John Wesley*. Nashville: M.E. Church, South, 1900.

Bradburn, Samuel. *A farther account of the Rev. John Wesley, M.A.* London: Samuel Bradburn, 1795.

Bradley, James E., and Richard A. Muller. *Church History: An Introduction to Research Methods and Resources*. Grand Rapids, MI: Eerdmans, 2016.

Brantley, Richard E. *Locke, Wesley, and the Method of English Romanticism*. Gainesville: University of Florida Press, 1984.

Cadman, S. Parkes. *The Three Religious Leaders of Oxford and Their Movement—John Wycliffe—John Wesley—John Henry Newman*. New York: Macmillan, 1916.

Cataldo, Chet. *A Spiritual Portrait of a Believer: A Comparison between the Emphatic 'I' of Romans 7, Wesley and the Mystics*. Newcastle upon Tyne: Cambridge Scholars, 2010.

Cell, George Croft. *The Rediscovery of John Wesley*. Lanham, MD: University Press of America, 1935.

Cherry, Natalya. "Wesley's Doctrinal Distinctions in Developing the Faith That Marks the New Birth." *Wesleyan Theological Journal* 52:1 (2017) 100–112.

Church, Leslie F. *Knight of the Burning Heart: The Story of John Wesley [With Plates, Including Portraits]*. London: Epworth, 1938.

Clairvaux, Bernard de. *De Diligendo Deo*. https://www.pathsoflove.com/bernard/on-loving-god_la.html.

Clarkson, G. E. "John Wesley and William Law's Mysticism." *Religion in Life* 42 (1973) 537–44.

Coke, Thomas, and Henry Moore. *The Life of the Rev. John Wesley, A.M.: Including an Account of the Great Revival of Religion in Europe and America, of Which He Was the First and Chief Instrument*. Salem, OH: Allegheny, 2008.

Colish, Marcia L. *Medieval Foundations of the Western Intellectual Tradition 400–1400*. New Haven, CT: Yale University Press, 1997.

Collier, Frank W. *John Wesley among the Scientists*. New York: Abingdon, 1928.

Collins, Kenneth J. *John Wesley: A Theological Journey*. Nashville: Abingdon, 2003.

———. "John Wesley's Assessment of Christian Mysticism." *Lexington Theological Quarterly* 28:4 (1993) 299–318.

———. "Real Christianity as Integrating Theme in Wesley's Soteriology: The Critique of a Modern Myth." *Asbury Theological Journal* 51:2 (1996) 15–45.

———. *A Real Christian: The Life of John Wesley*. Nashville: Abingdon, 1999.

Collins, Kenneth J., and Tyson, John H. *Conversation in the Wesleyan Tradition*. Nashville: Abingdon, 2001.

Cordero, Maria Jesus Fernández. *Juan de Ávila (1499?–1569): Tiempo, Vida y Espiritualidad*. Madrid: Biblioteca de Autores Cristianos, 2017.

Cunningham, Joseph W. *John Wesley's Pneumatology: Perceptible Inspiration*. New York: Routledge Taylor & Francis Group, 2014.

———. "Justification by Faith: Richard Baxter's Influence upon John Wesley." *Asbury Journal* 67:2 (2012) 8–19.

De Blasio, Marlon D. "Conversion, Justification, and the Experience of Grace in the Post-Aldersgate Wesley: Towards an Understanding of Who Is 'a Child of God.'" *Asbury Journal* 66:2 (2011) 18–34.

Depetris, Carolina. "Crossing Readings on Mysticism: Alejandra Pizarnik, Antonin Artaud, Miguel de Molinos, Simone Weil and Georges Bataille." *Revue de littérature compare* (2013).

Dobrée, Bonamy. *John Wesley*. London: Duckworth, 1933.

Dodge, Reginald J. *John Wesley's Christian Library*. London: Epworth, 1938.

Dreyer, Frederick. "Faith and Experience in the Thought of John Wesley." *American Historical Review* 88:1 (1983) 12–30.

Edwards, Maldwyn. *John Wesley and the Eighteenth Century*. New York: Abingdon, 1933.

English, John C. "The Cambridge Platonists in Wesley's 'A Christian Library.'" *Proceedings of the Wesleyan Historical Society* 36 (Oct 1968) 161–73.

Esquerda Bifet, J. *Introduccion a la Doctrina de San Juan de Ávila*. Madrid: Biblioteca de Autores Cristianos, 2000.

Faulkner, John Alfred. "Wesley the Mystic." *London Quarterly Review* 153 (1930) 145–60.

Fernandez, F. G. "Saint John of Ávila: An Opportune Grace in an Epoch of Crisis and Conflict." *Anuario de Historia de la Iglesia*. Pamplona: Servicio Publicaciones Universidad Navarra, 2012.

Gill, Frederick C. *In the Steps of John Wesley*. London: Lutterworth, 1962.

Green, J. Brazier. *John Wesley aund William Law*. London: Epworth, 1945.

Green, Joel B. *Reading Scripture as Wesleyans*. Nashville: Abingdon, 2010.

Green, Richard. *The Works of John and Charles Wesley: A Bibliography*. London: C. H. Kelly, 1896.

Green, V. H. H. *John Wesley*. London: Thomas Nelson, 1964.

———. *The Young Mr. Wesley. A Study of John Wesley and Oxford [With Plates, Including a Portrait]*. London: Edward Arnold, 1961.

Haddal, Ingvar. *John Wesley: A Biography*. New York: Abingdon, 1961.

Hammond, Geordan. *John Wesley in America: Restoring Primitive Christianity*. New York: Oxford University Press, 2014.

Harper, K. "Law and Wesley." *Church Quarterly Review* 163 (1982) 61–71.

Hattersley, Roy. *The Life of John Wesley: A Brand from the Burning*. New York: Doubleday, 2003.

Heitzenrater, Richard P. *Wesley and the People Called Methodists*. Nashville: Abingdon, 1994.

Herbert, Thomas Walter. *John Wesley as Editor and Author*. Princeton: Princeton University Press, 1940.

Hernandez, F. M. "Was Saint John of Ávila an Erasmian?" *Anuario de Historia de la Iglesia*. Pamplona: Servicio Publicaciones Universidad Navarra, 2012.

Houston, Joel. "A Change of Heart in Bristol? John Wesley's Doctrine of Election in Perspective, 1739–1768." *Wesleyan Theological Journal* 51:2 (2016) 68–78.

Hurst, John Fletcher. *John Wesley the Methodist: A Plain Account of His Life and Work*. New York: Eaton & Mains, 1903.

Hutton, William Holden. *John Wesley*. London: Macmillan, 1927.

Jones, Rufus. M. "Quietism." *Harvard Theological Review* 10 (1917) 1–51.

Kallstad, Thorvald. "John Wesley Och Mystiken." *Teologisk Forum* 2:2 (1988) 7–42.

Kisker, Scott. "Justification, the New Birth, and the Confusing Soteriological Passages in John Wesley's Writings." *Wesleyan Theological Journal* 52:2 (2017) 47–62.

Koskela, D. M. "The New Birth and the Knowledge of God." *Wesleyan Theological Journal* 52:1 (2017) 7–22.

Kroll, Harry Harrison. *The Long Quest: The Story of John Wesley*. Philadelphia: Westminster, 1954.

Lawson, A. B. *John Wesley and the Christian Ministry: The Sources and Development of His Opinions and Practice*. London: SPCK, 1963.

Lawton, George. *John Wesley's England: A Study of His Literary Style*. London: George Allen & Unwin, 1962.

Lee, Umphrey. *John Wesley and Modern Religion*. Nashville: Cokesbury, 1936.

———. *The Lord's Horseman: John Wesley, the Man*. New York: Abingdon, 1928.

Lelièvre, Matthieu. *John Wesley, Sa Vie et Son Oeuvre*. Paris: Librairie Evangelique, 1992.

Lopez, D. Damaso Delgado. *Cronica de los Festejos en Montilla por la Beatificacion del V. Maestro Juan de Ávila*. Montilla: Establecimiento Tipografico de El Progreso, 1895.

Losa, Francisco de. *The Holy Life of Gregory Lopez, a Spanish Hermite in the West-Indies, Done out of Spanish, The Second Edition*. 1675.

Macconnell, Francis. J. *John Wesley*. London: Epworth, 1939.

Maddox, Randy L., and Jason E. Vickers, eds. *The Cambridge Companion to John Wesley*. Cambridge: Cambridge University Press, 2010.

Marshall, D. *John Wesley*. Oxford: Oxford University Press, 1965.

Martyn, Stephen. "The Journey to God: Union, Purgation and Transformation within the Ascent of Mount Carmel and a Plain Account of Christian Perfection." *Asbury Journal* 67 (2012) 138–57.

Mateo, R. Garcia. "Saint John of Ávila, a Master of Prayer." *Anuario de Historia de la Iglesia*. Pamplona: Servicio Publicaciones Universidad Navarra, 2012.

Meistad, Tore. "To Be a Christian in the World: Martin Luther's and John Wesley's Interpretation of the Sermon on the Mount." PhD diss., Norway, University of Trondheim, 1989.

Mercer, Jerry L. "The Centrality of Grace in Wesleyan Spirituality." *Asbury Theological Journal* 50:2 (1995) 223–34.

———. "The Centrality of Grace in Wesleyan Spirituality." *Asbury Theological Journal* 51:1 (1996) 223–34.

Molinos, Miguel de. *Guia Espiritual: Que Desembaraza el Alma, y la Conduce por el Enterior Camino, para Alcanzar la Perfecta Contemplacion, y el Rico Tesoro de la Interior Paz*. Barcelona: for Rafael Urbano, 1675.

———. *The Spiritual Guide*. Edited by R. P. Baird and Bernard McGinn. New York: Paulist, 2010.

———. *The Spiritual Guide Which Disintangles the Soul, and Brings It by the Inward Way: To the Getting of Perfect Contemplation, and the Rich Treasure of Internal Peace*. 2nd ed. London: printed for Tho. Fabian, 1688.

Monk, Robert C. *John Wesley, His Puritan Heritage: A Study of Christian Life*. Diss., Princeton, NJ: University of Princeton Press, 1963.

———. *John Wesley: His Puritan Heritage, a Study of the Christian Life*. London: Epworth, 1966.

Oden, Thomas C. *John Wesley's Scriptural Christianity: A Plain Exposition of His Teaching on Christian Doctrine*. Grand Rapids, MI: Zondervan, 1994.

———. *John Wesley's Teachings*. Grand Rapids, MI: Zondervan, 2012.

Olson, Mark K. "The New Birth in the Early Wesley." *Wesleyan Theological Journal* 52:1 (2017) 79–99.

———. "The Stillness Controversy of 1740: Tradition Shaping Scripture Reading." *Wesleyan Theological Journal* 46:1 (2011) 120–33.

Oord, Thomas J. "Prevenient Grace and Nonsensory Perception of God in a Postmodern Wesleyan Philosophy." In *Between Nature and Grace: Mapping the Interface of Wesleyan Theology and Psychology*, edited by Bryan P. Stone and Thomas J. Oord. San Diego: Point Loma, 2000.

Overton, John Henry. *John Wesley*. London: Methuen, 1891.

Peers, F. Allison. *Studies of the Spanish Mystics*. Vol. 2. London: Sheldon, 1960.

Piette, Maximin. *La Réaction de John Wesley dans l'évolution du Protestantisme*. Paris: Picard, 1927.

Rack, Henry D. *Reasonable Enthusiast: John Wesley and the Rise of Methodism*. London: Epworth, 1989.

Rattenbury, J. Ernest. *Wesley's Legacy to the World: Six Studies in the Permanent Values of the Evangelical Revival*. Nashville: Cokesbury, 1928.

Rey, Arsenio. "Caracter Ideologico y Literario del Quietismo de Miguel de Molinos en su *Guia Espiritual.*" Diss., New York University Press, 1974.

Rodriguez, Gonzalez, and Maria Encarnacion. "San Juan de Ávila, doctor de la iglesia universal." Madrid: Biblioteca de Autores Cristianos, 2012.

Rodriguez, M. E. G. "Saint John of Ávila: From Master to Doctor." *Anuario de Historia de la Iglesia.* Pamplona: Servicio Publicaciones Universidad Navarra, 2012.

Rogal, Samuel J. *The Wesleys in Cornwall, 1743–1789: A Record of Their Activities Town by Town.* Jefferson, NC: McFarland, 2015.

Roldan-Figueroa, Rady. *The Ascetic Spirituality of Juan de Ávila (1499–1569).* Brill: Leiden, 2010.

Rupp, E. Gordon. *Religion in England, 1688–1791.* Oxford: Clarendon, 1986.

Schmidt, Martin. *John Wesley: Leben und Werk.* Zürich: Gotthelf Verl, 1953.

———. *John Wesley: A Theological Biography.* Nashville: Abingdon, 1963.

Simon, John. S. *John Wesley, the Last Phase.* London: Epworth, 1934.

———. *John Wesley: The Master-Builder.* London: Sharp, 1927.

———. *John Wesley and the Religious Societies.* London: Epworth, 1921.

Smith, Warren Thomas. *John Wesley and Slavery.* Nashville: Abingdon, 1986.

Snyder, Howard A. *The Radical Wesley.* Downers Grove, IL: InterVarsity, 1980.

Southey, Robert. *The Life of John Wesley.* Hutchinson, 1820.

Tomkins, Stephen. *John Wesley: A Biography.* Grand Rapids, MI: Eerdmans, 2003.

Turner, E. E. "John Wesley and Mysticism." *Methodist Review* 113 (1930) 16–31.

Tuttle, Robert G. "The Influence of Roman Catholic Mystics on John Wesley." Diss., University of Bristol, 1969.

———. *John Wesley: His Life and Theology.* Grand Rapids, MI: Francis Asbury, 1978.

———. *Mysticism in the Wesleyan Tradition.* Grand Rapids, MI: Francis Asbury, 1989.

Tyerman, Luke. *The Life and Times of the Rev. John Wesley, M.A.* 3 vols. London, Hodder & Stoughton, 1890.

Tyson, John R. "John Wesley and William Law: A Reappraisal." *Wesleyan Theological Journal* 17:2 (1982) 58–78.

Van Valin, Howard F. "Mysticism in Wesley." *Asbury Seminarian* 12:2 (1958) 3–14.

Virvidakis, Stelios, and Vasso Kindi. "Quietism." *Oxford Bibliographies,* last updated Feb 26, 2013. https://www.oxfordbibliographies.com/display/document/obo-9780195396577/obo-9780195396577-0184.xml.

Wakefield, Gordon Stevens. "'A Mystical Substitute for the Glorious Gospel'? A Methodist Critique of Tractarianism." In *Tradition Renewed,* edited by Geoffrey Rowell, 185–98. Allison Park, PA: Pickwick, 1986.

Watson, Richard. *The Life of the Rev. John Wesley to which are Subjoined Observations on Southey's Life of Wesley: Being a Defence of the Character, Labours, and Opinions of the Founder of Methodism, against the misrepresentations of that publication.* London: J. Mason, 1835.

Wesley, John. *The Character of a Methodist.* Bristol: F. Farley, 1742.

———. *A Christian Library: Consisting of Extracts from and Abridgments of the Choicest Pieces of Practical Divinity, which have been Publish'd in the English Tongue. In Fifty Volumes. By John Wesley.* Vol. 38:249–93 (Miguel de Molinos). Bristol: printed by Felix Farley, 1754.

———. *A Christian Library: Consisting of Extracts from and Abridgments of the Choicest Pieces of Practical Divinity, which have been Publish'd in the English Tongue. In Fifty*

Volumes. By John Wesley. Vol. 46:252–329 (Juan de Ávila). Bristol: printed by Felix Farley, 1755.

———. *John Wesley.* Edited by Albert Cook Outler. New York: Oxford University Press, 1964.

———. *The Journal of the Rev. John Wesley, A.M., Sometime Fellow of Lincoln College, Oxford: Enlarged from Original MSS., with Notes from Unpublished Diaries, Annotations, Maps, and Illustrations.* Edited by N. Curnock. 8 vols. London: Epworth, 1938.

———. *The Letters of John Wesley, Standard Edition.* Edited by John Telford. 8 vols. London: Epworth, 1931.

———. "Notes on the Song of Solomon." Wesley Center Online. http://wesley.nnu.edu/ john-wesley/john-wesleys-notes-on-the-bible/notes-on-the-song-of-solomon/.

———. "Notes on St. Paul's Second Epistle to the Corinthians." Wesley Center Online. http://wesley.nnu.edu/john-wesley/john-wesleys-notes-on-the-bible/notes-on-st-pauls-second-epistle-to-the-corinthians/#Chapter+IV.

———. *A Plain Account of Christian Perfection.* Edited by R. Maddox and C. Chilcote. Kansas City: Beacon Hill, 2015.

———. "Preface to the Old Testament Notes." Wesley Center Online. http://wesley. nnu.edu/john-wesley/john-wesleys-notes-on-the-bible/preface-to-the-old-testament-notes/.

———. *The Works of John Wesley.* Vol. 1, *Sermons I, 1–33,* edited by Albert Cook Outler. Nashville: Abingdon, 1984.

———. *The Works of John Wesley.* Vol. 2, *Sermons II, 34–70,* edited by Albert Cook Outler. Nashville: Abingdon, 1985.

———. *The Works of John Wesley.* Vol. 3, *Sermons III, 71–114,* edited by Albert Cook Outler. Nashville: Abingdon, 1986.

———. *The Works of John Wesley.* Vol. 4, *Sermons IV, 115–151,* edited by Albert Cook Outler. Nashville: Abingdon, 1987.

———. *The Works of John Wesley.* Vol. 7, *A Collection of Hymns for the Use of the People Called Methodists,* edited by Franz Hildebrandt and Oliver Beckerlegge. Nashville: Abingdon, 1983.

———. *The Works of John Wesley.* Vol. 9, *The Methodist Societies I: History, Nature and Design,* edited by Rupert Davies. Nashville: Abingdon, 1989.

———. *The Works of John Wesley.* Vol. 10, *The Methodist Societies: The Minutes of Conference,* edited by Henry Rack. Nashville: Abingdon, 2011.

———. *The Works of John Wesley.* Vol. 11, *The Appeals to Men of Reason and Religion and Certain Open Letters,* edited by Gerald R. Cragg. Nashville: Abingdon, 1989.

———. *The Works of John Wesley.* Vol. 12, *Doctrinal and Controversial Treatises I,* edited by Randy Maddox. Nashville: Abingdon, 2012.

———. *The Works of John Wesley.* Vol. 18, *Journals and Diaries I, 1735–38,* edited by W. Reginald Ward and Richard P. Heitzenrater. Nashville: Abingdon, 1900.

———. *The Works of John Wesley.* Vol. 19, *Journals and Diaries II, 1738–43,* edited by W. Reginald Ward and Richard P. Heitzenrater. Nashville: Abingdon, 1990.

———. *The Works of John Wesley.* Vol. 20, *Journals and Diaries III, 1743–54,* edited by W. Reginald Ward and Richard P. Heitzenrater. Nashville: Abingdon, 1991.

———. *The Works of John Wesley.* Vol. 21, *Journals and Diaries IV, 1755–65,* edited by W. Reginald Ward and Richard P. Heitzenrater. Nashville: Abingdon, 1992.

———. *The Works of John Wesley*. Vol. 22, *Journals and Diaries V, 1765–75*, edited by W. Reginald Ward and Richard P. Heitzenrater. Nashville: Abingdon, 1993.

———. *The Works of John Wesley*. Vol. 23, *Journals and Diaries VI, 1776–86*, edited by W. Reginald Ward and Richard P. Heitzenrater. Nashville: Abingdon, 1995.

———. *The Works of John Wesley*. Vol. 24, *Journals and Diaries VII, 1787–91*, edited by W. Reginald Ward and Richard P. Heitzenrater. Nashville: Abingdon, 2003.

———. *The Works of John Wesley*. Vol. 25, *Letters I, 1721–39*, edited by Frank Baker. Nashville: Abingdon, 1980.

———. *The Works of John Wesley*. Vol. 26, *Letters II, 1740–55*, edited by Frank Baker. Nashville: Abingdon, 1982.

———. *The Works of John Wesley*. Vol. 27, *Letters III, 1756–1765*, edited by Ted A. Campbell. Nashville: Abingdon, 2015.

———. *The Works of John Wesley*. Edited by T. Jackson. 14 vols. Grand Rapids, MI: Zondervan, 1872.

Wesley, John, and Edward Sugden. *The Works of Wesley*. Vols. 1 and 2, *Wesley's Standard Sermons*. Grand Rapids, MI: Zondervan, 1955.

Whitehead, John. *The life of the Rev. John Wesley: Collected from his Private Papers and Printed works; and Written at the Request of his Executors. To which is Prefixed some Account of his Ancestors and Relations; with the Life of the Rev. Charles Wesley, Collected from his Private Journal, and Never before Published. The Whole forming a History of Methodism, in which the Principles and Economy of the Methodists are Unfolded. Complete in One Volume*. London: Printed by Stephen Couchman, 1857.

Wilson, D. Dunn. "The Influence of Mysticism on John Wesley." Diss., Leeds University, 1967.

———. "John Wesley, Gregory Lopez and the Marquis de Rentry." *Proceedings of the Wesley Historical Society* 35 (1966) 181–84.

———. "John Wesley and Mystical Prayer." *London Quarterly and Holborn Review* 193 (1968) 61–69.

———. "John Wesley's Break with Mysticism Reconsidered." *Proceedings of the Wesley Historical Society* 35 (1965) 65–67.

Winchester, Caleb Thomas. *The Life of John Wesley*. New York: Macmillan, 1906.

Wood, A. Skevington. *The Burning Heart*. Grand Rapids, MI: Eerdmans, 1967.

Wood, Lawrence W. "Conflicting Views of New Birth between John and Charles Wesley." *Wesleyan Thological Journal* 52:1 (2017) 40–78.

Zangwill, Nick. "Quietism." *Midwest Studies in Philosophy* 17 (1992) 160–76.